Janet D. Smith,

'4, Hilary Crescent,

Ayr.

14ᵗʰ May 1942.

With best wishes from Isabel.

Best Foot Forward

By the same author

SHOES WERE FOR SUNDAY

To my mother, and to all of that gallant
band who were sojer-clad, but major-minded

'How sweet to remember the trouble that is past.'
EURIPIDES

I

I CAN remember with particular exactness the day that I left childhood birthdays and went into my teens. 'Into my teens.' What a strange, grown-up sound that had. Nobody else seemed at all impressed by this milestone in my life. But I remember it. Because on the previous day, when I was jumping down the long school stairs two at a time, the eccentric Highland schoolteacher had stopped me and had asked, 'How old are you now, Molly?' 'Twelve,' I replied. And I realised, with a surprising pang, that this was the last time I would be able to say that with truth. In school, people didn't usually go about asking your age. Your age-group dictated what class you were in, and everybody knew almost to the month what age everyone else was. I remember being very surprised that Mr. McAllister didn't know how old I was, and thought maybe he had asked that question on that special day so that I should remember forever the last time I had told anybody I was twelve.

I was in no hurry to grow up. Schoolgirl heroines were far and away my favourites in the whole world of literature, which I explored to the full, and I had been haunted for months by the harrowing tales of a little girl who had died at the age of thirteen. She had been thrown from her horse, and knew she was mortally afflicted, and I could hear her rebellious cry, 'How would you like to die at thirteen?', ringing in my ears. The book ended with her sobbing, 'I don't want to die. I am only thirteen.' I was sure I was to share her fate, although the only horses I ever saw in Springburn were those which drew the milk-carts, or the coal-carts, or which thundered down West Nile Street between the Railway Station and the Post Office, with cheery wee trace-boys perched negligently on the animals' arched necks, caps pushed to the back to their heads, monarchs

9

of all they surveyed. I could possibly be knocked down by such a horse, but it was quite certain I would not fall off its back!

And yet I almost did share the fate of the little schoolgirl heroine with whom I had so closely identified. And it was from no outside danger that the hazard came, but from my own intense and emotional temperament. Grannie, who had shared and guided my every waking thought for as long as I could remember, had died, and my grief transformed me from a bright, eager, happy child, who had complete confidence that everything would go on forever, to a frightened, trembling wisp of a girl who jumped at every shadow, and who stood poised for terrified flight at every sound. When I came back with a message for my mother, instead of jumping up and down on the mat outside the door, as I used to do before diving instantly into the kitchen, I would post myself half-way across the landing, in case Grannie's ghost should leap out at me when the door opened. 'What are you standing away back there for?' my mother would ask irritably as I stared at her, not venturing a step forward until I'd made sure it was really my mother. 'Come in for goodness' sake, and keep the draughts out.' How could I tell her that it was Grannie's ghost I was frightened of? 'She looks haunted,' I heard a neighbour say to my mother, and I jumped in fright. Was Grannie haunting me? Grannie, who had left such a void in my life that I didn't know how to fill it?

Even worse to bear than the thought of her ghost was the awful emptiness of the house when I came home from school. My brothers and I would sit and stare at each other in the silence until it was time to set the table for my mother, so that it would all be ready when she came in from her work. She still seemed to be able to eat, and so did my brothers, but I had lost my appetite with my grannie and never felt hungry at all nowadays, not even for sweeties. With the habit of years, I would set the table for five, and then realise with a pang of anguish that the fifth place, Grannie's, would never be needed again. The terrible finality of it, the endless silence, nobody to tease and torment me and keep me right, all this I locked inside me. I dwindled, and grew thin, and was down to three stones and twelve pounds at the age of thirteen, and a terrible lassitude stole over me so that I seemed to be walking in a dream world where people walked and talked all round me, but left me isolated in this aching void of stillness.

One day a neighbour called, who hadn't seen me since Grannie died, and for whom I used to dance and recite whenever she asked me. She took one look at me, and, with the involvement we all felt for each other in the tenements, immediately tackled my mother. 'My Goad, Jeanie, that wean's away tae a shadow. Is she eatin'?' 'Nut a bite will she take!' said my mother, 'but she sleeps like a log, and sleep's life tae weans, you know.' 'It's no' life at that age, Jeanie,' and she went on to whisper urgently to my mother and I caught the dramatic words 'fatal melancholy'. They had a great love for the dialogue from *My Weekly* in our tenements, and both women seemed almost overcome by the thrilling words 'fatal melancholy'. I began to be quite stirred myself, but I wasn't so pleased when my alarmed mother dragged me on unwilling feet along to the doctor's surgery the very next night. The surgery was packed, as usual, and there was the smell of wet clothes, and engine grease from the men's dungarees, and quite a sociable atmosphere as people recognised a neighbour and started a whispered conversation. The men disdained to talk, and picked up one of the dog-eared magazines and started to read, or turn the pages to look at the pictures, while the chairs squeaked as we each moved along one with the disappearance into the doctor's room of the next patient.

Children were 'shushed' to silence if they dared to make a noise, or attempted to crawl under the table to start a game of hide-and-seek. 'Whit?' an outraged mother would hiss. 'Ye don't play in the doactor's surgery, so ye don't. Ye sit still and behave yersel'.' My mother had found a listening ear, and settled down to explain that she wasn't here for herself, but it was Molly who wouldn't eat and couldn't get over losing her grannie. So that was why I couldn't eat, I thought in surprise, it was because Grannie wasn't there to tell me what to do. When I remembered how often I had said 'Och but, Grannie, I don't *want* gruel', and she had said 'Sup it up, for it'll gi'e ye strength', I wished, oh how I wished, that she could give me a plate of gruel now. Oh I'd take it, and never a word of argument out of me. My longing for my grannie was so intense that it completely exhausted me, and I sat down on the surgery floor—for the seats were for the adults—and went to sleep.

'Come on, hen, it's oor turn,' and my mother pulled me up and took me into the surgery. The doctor drew me towards him, his eyes full of troubled sympathy, while I stared tiredly past him. 'My, my, Molly,' he teased gently, 'where's the wee girl who used to run to open the door to me when Grannie had one of her attacks of bronchitis, eh? And a fine cup of tea you used to make for me too.' At that memory of Grannie sitting up in bed, checking that I had everything in readiness for the visit, my lips trembled, but my grief was too deep to find words for it, and too paralysing to be endured. My mother was explaining that all I wanted to do was sleep, and she had thought that would be a fine cure, for didn't everybody know that sleep was life? 'But not this type of sleep Mrs. Weir,' said the doctor, just as that neighbour had said. 'She must be roused or she will simply slip away in her sleep.' My mother's eyes widened in fear. 'You see,' went on the doctor, 'for the moment, strange as it seems in such a wee lass, she has lost the will to live.' The words seemed to be coming from a long way off, and I listened with a sort of detached interest.

Exercise was prescribed. A walk to the park every day without fail, whatever the weather, so long as I was warmly wrapped. Red wine to stimulate my appetite and improve my blood condition. Brown wholemeal bread for nourishment. Liver and tripe for easy digestion, and to correct my anaemia. It would be a terrible struggle for my mother to provide such luxuries, he knew, but he was sure she would do her best for me.

From that minute I knew no peace. I was dragged, whimpering and miserable, from my warm bed, my only refuge from the world which was so empty for me without my grannie. Every day I was forced to walk up Springburn Road to the Public Park, my feet dragging at every step. If we met a neighbour I would stand in silence, tears trickling down my white face, until the cold forced me to whisper, 'Come on, Mother, come *on*!' The neighbour would look at me, baffled, wondering aloud where Grannie's wee girl Molly had gone, and then would whisper to my mother that she doubted I would make old bones. 'She looks as if she is going into a decline,' she would whisper to my mother, who by this time was distracted out of her mind at the change in me. 'People don't go into declines nowadays,' she would declare stoutly, more to comfort herself than in defiance, and I would be trailed round every path in the park, and in and out the hot-houses, and my face examined to see if the blood had whipped up some roses.

When we got back, frozen almost to the bone, for it was bitter January weather. I would crouch on the fender stool in front of the fire, and my mother would pour out a glass of that horrible red wine, which I sipped while I nibbled a thin tea biscuit, to ease the bitter taste. That wine was like poison to me. It was worse than the port Grannie's chum used to give me on New Year's Day, but it had been bought for my good and I forced it down my throat, knowing what a sacrifice it had been for my mother to buy it. My mother would watch me shudder at the bitter brew and would say sympathetically, 'I couldnae drink it masel', hen, but the doctor said you have to take it or ye'll no' get better.'

The slighest noise in the house became intolerable. I, who had raced, and leaped and sung with the children of the teeming tenements, regarding noise as the normal accompaniment of living, was driven to the edge of hysteria by every high laugh, by the noisy caperings of my brothers, by the chattering of the visiting neighbours who came in nightly for a cup of tea and all the latest news. In the end, to give everybody else peace, I was sent down to sleep in old Grannie's downstairs. The quietness of her single end was bliss. It faced the front too, whereas our kitchen looked into the back court, and I enjoyed the novelty of the big street-lights shining in the windows. There was just the one room, with a shining, immaculate range, which was kept as perfect as my grannie kept ours, a neat and tidy dresser with no toys or clutter like ours, which had to keep all the junk of five people, and a high double bed set into the recess, with curtains to screen it off during the day. Very posh, this last touch, and I admired it very much. The curtains were of gold-coloured chenille, and were looped back at night, and the matching gold-coloured chenille bedspread carefully folded and laid on top of the stool, before we climbed into bed.

This grannie slept at the front of the bed like my own grannie, and I at the back, but I couldn't coorie into her back, for she had high blood pressure and had been recommended to lie almost upright against banked pillows. When I would turn during the night I was terrified to see her sharp face in ancient profile against the ghostly light shining in from the street. Her breathing was so shallow I thought this was another grannie who had died, and if she was dead I would have to climb over her, and I knew I would never be able to do it, and I would be trapped beside a corpse until somebody thought to come to the door to see what had happened to me. Heart hammering with fright, I would tug at her flannel nightgown to make her start and mutter, just to reassure myself she was still alive, and oh the blessed relief when she told me to be at peace and lie still.

My teachers, those dedicated creatures who knew us as well as our own mothers did, were getting worried. What had happened, they wondered, to the industrious wee girl whose hand had always been the first to shoot up to answer their questions? Where was the mental alertness of yore? Worst of all, what business had a girl of my age to have such lacklustre eyes and apathetic mien?

There was a consultation among themselves, and a note was sent to my mother, suggesting that they apply for a place for me in Kilmun Seaside Home, a convalescent home run by a temperance charitable organisation. They were sure a holiday in the country was what I needed, a complete change from my usual surroundings, and a chance to build up my strength. My mother had a great respect for the wisdom of those in authority, and she certainly didn't know what else to do with me, and couldn't afford to give me a holiday or take time off work in the month of March, which was still regarded as winter in Glasgow. Nobody went for holidays at any other time than the Fair, everybody knew that. But we'd all heard of convalescent homes, and greatly envied those who belonged to the Masons, or to the Co-operative staff, and who were sometimes lucky to be nominated for such a holiday at no expense whatsoever. We'd never dreamed of such a thing for ourselves, and never imagined the directors of any holiday home would look sideways to help us, even if we'd dared to ask them. But an application went in signed by the headmaster, and in due course the Board were pleased to inform us that I would be granted two weeks' stay at Kilmun Seaside Home from 2nd March. At any other time the mere idea of a holiday by myself would have had me lost in delighted wonder, but not this time. It was all part of the nightmare I was going through.

The seaside in March. There would be nobody there. It would be empty. There would be just me and the sea. I was still only thirteen. Maybe my fate was going to catch up with me there, and I would share my story-book heroine's early demise far, far from my home.

It was a peculiarly hard spring that year, and the loch was frozen over in a sheet of glittering silver when I got off the bus. I caught my breath. I had never seen the icy beauty of a winter landscape before, and in spite of the dull ache in my heart, and the strangeness of solitary travel, interest stirred. Bare trees cut from ice stood motionless. Grey skies were heavy with more snow to come. The Home stood by itself in a beautiful empty landscape, so different from the crowded silhouette of the tenements, and suddenly I felt for the first time for months that I could breathe. It was exactly three months since Grannie had died, three months since I had drawn a breath free from wretchedness.

I can't remember how I got there. I think I travelled alone, seen off by some official of the charity. Certainly no member of my family came with me, for who had money for fares for such coddling, and anyway I would come to no harm. I had taken my brief farewells of them at home, certain I would never see them again, and I wondered if they would miss me very much, and say to each other: 'She never made old bones. She was only thirteen.'

After our room and kitchen tenement house I had never seen such space. Fancy having rooms devoted entirely to *sleeping*? A huge room with four beds in it, with real wardrobes to hold our clothes, was shared with three women. I had always been used to sharing, so this was no hardship, and we had each a bed to ourselves! What a waste it seemed. Fancy a whole bed for each of us when we could easily have managed two in each bed. It would have been warmer too. I had always been used to the comfort of a warm body to coorie into in bed, and it seemed chill and strange to find only draughty spaces in front and behind me when I tried to go to sleep.

The three women with whom I shared were a bit taken aback to find a wee lassie in their midst. 'Whit wis wrang wi' ye, hen?' they asked sympathetically. When they heard it was just something vague like not being able to eat, tiredness, anaemia, all lumped into the term 'nervous debility', they lost interest.

They had had far more interesting illnesses. They told terrible tales of operations, which fascinated and horrified me at the same time, and I had wild visions of adult life being a succession of near-fatal illnesses from which I would be lucky to be rescued in the nick of time, and certainly with some vital part of me missing after a butcher of a surgeon had done his dire work. I began to think my grannie and my mother had surely been exceptionally lucky to have gone through life with every bit of themselves complete, and nothing left of their precious insides in pickle jars in hospitals. I shuddered at the prospect of my own insides being on exhibition for students at some future date, for my companions assured me cheerfully, 'Och it happens to everybody at wan time or another.'

These morbid conversations did nothing for my mental state, but I thoroughly enjoyed their tales of their romances. This was even better than Grannie's *My Weekly*, for I was getting it at first hand, and no inhibitions about my being 'far too young to understand'. Two of the women were spinsters, a name which intrigued me very much, for I'd never heard the word before. The other was a widow. Both spinsters had been engaged to soldiers who had perished long years ago for king and country; how sad and how romantic they seemed, in spite of honest faces scrubbed clean with soap and water, metal curlers in their sparse hair, and pink flannelette nightgowns covering them modestly from neck to feet, and sleeves which came down to thin wrists. We speculated for hours on how many children they might have had had their lost loves returned from Flanders field, and what sort of houses they might have lived in. It was all most thrilling and enjoyable until the widow, for some strange reason, would interrupt to say, 'Aye, they're the best kind o' weans to have, the wans that never made ye greet, even if they never made ye laugh.' This effectively quenched all conversation, the light was put out, and I fell asleep furnishing the never-never-land houses of the poor husbandless spinsters.

The Home took men as well as women, and there was strictly no integration. Two long tables ran the length of the dining room. This was another source of amazement to me. A whole big room devoted entirely to eating, and the tables standing there all the time just to hold our plates and food, and never cleared to play at cards, or for homework, or games. I felt I was in a castle when they could afford such a room to stand empty except at meal-times. I had never dreamed of such space or luxury. At one long table the women were ranged down both sides. At the other table two rows of men faced one another. I wasn't in the least interested in those dull men, and never even looked at them, for I thought the women were far more exciting, but I noticed some of the women seemed very curious, and kept stealing little glances across the no-man's-land between the tables. At the top of the room the matron and her assistants sat at a small separate table, keeping an eye on the proceedings, and two local women served the food.

I still had little appetite, and can't remember much about the food, except on one terrible night when the cook burnt the scrambled eggs, and the smell filled the whole house. We all came into the dining room holding our noses, but, burnt or not, the horrible mess was served up to us. I tried to swallow it, remembering Grannie's wrath if any food was left, but I just couldn't force it down. I may say it successfully put me off scrambled eggs for many a long day. The adults were loud in their condemnation of the cook, and furious at not being offered a substitute dish in place of the spoilt eggs, but I thought it quite reasonable, for, after all, on a Sunday night they wouldn't have been able to get anything from the shops, which in any case were miles away, and anyway no buses ran on Sundays from the Home.

The authorities must have been terrified there would be any fraternising of the sexes, because for our morning walks the females turned left on leaving the Home, and followed the loch-side, while the men turned right and meandered towards the hills.

The afternoon walks saw the routes reversed, the men taking the loch walk, and the females the hill route.

Not a word was exchanged as the groups set off in opposite directions, but many a surreptitious glance was exchanged over a shoulder before the distance grew so far between them that it was no good hoping to discover whether somebody had found them interesting enough to become flirtatious, albeit in silence.

As for me, my appetite was returning with the caller air, and my meagre pocket money, scraped together by my mother, was enough to buy me ginger beer in a stone bottle from a wee shop half-way between the Home and the furthermost point of our walk. I had never tasted ginger beer from a stone bottle before and thought it absolutely delicious. And there was Cadbury's chocolate too, narrow thick bars all joined together in a row which had to be broken by the shopkeeper to detach my penny bar, and sometimes if she was clumsy I got a wee bit from the bar next in line. I never stopped to think of the sense of being cheated which must have been felt by the next purchaser, as I stood there silently willing the girl to break the chocolate in my favour. No gambler watched the turn of a roulette wheel more breathlessly than I watched the breaking of those chocolate bars. I was obviously getting better in health when I could turn my mind to such cunning, with my taste for sweeties coming back unimpaired. I never realised how lovely it could be to feel appetite for food—and for life—slowly steal back.

The stone monument at the end of our morning walk carried words which I carefully memorised, and used to chant to myself:

> 'Lives of great men all remind us
> We can make our lives sublime,
> And departing leave behind us,
>   footprints on the sands of time.'

I puzzled and puzzled over the meaning. Why wasn't it 'footsteps'? I wondered. Well of course, you could *hear* footsteps, but the minute they were out of earshot they wouldn't be left behind. That was it. But then footprints wouldn't stay on sand very long either. The next tide would wash them away. Departing must mean death. I was much preoccupied with death just then. Slowly I came to the conclusion that it must mean that whatever you did in life, even if you made it sublime, you wouldn't make more impression on the rest of the world than a footprint would make on wet sand. But even that was a lot when you thought of all the people there were hurrying about trying to be famous, who would leave no impression at all. That must be it. I determined to make that my goal, and leave a wee footprint of my own. I wasn't sure how. I'd always wanted to be an actress—maybe that would be it. Or a writer.

the lumpy porridge. My grannie would have had plenty to say to the cook in that Home. I had seen Grannie making our porridge every morning in life, and I knew fine that the cook hadn't had the water boiling, and that she hadn't sprinkled in the meal slowly enough, or kept stirring as she should. Grannie was scathing of people who wasted good food, and who were too lazy to do things properly. But fancy that big house, with its posh dining room, and its rooms devoted entirely to sleeping, not having such tasty food as we enjoyed in our wee room and kitchen in Springburn. I had thought that the richness of a house ran like a thread of pure gold through every part of it. But it seemed it could stop short of the kitchen, whereas our wee room and kitchen had had a treasure of pure gold in my grannie. I was pleased at the picture of my glittering grannie, and then laughed at the very idea. I was getting fanciful, and would have to be careful, for Grannie always said day-dreamers just wasted their lives, and the happiest folk in all the world were those who knew how to work for their living.

Because of the extra two weeks I was staying at the Home, I spent my fourteenth birthday there, and on that icy March morning I realised I was maybe going to make old bones, after all, for I had come through this dreaded thirteenth year and I hadn't followed my schoolgirl heroine to an early grave. Usually birthdays meant very little in our house, maybe a wee hankie, or toasted cheese for tea, but this time, because I had been away from home for such a long time, my mother must have rallied all my chums to mark the occasion, and I was almost overwhelmed by the letters and cards which tumbled in the letter box at the Home for me. A huge pile stood by my break-fast plate, and I flew to the lounge to open them all. How beautiful they were. Fairies with glitter on their wings, flowers in impossibly beautiful vases, bluebirds flitting through blos-som, violets for March, and shamrocks because I was born on St. Patrick's Day. And *all* the chums had told me the end of the 'following-up' serial which I had missed by being away. We had followed the heart-breaking adventures of our screen heroes and heroines for endless weeks, and I fell into a day-dream of delight, imagining them walking together into a golden unset at the end of all their sufferings, to 'live happily ever after'. Oh I wished I could have seen it all for myself, but the words in every letter, 'She gets him in the end', told me all.

Somehow my mother had managed to send me a box of chocolates, and I handed them round to my room-mates after our supper. We had a concert that night among ourselves, and because they knew it was my birthday, I sang for them 'I passed by your window' and for an encore 'Mother Machree'. Unaccompanied, of course, for nobody knew how to play those pieces on the piano. But I didn't care. I had sung them dozens of times at our back-court concerts, and knew every note, and how to start on a key which wouldn't be too high for me when I came to the top notes. In fact when one of the old ladies marvelled at my confidence, and had been afraid I'd never get up to the high 'Oh God Bless you and keep you, Mother Machree' phrase, I said, with shattering belief in myself, 'Och I *knew* I would get up, I've done it before.' I spoke in all innocence, not having learned that there are times when breathing and vocal chords don't always work in harmony, and when fear of an audience can do strange things to a performer.

We got a bedtime cup of tea on my last night, because so many of us were leaving in the morning, and even the staff stayed to sip theirs with us and nibble daintily at their biscuits. I was coaxed to sing again, and gave them Grannie's chum's favourite. 'Bonnie Mary of Argyle'. I had started on it before I remembered that the last time I had sung it had been for Grannie and her chum on what was to be her last visit on New Year's Day the year before. Now I was singing it to a room full of strange old ladies, and my own grannie would never hear it again. My voice faltered. Grannie's voice was suddenly real to me, and I could hear her saying as she had said a hundred times when I was tackling a difficult task which had me pechin' with annoyance, 'Come on noo, hen, pit yer best foot furrit'. And, magically, I felt my voice strengthening and growing firm and clear, just to please her. I sat down to warm applause, and I heard the voices of my adult room companions saying, 'Ye got a rer clap, hen. That wis awfu' nice. By jings, ye fairly mind a' the words.' I paid no attention. I was absorbed, wondering if this was a new kind of haunting Grannie was going in for. A curious sort of peace stole over me. I wasn't frightened any more. I think it was at that moment I truly realised Grannie's spirit would never never leave me.

2

I T was marvellous to be home again, but how wee and neat and tidy our room and kitchen seemed after the vastness of the Home. My mother had put a clean tablecloth on the table, just as if I was a visitor, and there was home-made jam, and cakes from the City Bakeries, and a wee print of my favourite fresh butter and, unbelievably, even a wee drop of cream in the tiny jug with 'A present from Girvan' written on it in gold.

For some reason I felt strange and shy. Maybe it was the tablecloth, or maybe just the shock of seeing our house with new eyes after being away such a long long time. I sat with my feet neatly placed together under the big chair, where I was perched right on the very edge, my eyes running round taking everything in, from the flaming coals in the range to the reflections in the brilliantly polished brass kettle on the mantelpiece. It was just like the New Year. I was frightened to move in case I dirtied anything. Even my mother seemed different. Not tired. Not in dungarees, but in a nice white blouse (*white*, and it a week-day, and us not expecting company—what could it mean?). After being with the old ladies in the Home, and sharing life with my spinster room-mates and the elderly widow, I had forgotten how young my mother was. How bright and wavy her red hair, how clear her pink-and-white complexion, and how small and slim her build. I was puzzled why I had never noticed all this before, and wondered if it was because I had never taken time to sit and look at anybody very much in our house before I had gone to that Home, for I had always been too busy out playing, and in the rush and stir of our tenement life we never actually sat and *looked* at each other.

My mother was full of questions. 'Whit wis it like, hen?',

'Were the folk nice tae ye?', 'Did they gi'e ye enough to eat?' She had heard it all from my letters, for I had written to her every week, but she wanted to hear it all over again. After all, it wasn't everybody's wean in the tenements who had been away in a great palatial Convalescent Home for a whole month. If it had been Buckingham Palace she couldn't have been prouder or more impressed. She hadn't even seen it, but she took my word for its size and its richness, and she even embroidered an extra here and there later when she was telling the neighbours about it. She kept exclaiming over my rosy cheecks, and how well I had filled out, and declared she was sure I would have forgotten all about them I had been away such a long time.

It was said in jest, but I very nearly had. In fact I had almost forgotten I had two brothers until they came charging in for their tea, then stood staring at me, kicking their feet awkwardly. 'Hullo,' they said. 'Hullo,' I said. Then they took in the laden table. 'Ohhh! Cakes!' 'I want the Fern cake,' said Tommy. 'And I want the coconut one,' said Willie. 'You'll give Molly her pick first,' said my mother, 'for I bought them seeing it was her first night home.' They grinned, for they had seen the chocolate liqueur cake which they knew was my favourite, and they knew there was no competition for the cakes they preferred.

And then I remembered what was puzzling me. 'Why are ye no' at yer work, Mother?' I asked. She paused briefly as she poured boiling water into the teapot. 'Oh, the job feenished. They put a' the women off, even the widows, and took men on.' I stared at her. I knew this was serious, for we needed every penny she earned. 'Ur ye on the Buroo, then?' 'Juist for a wee while. I've been promised they'll take me on at the Co-operative offices, cleaning, as soon as there's a place.' I opened my mouth to say something, for I knew how proud she was of her skill as a fitter in the Railways, and as a machine operator in the big workshops. 'Come on, come on, sit doon to yer tea, and don't bother yer heid the night about jobs for me.'

It was like a party after all the solid food at the Home. It was the sort of tea we all loved. Lashings of bread and jam and cakes and biscuits, and the richness of cream to trickle on top of the tea, to form strange patterns and then transform the brew to a satisfying fine beige colour. Neighbours knocked at the door and came in to see me, and to rejoice in the sight of rosy cheeks, a phenomenon in the tenements as far as the girls were concerned. The boys sometimes acquired this healthy glow, racing up and down stairs delivering milk on frosty mornings, but the girls were mostly pale and on the thin side, like me. One neighbour brought her wee boy, who had very bad rickets. My mother had told me that this was because wee Eck's mother had been too poor to give him real milk when he was an infant, and had given him weak tea in his bottle and his bones hadn't developed. I gazed with interest at his wizened little face, and at his poor bent legs, and I wondered if it would straighten them out now, if he were to drink nothing but milk forever and ever. He saw me looking at his legs, and I quickly looked away, but I needn't have worried, for he wasn't self-conscious about them. I had just learned those finicky ways with all those adults at the Home, who seemed mad if their pecularities were pointed out, whereas we saw nothing cruel about singing about a wee humpty-backed man who roamed our streets:

'Wee Johnnie Morrie,
Fell ower three storey',

in explanation of his deformed back. Johnnie himself didn't mind, and seemed proud to be the subject of a song. But I had found out already that everybody wasn't like us.

It was great to be back to a world which held children and folk of all ages again, and I found myself slipping back into the easy acceptance of childhood with every passing minute.

Then it was bedtime and I lifted the bed-pawn to pull out the hurley bed, where I had slept all my life with Grannie. There was nothing there! Nothing but the clothes basket, and the bath, the zinc bath where we splashed on Sunday mornings in front of the fire, and which was usually stored by our next-door neighbour, who had the privilege of using it for her own four children for providing this service. 'Where's the bed?' I cried out in alarm. Was everything changing now Grannie had gone? I wanted things to be as I remembered them, especially my bed.

My mother laid down the paper she was reading. She loved reading the papers 'from batter to batter', as she graphically put it, and not even my homecoming interrupted this luxurious devouring of the world news. 'Oh we gave it to the McPhersons. They've a new wean, and they needed the extra bed.'

That awful empty sickness of thinking of the hurley without Grannie threatened to rise and engulf me again, but my mother was going on: 'Aye, you'll have to go along and see the new wean. You'd think it was the first wean that had ever been born. Mind you, it's nine years since she had Ella, and she's fairly taken on wi' hersel'.' My wise mother, knowing of my passionate interest in babies, held my attention. 'When was it born?' I demanded. I loved seeing infants practically as soon as the doctor left the house (or, more often than not, the midwife, for doctors were only brought in in our tenements if there were complications, which there seldom were). I loved their wee red crinkled faces, and the way they fastened on to their mothers, like kittens, when they were hungry. Bottle babies were practically unknown in our world, and seemed a terrible waste of money, when the mothers had all that good milk themselves and it not costing a penny. I thought that mothers had this magic milk supply all the time, and wondered why they didn't feed anybody else's baby when it screamed with hunger as they held it. I realised there might be a little mystery somewhere, for I had heard a neighbour say with a laugh, when holding a baby which butted her in search of food and comfort, 'Aw there's nothing there for you, hen.' 'Why wasn't there?' I wondered. 'She's got bumps the same as all the other mothers.' Something held me back from asking, though. But I kept a watchful eye afterwards and realised that only the ones with babies had milk. The others just had the bumps in readiness for when they were needed! The more I thought of it, the more sensible it seemed, for it could be very uncomfortable to have had pints of milk slurping about if no baby had come along to use it up. Yes, a very good idea, I decided. God knew all about it and had arranged it perfectly.

The McPherson baby had arrived ten days ago, I learned, and it was so tiny that Ella's doll's hat had fitted its head. I drew an ecstatic breath. As wee as all that! Just like a doll. I couldn't imagine anything more perfect, and couldn't wait for tomorrow to rush along to see it. The hurley was almost forgotten, and my mother was taking the cover off the big bed in the recess where she slept, and telling me to get in. So I was to coorie in at her back now, instead of Grannie's. How high the bed seemed, and what activity seemed to be going on in my sleeping quarters after the stillness of the Convalescent Home, where nothing went on in a bedroom but undressing, some quiet chatter and sleep. The boys were playing with their football cards, covering up the names of the teams at the foot of the painted cards, and guessing the number of letters which made up the title. A correct guess meant surrendering the card, and howls of anguish went up when a favourite card was lost. My mother was rinsing out some clothes. A neighbour popped a head in to borrow a cup of sugar. Another neighbour came in on her way home from the pictures, her eyes red with tears over Norma Talmadge's parting from her lover. My head was spinning. Had it always been like this? Would I ever be able to sleep in this kitchen, humming with life and excitement. Oh it was lovely to be home, but a treacherous corner of my heart yearned for the tranquillity of that still bedroom in Kilmun.

But the space below the bed, where the hurley used to be, provided marvellous extra storage and we felt a heady sense of tidiness at being able to lay our boots and shoes there in a neat row, hidden behind the bed-pawn. The dirty washing could be kept there too, and my skipping ropes, and the bools and the jawries we used for our games at moshie, and the big doll Auntie had sent from Australia, and the jeely pan, and the girdle. How had we ever managed without it? The dirty washing was stowed neatly in the bath, for we only used the bath on Sunday mornings. It was nice to have it in the house all the time, though, but I learned it had caused a great feud when my mother asked politely if she could have it back now as we had room to keep it ourselves. While the hurley had been used, our next-door neighbour had kept our bath under her bed, and she had grown so used to doing her washings in it, as she hated to use the wash-house, that she had come to think the bath was hers, and that *she* was lending it to *us* when we had it for our Sunday bathing. She had been astounded at being asked to return it, my mother told me, and had actually cast doubts as to who had bought it in the first place. 'My Goad,' said my mother, 'her that hisnae two pennies tae rub the-gither trying to tell me that she had ever bought a bath!' She sighed with righteous indignation. 'I've aye been feart she would try to pawn it, for as sure as daith she's pawned everything else in the hoose except the weans.' The mere idea of pawning her children sent me off into peals of frightened laughter, but my mother said sadly, 'Och that man never knows if he'll have tae staun' up for his dinner when he comes hame or if the table will be away at the pawn. Ah don't know whit she does wi' her money, and her wi' a man's wages comin' in.'

To my mother, a man's wages represented the peak of prosperity. She was horrified at the fecklessness of those who let all that easy money slip through their fingers, for she herself had had to work for every penny, and she would say, shaking her head at their foolishness, 'Aye, Mrs. So-and-So's an awfu' bad manager.' To her it was crystal clear that money had to be managed wisely or it would be like fairy gold—gone when it was needed most.

She had every sympathy for wives who were left staring at empty purses while their husbands squandered the best part of their wages over the pub counter, and she had not the slightest commiseration for the man compelled to drown his sorrows. One night we heard a terrible bang outside our door, and when we had all rushed out to see what had caused it, could hardly make out anything but a black shape on the landing and clouds of dust rising to choke us. 'My heavens,' gasped my mother, 'it's Mr. Irvine. He's fallen ower the banisters.' Mr. Irvine was a notorious drunkard, and my mother decided he'd taken a dive over the banisters, blinded by whisky. Then as the dust cleared we saw we were staring at the Irvines' bass mat and not the body of the drunkard. At that moment his daughter came down to recover the missile, which she had thrown at her father in fury because all they had had to eat for their tea was bread and margarine, and her father had come staggering home from work drunk. 'You might have murdered him,' said my mother looking at the size and thickness of the mat, and judging the height from which it had been thrown, for by this time she had learned that the mat had been aimed at the vanishing figure of Mr. Irvine as he'd reeled downstairs to get away from his family's wrath. 'A good thing if I had,' said his daughter through gritted teeth. We were very shocked at this savagery, but not really surprised. Far better to be without a man at all than to have one who thought his wage packet was to satisfy his own selfish drouth. But my mother sent me up afterwards

with a pot of her home-made black-currant jam to add a wee
bit of luxury to the bread and margarine.

Everybody envied the wife who enjoyed the rare novelty of
having a pay packet handed to her, unopened, and whose husband meekly accepted a small portion of it as pocket money.
We had one on our stair, and although she looked, as my
mother described it, 'as if butter widnae melt in her mooth',
she obviously held her pale husband in terrorised thrall. Whatever she spent her unopened pay packet on, it wasn't on food,
for her four small children were thin and white and listless, and
her husband much the same. She, however, continually sported
new hats, and 'peerie heels' on her smart shoes. The tenement
women may have envied the pay packet, but they clearly despised the husband. 'Nae spunk at a'',' they declared. 'A moose!'
And, final damning words, 'Of course he's English. Saft, that's
whit he is. A damned good feed would dae him the world of
good.' I would have thought a soft Englishman who handed
in every penny of his pay was a far better bargain than a Scotsman who drank away half his earnings, but the women seemed
to find something in their own dour men which satisfied them.
I decided adults were sometimes hard to fathom.

And one of the strangest things to understand about adults
was how difficult it seemed to be for them to write a letter. I
was always scribbling. I even made up the words on my Christmas cards, and I wrote the words for our children's concerts
in the back courts, and anybody would have thought I was
doing something special the way the neighbours respected this
trick with the pen, for it was to our door they came if they
wanted a letter of importance sent or read.

Even at the age of ten I was asked by an aunt to write a
letter for her to a lawyer. A lawyer! I was terrified, but most
impressed. She told me the gist of what she wanted to say, I
phrased it in what I decided was formal language, she was
delighted, and the lawyer apparently never raised an eyebrow.
That, maybe, laid the foundations of my career as the tenement
scribe.

When unemployment was rife in my native city, shabby boys
and men would come to our door, and would sit with pathetic
humbleness while I wrote out cogent reasons why their unemployment pay should be continued. I'd drum up proof of
having 'genuinely sought employment', giving names, addres-

ses and times of application. Great was the mutual rejoicing when it was agreed the few shillings a week would continue to be paid, and the children could eat a sausage with their stark diet of potatoes and bread.

For another I'd make earnest application for a job at sea, with recommendations from the Minister, and from our local J.P. as to the character of the man sitting so bright-eyed and hopeful watching me writing. I'd copy out references in my best handwriting, in ink, of course, with a brand-new pen-nib given to me by the girl in the Co-operative—a nib which helped to make my childish hand seem more impressive and grown-up looking.

When a letter was required to impress upon the factor the urgency of a particular claim to have a sink repaired, or a leaky pipe mended, or a new pane put in a draughty window, the irate tenant came to me first, so that I could put it as forcefully and yet cunningly as possible. What the factor must have thought at receiving so many letters of complaint in the same handwriting, nobody stopped to think. It was enough if we could frighten him into doing the repairs, for we felt he would be far more likely to remember to alert plumber or glazier if a complaint was made in writing than if it were given verbally when he was collecting the rents.

I was so successful in getting pipes mended and the communal lavatories unstopped that I was in danger of getting no homework done at all, with the stampede of tenants eager to make use of me as a scribe. Nobody cared a scrap that it was my time they were using. What was time to a wee girl? And if I had the ability it was only correct I should use it to help them.

The Scots are great settlers, and everybody in our tenements had relatives in all parts of the globe. Many a letter I'd pen to cousins in Canada, or New Zealand or Australia, telling them that John, or Helen, or Nessie would soon be joining them, travelling on the S.S. so-and-so, and arriving on such-and-such a date, and would look forward to the reunion at the port of arrival. I even wrote letters for the emigrants to take with them, to be handed to their new employers, and copies by the dozen of the appropriate character references. I sometimes felt I was sending the whole of Scotland's young manhood and womanhood overseas on a tide of my letters.

And when we went down to the quay-side to wave them off,

and enjoy a last eightsome reel before the tearful singing of 'Will ye' no' come back again', as often as not they'd pat an inside pocket and say, 'Aye, we've got yer references here hen, you're a rare wee writer, so ye are.' I just hoped they would find somebody in Australia or New Zealand or Canada who would be able to write for them, or we'd never hear if they prospered or failed in those far-away places which held out such high hopes for them.

We seldom did hear. The usual dramatic intimation of prosperity was when we found them in our midst, dressed up to the nines in light-coloured clothes which would have dirtied in five minutes in the smoke of Springburn, eyes filled with wonder that they could ever have lived among us. This laconic habit of just getting on to a boat and heading for Scotland without so much as a letter was carried to extremes by an aunt and uncle of mine. He had landed in Australia at the end of the first world war, my mother told me, and kept promising to send for his wife as soon as he had gathered enough money for the fares. This went on for a year or so, until she became thoroughly fed up, and went down to consult the authorities as to how she could join him. To her delight, she was able to get a passage for herself and the three children under a special ex-servicemen's scheme, the small amount charged to be repayable by her husband from Australia. No sooner the word than the blow. Without a word to him, she packed up and set off for Sydney. He for his part had decided to give her a wonderful surprise and come home and take them all back to Australia. He never dreamed of sending a letter, for where else would a wife and three children be but at home?

My mother told me she had nearly collapsed with shock when she met him walking up Springburn Road. 'Whit are you daein' here?' she screamed when she was assured he wasn't a ghost. 'Jessie and the weans will be in Australia by this time.' Now it was his turn to lean on the shop door to steady himself. As my mother told me dramatically, 'They had passed each other on the way.' I had a vivid mental picture of their ships barely grazing one another and couldn't understand why they couldn't have *seen* one another, and joined parties in mid-ocean.

I wasn't a bit interested in a distraught auntie arriving in a strange country with three children and no home or husband to go to, or hearing how the ex-service association cared for her in a hostel until her husband joined her. He, fortunately, had taken a round ticket, so there was no problem of finding his fare to get back to Sydney.

No, what thrilled me was the drama of those ships passing each other, and when I later heard the expression 'like ships that pass in the night', I felt it was surely invented to fit the story of my auntie and uncle who could have saved themselves a whole lot of trouble if only they'd written a wee letter to each other, telling of their intentions.

We thrived on drama in the tenements, where each knew everybody else's business, and another sea adventure we all sighed and thrilled over was that of the girl in the next close who went out to join the lad who had emigrated to Australia a few years earlier. She was only nineteen, had never been away from home before, and was put in the care of an emigrating couple, middle-aged, who had promised to keep an eye on her. Marion and Peter were to be married as soon as the ship docked, and we all nearly swooned with delight as she described to us, before she left, how Peter would come rushing up the gangway with his best man and the bridesmaid, and they would go straight to the church and be married. He had a house for her, was in a marvellous job, and they would live happily ever after. She could see it all, and so could we. It was far better than the pictures, for it was happening to us.

We all went down to the Broomielaw to see the ship off. Melodeons played while we danced the reels, bagpipes droned sadly, 'Will ye' no' come back again', but this time it was all excitement, for it was a wedding celebration we all dreamed of, and the elderly couple were caught up in all the joy, and felt it was their own daughter who was the centre of all this attraction.

We heard nothing for months. Then Marion's parents had a letter from the elderly couple. This was a letter which had to be written, and it told how the atmosphere of the ship had completely turned Marion's head, and they had been able to do nothing with her. She'd been the maid-of-all-work at home, while her older sisters went out to work, and she'd never been used to being dressed in nice clothes every single day and to living what seemed to her the life of a millionairess. She was only travelling steerage, but it was all unbelievable bliss.

The Australian accent was glamorous as Hollywood to her

simple ears, and she'd fallen madly in love with one of the ship's officers. She refused to listen to the old couple's advice to wait till she got to Australia, for the man might be a married man, and not to do anything she'd regret. We heard all the full details later when the old couple came home for a holiday. When they had got to the port where Peter was to meet them he'd rushed up the gangway, just as we'd imagined he would, with his best man and bridesmaid, and Marion had drawn aside and said, 'I'm not getting off, Peter. I'm not getting married.' The old lady who was telling us the story said he turned white as a sheet, and begged her to come off and at least talk it over. She wouldn't. Peter left the ship. They sailed on to Sydney. And, in the end, the ship's officer did turn out to be married. The old lady said he had been as dismayed as Peter at this turn of events, for, of course, it had only been a ship's flirtation to him and he didn't dream Marion would expect him to marry her.

My mother was on night-shift when this old lady had called to tell us all this, and she was nearly late for her work following all the details of the broken romance. 'What happened to Marion?' she asked as she scrambled into her dungarees. 'Did she stay in Sydney?' 'No,' said the old lady, 'I think she was too ashamed. She went up country and worked in a fruit farm, and she ate so much fruit she got a sort of blood disease and had to be taken to hospital. And, believe it or not, she married one of the doctors.'

'My goodness,' I thought. 'Marion, who used to take me down to the Tally's for a pokey hat. Who used to sing to me when I sat on the dresser and watched her scrub the kitchen floor. Abandoning Peter. Falling in love with a married ship's officer. Getting poisoned. And then marrying a doctor!'

Gosh, the penny matinée would have to be good on Saturday to beat all this.

3

THE only time we ever went to the pictures was on Saturday afternoons. The evenings were totally undreamt of by us, for who could possibly have afforded sixpence or more to see the same show at night that we could see for a penny on a Saturday? It cost tuppence for the balcony, but I only knew of this from the prices written on the ticket window—I never had tuppence to patronise this exclusive part of the cinema, nor had anyone else I knew. Downstairs was good enough for us, and we queued patiently the moment we had swallowed our dinner, which was our name for the glorious feast of ham and a shared fried egg which we always had on Saturdays, and which represented for us the tastiest and best dinner we could imagine. What a marvellous day Saturday was. No school for a start, and even when Grannie was alive, hardly any messages, for all the week-end food was laid in by Friday afternoon when I came home from school, and the only thing I was likely to be sent for on Saturday were some mutton pies from Torrance's the bakers, if there was enough money for them, after I came home from the pictures.

We didn't even play in the back courts on Saturday mornings. Those with enough pennies tore along to the newspaper shops to make careful selection of their favourite comics, and the rest of us breathed down their necks to follow the adventures of colourful boys and girls who led such stirring lives compared with ours. The purchasers of the comic papers were cocks of the walk on Saturday mornings, and would often be carried to the shops shoulder high by some penniless volunteer who would cry, 'Gi'e ye a cerry-coad doon to the shop, if I get first read of your comic efter you've read it yoursel'.' This offer was often taken up, and it was like some Eastern ceremony, with the rich one perched high above the head of his human

34

beast of burden, arms held out to balance himself, fists gripped securely by the trotting boy, the rest of us racing alongside to take part in the thrilling purchase, and enjoy the sight of a brand-new clean comic. Comics changed hands again and again from one Saturday to the next, their value going steadily down with each exchange, and their colours getting grubbier and grubbier, as unwashed hands smoothed them out and drooled over their contents. Once read, they could be exchanged for another second-hand comic, and in this way we all managed to read every comic published, although the original purchasers were a mere one apiece.

Sometimes I helped a chum deliver greengroceries. She had left school and landed an enviable job as message girl in a greengrocer's shop for the splendid salary of nine shillings a week. It seemed an odd sum to me, somehow. Why not ten shillings, I wondered? That was a nice round sum. My chum was indignant when I mentioned this. 'Well, it's more than the seven-and-six Nellie is getting in the dairy,' she exploded, 'but if you think nine shillings is so funny, then you needn't bother to come and help me deliver the baskets on Saturday.' 'Oh I don't think it's funny,' I assured her, seeing my treasured peep at the 'toff's houses' vanishing under her rage. 'It's just that I thought you were worth ten shillings.' Oh! cunning one that I was. It worked, as I hoped it would. And I was instructed to wait up the road, out of sight of the shop, for she didn't want her boss to think she couldn't manage the heavy baskets herself. That nine shillings meant potatoes and cabbage and ham for their Saturday dinner, for her mother, unemployed dad, and three brothers and sisters, instead of potatoes and oatmeal and a bit of margarine. Besides many a wee 'extra' for their teas during the week.

So I would hide in the doorway of the Maypole Dairy until I saw Maggie stagger up the road, the big brown shiny basket grasped tightly in both hands. It was a grand basket, and we both approved and admired its fine quality, even if it was a ton weight to carry. We balanced it methodically between our crossed hands, and headed for Balgray Hill and the houses of people who seemed to us rich beyond the dreams of avarice. I had often run along the narrow alleyways between those big houses, on my way to the Public Park, and had never dreamed that those brick walls actually represented the ends of gardens, and that once through the little door in the wall, one found real green grass, and flowers, and *back doors* to the houses. I had once heard a man in the butcher's, ordering two chops, say to the assistant, 'Tell the boy the back door', and wondered what he could have meant. Now I knew. Deliveries were made at the back doors, straight into the kitchens, so that the posh fronts of the houses wouldn't be dirtied or made untidy. I was very impressed. Maggie and I would lug the big basket into back porches, bang the knocker and wait until we heard a voice say 'Come in', or have the door opened to us. We would tip the potatoes into big boxes, lift out tomatoes and fruit carefully, stand by patiently until everything was checked to make sure the greengrocer had sent only goods of perfect quality, and, if we were lucky, be given a biscuit at some houses, or even a ha'penny. But we hardly ever got money, for these posh people settled their accounts monthly, and so didn't have to hand money over to the delivery girls. We were especially fond of one house which employed a cook—fancy, a cook!—and if this large-hearted creature had time, she'd make us a cup of tea, or, better still, some hot cocoa if it was a chilly morning. She made delicious rock cakes, and it was a field day for us if we were given one of those to nibble with our hot cocoa. Then we had to run the rest of the way to catch up, for Maggie's boss knew practically to the minute how long she should take to return with an empty basket. I thoroughly enjoyed this glimpse of how the other half lived, and my mother and Grannie seemed highly amused at my descriptions of the fine kitchens, and gratified that I found no cooking range which was as shining as our own. It was a sad day for me when Maggie was promoted to serving behind the counter and my Saturday morning deliveries to Balgray Hill came to an end.

While the job lasted, though, these deliveries filled my Saturday mornings, and then it was a sprint home for my dinner, then out to queue for the pictures. We had a grand choice. The Princes was my favourite. Clean and comfortable, and just out of the wind for queueing. The wee Ideal was favoured by a lot of other children, especially as there was a well-tried method for 'skipping-in' without paying. An unguarded door was stealthily opened by the one who had paid, and his pals slipped through for nothing. It was a terrible risk, and an awful showing up if you were caught, and I never knew any girls who did this. Only the boys had the daring, or the cheek, depending on how you looked at it. Anyway, as I was an ardent member of the Church, Sunday School, Bible Class, Guides and Band of Hope, I was sure God would have struck me dead if I had tried it!

The Kinema, or the 'Coffin', as it was called because of its shape, was up the High Road, but was not among the favourites of the children. It was a concrete building, cold and cheerless, and far too near the cemetery for comfort, although the grown-ups didn't seem to mind, and it was usually packed in the evenings.

The Public Hall had pictures too, strange films with French actors with dead-white faces and black lips, and frightening films about monsters, but they also had marvellous 'following-ups', as we called the serials, and once you'd seen the first episode you just *had* to go back for the whole twelve weeks.

Also, they had a rare wee man called Dougie who told us all what we could expect to see the following Saturday. He was a great character, loved by us all.

The lights would go up after the big picture, and wee Dougie, the projectionist, would make his stately way from the magic room where he worked the projectors, round the gallery, thence down a flight of steep stairs to the stage. We children waited in a state of eager anticipation—eager, but far from silent. At the first sound of his footsteps, we chanted in unison 'Here's Dougie, here's Dougie', a noisy chorus which may be thought to have been some embarrassment to the man. Not a bit of it. He was quite unmoved, and neither speeded his footsteps nor slackened his pace. He chewed rhythmically on a piece of tobacco and ignored our cries. He may even have enjoyed being the centre of attraction for this brief moment each Saturday matinée, for we were certainly never told to shut up.

Having reached the centre of the stage, he would hold up a hand for silence. He obtained instant obedience. You could have heard a pin fall. For weren't we to hear of splendours and thrills in store for us next Saturday? And on those special occasions, when the current serial had finished, wouldn't we be told what hair-raising adventures were to be ours for the next twelve weeks? Tucking the tobacco safely into a spare corner of his cheek, and in a voice which reached every corner of the cinema, he would give us a word picture of the attractions for the coming week. Names of our favourites were greeted with yells and cheers. The announcement of a lovey-dovey picture met with groans and cat-calls. He had us in the palm of his hands, and we responded vociferously to each announcement.

His brief moment of glory over, he took the long walk back to the projection room, accompanied this time by our chanting 'Good auld Dougie; good auld Dougie'. He would disappear through the little door at the back of the gallery, the lights would go out with a blinding suddenness which plunged us into dramatic darkness and made us catch our breaths almost in fear. Then the screen would spring to life, usually after a false start which we basely jeered. Dougie was in command of the projectors, and we were lost in the life pulsing on the screen for the next hour.

We were all very docile in this cinema, apart from our noisy reception of wee Dougie, maybe because it was the Public Hall during the weekdays. But in the Princes we always seemed to go wild with an excess of energy before the pictures started, and raced up and down the passages downstairs in the stalls, throwing oranges or apples to one another, and changing comics.

The plutocrats upstairs, though, enjoyed the luxury of fighting to place themselves within spitting distance of the wide beam of silvery light which shone from the window of the projection room to the screen. Within a certain strategic range they could send showers of quicksilver through that magic ray, never pausing to wonder what happened to their transformed spittle when it reached the heads of the unfortunates sitting underneath. I don't suppose I'd have given it a thought myself had I been lucky enough to be able to penetrate the mystery of the posh seats in the balcony. They didn't follow such actions to their conclusion. It was joy enough to be able to make silver showers with saliva, and how I envied those who could perform this miracle, even if it was often my luckless head which received the shower once it had gone through its silver beam. It was almost better than sparkling frost, for it cost nothing, but my mother would wrinkle her nose in disgust when I came home bearing only too obviously the evidence of the pastimes of the upstairs spitters, and my head would be plunged beneath the cold tap to rinse it clean, my yells of anguish completely ignored as the icy water hit my warm scalp. Sunday morning was for hair-washing, and I needn't think I was having kettles boiled up specially for me on Saturday at tea-time if I was silly enough to sit underneath people who had such bad habits. Bad habits! I kept quiet about my secret longing to be able to indulge in such things myself.

When the cinemas emptied after the matinées, the boys, like the innocent, unconscious animals they were, immediately relieved themselves. Now that *was* a bad habit, I quite agreed. We girls turned our faces away delicately, and pretended we were unaware of the fierce jets battering the corrugated fence which lined the side exits. If the male and female adults in Kilmun were forbidden to mix, we needed no such embargo. We didn't choose to mix. Girls went with girls, and boys enjoyed the company of boys. When boys were very small they were looked after by older sisters or bigger girls, but the moment they realised that boys had far more exciting games like 'buckety-buck-buck-buck' played with a tin can, and involving fast races through the closes, and back courts, and that boys had far higher jumps from the dykes than mere girls, they were off. They would have been regarded as Jessies if they had behaved otherwise, and even mothers and sisters accepted this, though sometimes with sighs of misgiving when the toddlers were very wee.

We hated having to take any of the wee boys with us to the matinées, for they often became frightened, and started to yell, and an attendant would race down the passage, jerk a thumb in the direction of the screaming boy and shout, 'Who's wi' this wean? You? Right, oot wi' him.' There was no possibility of argument. If you dared protest he simply charged along the row, lifted both noisy child and his accompanying sister or bigger girl bodily, and put both outside the door. Nobody came to the rescue, for one word from anyone only resulted in him or her being hauled from the seat and pushed outside with the others. And, of course, we all wanted to see the end of the big picture.

When I came home I used to re-enact every bit of the fantasy I'd seen on the screen for my grannie, or my mother, and later for any neighbours who came in for their bedtime cup of tea with us. Old Mrs. Peebles used to declare, 'My Goad, it's as guid as being there masel'.' Grannie and my mother would frown at her, for they felt I needed no encouragement in this direction, since I play-acted far too much as it was. Mrs. Peebles had been frightened off the cinema for life because one night, years before, she had gone when there was a film showing a terrible storm of rain, thunder and lightning. She had jumped to her feet and shouted, 'My Goad and I've left ma washin' oot.' She'd run from the pictures, only to find the streets outside bone dry, for, of course, the storm had been on the screen. Not only had she made a perfect fool of herself in front of everybody, but she didn't even get back inside again to see the end of the picture. If you wanted to go out for any reason you had to obtain a 'pass-out' ticket, and Mrs. Peebles in her passionate rush to rescue her washing had no such thought in her head. So, no pass-out ticket, no re-entry. How unjust that seemed to her, and to us when she'd told her story for the hundredth time. But her dramatic rush from the 'Coffin' cinema passed into Springburn lore, and was related with tears of laughter to every newcomer to the tenements. But the cinema never got another penny of her money as long as she lived. She learned of all the plots and dramas through me, and in her I had my perfect audience. If it was a comedy, I was 'faur better than wee MacGreegor'. If it was a drama, I was 'faur before yon Garbo wumman'. She heard of every single episode of the serials from me, and was just as eager to hear how the heroine or hero had been rescued as I was to tell it. I hadn't realised I was maybe beginning to feel superior to this simple woman until I came in from Sunday School one day and began memorising the text we'd been given. Mrs. Peebles was in having a cup of tea when I came home from Sunday School. 'How beautiful upon the mountain,' I intoned, and then stuck. To my amazement Mrs. Peebles continued: 'Are the feet of them that trespass not.' I stared at her open-mouthed. 'Do you know that, Mrs. Peebles?' I asked. 'How do you know that? We just got it in the Sunday School the day.' Her eyes twinkled at me knowingly. 'Aye, I know it weel, lassie,' she said. 'Ah'm no' juist a heathen, ye know, even if I don't gang tae the pictures.' I could feel my face getting scarlet. 'Och, I didnae think ye were a heathen, Mrs. Peebles,' I protested. 'It was just . . .' and my voice trailed away. 'Aye, it was just ye didnae think I wid ken a thing like that.' I was thankful when my mother said, 'Don't scuff your good shoes. Put on your slippers and sit doon at the fire.' But I looked at Mrs. Peebles with new eyes after that, and I realised it wasn't only my teachers who knew far more than I did, but the tenement women knew a thing or two as well.

They took note of every change in our appearance, those neighbours of ours, and when I came back from Kilmun they noted with pleasure that I had grown rounded and healthy, and that I had a 'fine fresh colour'. They weren't the only ones who noticed me. To my annoyance and slight dismay, the boys began taking an interest too. I had absolutely no interest in *them*. I was astounded when a chum's brother slid a little note into my hand as I stood on the mat outside their house waiting for Lizzie to join me. When I opened it I read: 'Dear Molly, I was asking for you.' I screwed it up and threw it back at him. 'What a stupid thing to write,' I thought, angrily. And then, at the very idea of his regarding this as a letter, I began to laugh. His face grew scarlet, and then in mounting amazement I noticed him mouthing something. What was he trying to say? I stared at his contorted lips. 'Give us a kiss,' he was miming. I pretended I couldn't understand his fierce grimacing and mouthing, and marched out of the close. 'I'm not coming for you again, Lizzie,' I informed his surprised sister. 'You'll just have to climb the stairs and come up for me.' 'But why?' she protested. 'It's easier for you to come for me, because I live in the close and you've to come downstairs anyway.' 'I don't care,' I said. 'Your brother's daft, and I'm not coming to your door again.'

And I didn't. Every time I saw him afterwards I burst out laughing to cover my embarrassment at the mere thought of kissing that contorted mouth. I was probably influenced by Grannie's short sharp treatment of one schoolboy who had tried to make me a present of a puppy. He had brought it to our door, and Grannie had seized the broom and swept him from the mat, puppy and all. Poor David. I didn't dare look at him in school after that. He was English, his father having been transferred to our Railways, and he didn't realise it was soft to carry on like this, especially as I was about ten at the time. I didn't reason that Grannie wanted no truck with a puppy which would have to be fed and exercised and which would add to her work. I just took it that I was not to bother my head

41

with boys, who were only a nuisance anyway, so Lizzie's brother received only scorn from me. I didn't even like being teased about boys. One sure way of rousing me to fury, as he well knew, was for a neighbour of ours to pretend he had seen me from his kitchen window playing in the playground at school with a wee bandy-legged boy. 'Aye,' he would say dreamily, 'I saw ye tak' yer cheuch Jean from yer mooth, and gi'e him a wee sook at it, and then take it back again.' 'I did *not*,' I would shout angrily. 'I widnae dae any such thing.' 'Och aye, I saw ye a' right,' the old man would say, 'and a bonnie sicht it wis. He's a nice wee fella in spite o' his bandy legs.' I would be near to tears by this time, and baffled by the impossibility of making anybody believe me when an adult said such untrue things. Then he would relent and say, 'Och weel, maybe it wisnae you efter a', maybe it wis Ellie Cairns.' As Ellie Cairns was about six inches taller than I was, and twice as fat, I felt everybody would think the old man was just letting me down lightly, pretending to mistake somebody so different for me, and that in the end they *would* believe I'd been playing with the bandy-legged Joe, and sharing my toffee ball with him. When I complained about this to my mother, protesting, 'But, Mother, it's such *lies* Mr. Simpson tells,' she just laughed. 'Och it's only his fun. What does it maitter. You should just laugh at him and he would soon stop tormenting you. It's because he kens you'll get your dander up that he does it.' But her words fell on deaf ears. I wasn't wise enough to pretend I didn't care, and had to content myself with dodging Mr. Simpson when I could.

How betrayed I felt one night when I came in from playing up the High Road, when Grannie was still alive, and had found Mr. Simpson actually sitting in our house chatting to her. He'd called on somebody upstairs with a messege, and Grannie had been at the door when he was on his way down again. He had marched in and sat himself down at the fire, and produced his whisky bottle and poured out a glass for Grannie. When I appeared she handed it to me, with a whispered, 'Put it in the press, hen, I canna drink a' this whisky.' I, as a Rechabite, was horrified at the idea of my grannie sitting consuming whisky with this torment of an old man, and neither of them ill, for the fiery spirit was only consumed in our house in case of ill-health. 'Will I pour it doon the sink, Grannie,' I asked eagerly, seizing the glass from her hand. 'You'll dae nothing o' the kind,' she'd answered fiercely, forgetting to whisper. 'Pit it in the press as ye're tellt, and it'll dae us as medicine for the rest o' the winter.' I wanted to pour the hated Mr. Simpson's whisky down the sink in front of his very eyes, but I didn't dare rebel against Grannie's wishes, so I put it in the press beside the sugar, and hoped somebody would knock it over when they went in to get the things to set the table.

I felt there was no end to the mischief this wicked old man could make, what with tormenting me and then encouraging my own grannie to indulge in the evils of strong drink. I couldn't think of a single way of getting my own back, unless maybe I wouldn't go to see him when he was dead and lying in his coffin.

4

In our childhood, death wasn't hidden away as an obscenity from which we must all be protected. It was on calling terms in the tenements, and came at any age and at any time, and not just in old age. It was always good for a bit of drama to brighten up all our lives, not least being the details of how the loved one had passed away.

We would listen, enthralled, to tales of 'She sat up and gazed at the ceiling, as if she was seeing something we couldn't see, and then she gave a beautiful smile and breathed her last.' Oh how marvellous, we felt, how peaceful! We hoped we would be lucky enough to pass to the other side with such a welcome smile on our own lips. When wee bedridden Donald had died his mother told us he had looked up over the top of the wardrobe and cried, 'Mammy, Mammy, I can see the children playing in the sky, and they've all got wings. Oh I'm so tired, Mammy, it will be lovely to have wings to lift me up and take me everywhere without walking,' and then he had held out his arms and laughed, and passed away. How could we be sad at wee Donald's release when he had been able to pass on to us what heaven was like before he had joined the angels?

I couldn't reconcile those stories with the sight of a neighbour's dying husband whom I had seen when I went in to deliver some messages for her, and which had so unnerved me that I had been unable to eat for days afterwards. That was an exception, I decided, the ones who happily left for heaven must be the rule.

We all believed with utter conviction that we would all meet again in heaven afterwards, and we were only too willing to be convinced by the dying visions that the happy land truly existed, and the sight of it to glazing eyes would make the

44

prospect of leaving home and family very easy to bear. This familiarity with the grim reaper who visited the tenements so frequently, and our trust and confidence in life after death, armed us against a too-consuming grief. Death seldom came as a bolt from the blue, to find us unprepared, so we were able to cope with it. And the rituals we followed helped the bereaved to get over their grief. Mourning neighbours would have been very hurt if we had shown no interest in the corpse which lay coffined on the big table in the best room, where no fire burned during the three days of lying in state, and where the chill air struck to the heart as we entered to pay our respects, especially in winter. Bodies were not hidden away in chapels of rest in our childhood. They were on view for everyone to visit, and we went to see every corpse in our tenement, from babies to old men, and nobody thought it might be unseemly for children to have to face such things in the midst of play. Life had to be faced, and death too, and we thought it right that our loved ones stayed under our roof until the moment came for burial, and that everyone should want to gaze on their faces for the last time before they went from us to the cemetery. The quality of the coffins was a subject of much comment, and the women would agree that 'she had given him a beautiful send-off, with that polished mahogany coffin with the lovely handles and pure silk cords'. Penny a week insurance policies were taken out even before a birth certificate was obtained, to make certain of a proper burial. To have to be buried on the parish was felt to be a great disgrace. The women pursed their lips over one old woman, too poor or feckless even to afford the penny insurance. 'Ah well,' she would say cheerfully, 'if they don't bury me for decency they'll bury me for stink.' This was a dreadful attitude, everyone said, and the remarks on beautiful coffins were very pointed when she was in the company. For didn't everyone know parish coffins were made from orange boxes? One of the famous phrases of our childhood, often used by music-hall comics in lighter mood, was, 'Wid onybody like a last look at the corpse before he's screwed doon?' We saw nothing funny in these words used by the undertaker before the final solemn carrying out of the body, but could recognise the humour of the situation, of course, when applied to a drunk man on the stage.

I was always struck with the chill dignity of people in death.

Their remote calm completely transformed them from the flesh-and-blood people I had known and perhaps played with. Adults lifted us children up to place a hand on the brow of the corpse, because this was said to prevent nightmares afterwards, but in my case it induced them, and I used to shudder with fear at actually making physical contact with those waxen faces. 'No, no,' I would whimper, 'I don't want to touch wee Jimmy's forehead. No, I don't care if I get nightmares. No, no, no.' If I were forced to lay a hand on a clammy brow I felt haunted for weeks afterwards. It was considered a terrible disgrace to be so reluctant to touch anybody's loved one, and nobody else seemed to mind. I couldn't understand myself why I didn't mind looking at corpses, but yet couldn't bear to touch them.

The Irish Catholics held wakes, which struck us as being very heathenish. Fancy sitting up all night, all those men and women and children, drinking and carousing as if it was a party! It was even hinted that bottles of whisky were put in beside the corpse in case he was buried alive, and he'd have a wee drop to comfort him when he found himself under the cold clay. 'Buried alive'! That haunted many of us, and we listened, trembling, to stories of coffins having been dug up and the corpses turned over on their faces, or eyes staring with terror, and clawed marks on the coffin lid where they had scrabbled to get out. Cremation was practically unknown in my childhood, and certainly unthinkable for working-class people, but those stories of people being buried alive so tormented me that I made everybody promise, especially during the period following Grannie's death when it was predicted I 'wouldn't make old bones', that when I died they would see to it, 'cross their hearts and hope to die', that I was well and truly cremated. Of course they all promised, and although I felt sure they wouldn't have the least idea how to go about it, I was reasonably comforted. Nobody had to invent terrors for us, we invented them for ourselves, and not a soul worried about the effect on our young minds of all those macabre tales. And they were right. For as time wore on we forgot them, and, apart from the Irish wakes, accepted all the rituals of the next funeral with undiminished zeal.

We had a lot of Irish people beside us, who had come over to work in Glasgow, and my mother always described them as coming 'from the bog'. I used to picture them walking with feet sucking at wet peat to get to us. They greatly amused us by taking a long time to get accustomed to tenement life, and it used to be many months before they realised they were walking on good linoleum, and that they mustn't just chuck down their tea-leaves on the kitchen floor to empty the pot, for there was no turf floor in Springburn to soak all the lees up.

Their vocabulary was a source of entertainment too. One of the mothers came charging into the back court one day and demanded, 'Hiv ye seen John's faddle?' 'His whit?' we asked. 'His faddle. He had it not ten minits ago, and one of you spalpeens has taken it, so ye have.' We stared at each other in perplexity. What could a faddle be? 'Whit is it like?' I asked her, inspired, for a description seemed the only way we could find out. 'It's a wee thing, made o' silver, and ye blow it like this,' and she stuck her comb into her mouth and blew out and sucked in. We rocked with laughter. 'Ye mean a mooth-organ,' we gasped. Oh these Irish were comics and no mistake. Fancy calling a moothie a faddle! And then I laughed even harder, for as I said the word, it dawned on me she was saying 'fiddle' with her Irish accent. She thought a mouth-organ was a fiddle. Aye, my mother was right, they came from the bog, all right, but you had to like them, they were so funny. They didn't even go down on their knees to wash out the closes, as the other women did, they stood upright, then bent over double from the waist so that we could all see their bloomers as they swished back and forth with a soaking wet cloth. 'My heavens, you could swim through the close when thae Irish have washed it,' the women would tut-tut in vexation, 'and the weans tramp a' that water right up to the top flat.' However often they were told, they refused to get down on their knees, for the cold stone struck them as hard and unyielding compared with the soft earth they had come from in Ireland. So we sighed and put up with it, glad that ours weren't the 'dirty Irish' and at least knew the value of soap and water.

We always thought we knew the best way of doing everything, from washing closes with well-wrung-out cloths, to making briquettes to stoke the fire from sugar bags filled with dampened coal-dust. But if there was one field where we felt we excelled above all others it was in the matter of home cures.

Doctors were only called in when all else had failed. Apart from the cost, we had great faith in the folk medicine which had been handed down to us from one generation to the next.

For whooping cough the favourite cure was to suspend the victim over a tar-boiler, or 'torry-biler', as we called them. During an epidemic of the 'whoop' it only needed a whiff of the boiling tar to send us rushing home. 'Mammy,' we would pant, 'the torry-biler's here. Do you want to haud Willie ower it to cure his whoop?'

Mothers would seize unwilling victims and drag them from the house—no one was keen on having this cure himself, but all thoroughly enjoyed the sight of others getting it. Soon there would be a procession of mothers, patiently queuing to hold the spluttering child over the boiling, bubbling inferno, smoking like hell itself.

'Take big breaths, son,' they would urge. 'Draw it right doon into yer chest, and you'll no' cough any mair.' The victim, gasping at the sudden rush of tarry smoke which threatened to choke him, would cease coughing from sheer fright. Mothers would nod with triumphant smiles at each other, well satisfied that this free cure had worked once more.

Mind you, there were terrible tales of butter-fingered mothers who had allowed wriggling children to fall right into the bubbling pitch, later to be extricated coated forever in a deadly black embalming jacket. We'd never actually *known* anyone to whom this had happened, but the mere thought that it *might* have happened, and could do so again, was enough to make us stifle the slighest cough whenever we had occasion to pass the tar-boiler in company with an adult.

It was this added risk which made the sight of other children held high over the tar take on the excitement of a horror film. We would watch them with our breaths held in suspense until each little victim had feet planted safely on the pavement again. Only then would we resume our play, finding some of the soft tar to make 'torry-balls', which we rolled between our palms. Hardened in cold water, we used them like marbles for our games.

Some more fanciful mothers, with influential relatives, managed to get a card which admitted them to the gasworks, and swore by the effectiveness of the fumes there. The children were marched into the retort chamber, then instructed to climb upstairs and inhale deeply, to allow the gas fumes to circulate in their wheezing chests. It seemed to work, too, in spite of the envious sneers of those who couldn't get cards to take them inside the gasworks, and who declared it was just the diversion of the journey and the excitement of getting inside this impressive building which cured the weans.

One horrible scourge in our tenements was ringworm. I caught it myself, because a wee girl in my class at school fancied the tammy knitted for me by Grannie. She snatched it off my peg and pranced around the playground with it the whole of playtime one day, before I could grab it back. I jammed it firmly over my own curls and wore it in school the rest of the morning in case she would run away with it, for I knew Grannie would be mad if I lost it. What I didn't know was that the cheeky wee girl had ringworm and the infection had found a new home in my scalp! Home cures were no good this time and I was hauled off to the doctor, where every curl was cut off, then my head was shaved, and a bottle of iodine poured over it. I was taken to that surgery every Sunday, which was the one day my mother could spare from work, and more iodine poured over until the infection was killed. Oh the shame and misery of that shaved head! To be a skinhead in our tenements meant only one thing—ringworm! It shouted aloud as though I had carried a bell, and intoned 'Unclean, unclean', and left such a mark on my mind that I could never again be persuaded to let anybody try on my hats, nor would I even try one on in a shop afterwards, in case anybody with ringworm had been there before me.

Another head invasion, almost impossible to avoid in the tenements, was nits and head lice. The sight of fingers scratching at our heads was the signal for my mother to send us down without delay to the chemist for some quassia chips. These wee wood-shaving-like things were boiled up in water and the liquor strained off, and then a comb was dipped in the brew and drawn from root to tip of our hair. This went on for days, till all the eggs were tracked down, but unlike the iodine, which was drastic on hair roots, the quassia chips brew gave the hair a lovely gloss.

Borrowed combs were said to be the cause of spreading nits from one to another, and for a while we'd remember never to lend anybody our comb, then freedom from itch would make us careless—we'd lend our comb, and the quassia chips went on to boil again.

Worms was another affliction of our infants. It was quite usual to hear big brothers or sisters asking the chemist for a 'worm powder for my wee sister'. 'How old is she?' the chemist would inquire, unmoved at the thought of a human being having worms. I used to shudder at the thought of those wriggly things in anybody's inside, and wondered how they got in there in the first place. It was whispered that pieces spread with oatmeal and sugar resulted in worms, but I liked this concoction so much I refused to believe such a tale.

We all believed implicitly that the huge jars on the chemist's shelves, filled with orange or royal-blue liquid, held the unborn babies till the mothers came into the shop to buy them. We'd stare intently at those bottles, imagining we could see the tiny infant shape swimming about in this glamorous liquid.

We were most interested in each other's purchases and could diagnose each ailment from the goods bought. Gregory's Mixture, declared by my mother as a marvellous cure-all, meant somebody's stomach was out of order. 'Enough to cover a sixpence' was the recognised dose. This was stirred in cold water and swallowed as rapidly as possible, for the smell was awful, and it helped to keep it down if the nose was held firmly as the nauseous drink was imbibed.

If the stomach wasn't too badly upset, and the discomfort could merely have been a touch of wind, then a pinch of baking soda in water was highly favoured by all of us. I quite liked this. It had a sort of flavour of puff candy, and the ensuing belches or 'rifts' were warmly encouraged, instead of being frowned upon as downright bad manners if heard at any other time.

For lazy bowels, my mother's favourite cure was senna pods, or 'seenie pods' as we called them. I liked to be allowed to float the flat dry shapes in the tumbler of water, and was fascinated to find it transformed to a nice tea-coloured mixture next day. And it took no coaxing at all to get us to take sugarally water. This was made by putting a wee piece of jet-black Spanish liquorice in the bottom of a medicine bottle, topping it up with water, and a spoonful of sugar, and shaking it for hours until the brew turned dark brown. We used to chant a wee rhyme as we shook the bottle:

> 'Sugar-ally waater,
> As black as the Lum,
> Gether up peens,
> An' ye'll a' get some.'

Sometimes we sat it on top of the range to let the warmth draw out the flavour more quickly. A lovely fine froth formed on the top, and we sucked the sweet black liquor through this. Mmmm, it was delicious, and it seemed impossible to believe it could be doing us good at the same time.

Castor oil was used only as a last desperate remedy, for we all hated it. Everybody had patent ideas as to how to make it more palatable. Some swore by a wee drop of milk sipped just before and after the oil, making a sort of buffer sandwich which would disguise the foul taste. The magic didn't work for me. I still 'reached' and 'boked' in misery. Others favoured disguising it in orange juice, but in my opinion the oil wasn't disguised by the juice, but the juice entirely ruined by the smelly oil, and a good orange was never sacrificed in this way in our house.

The only way I could stomach it was to hold my nose in a pincer-like grip, swallow it down, and then lie flat and avoid any unnecessary movement for about ten minutes. Grannie thought this excellent behaviour, especially as it ensured the oil staying down and not having to go through the whole drama again, as well as being a saving of a second lot of oil.

But I never minded the magic of castor oil in getting grit out of the eye. I'd be playing with my gird, or my peever, and whoosh! a lump which felt as big as a marble would land in my eye. I'd drop everything in my anguish, and, eye red and puffy, sniffing and squinting, run upstairs. Grannie would take one look at me and reach for the castor oil and one of her steel knitting needles. I'd lie back in the big chair, head tilted over the side of it. 'Noo don't move,' Grannie would command me, 'or you'll get the needle in yer eye.'

Still as a mouse I'd crouch, while Grannie inserted the knitting needle in the castor-oil bottle. Then, holding the needle above my eye, which I was holding open as wide as I could, the drop of that blessed oil would be skilfully guided by Grannie's steady hand right under the lid, and in a second came relief. The rock had floated out, the raw eyelid was soothed, and I was ready for play again.

Sometimes it was my turn to administer our home cures to Grannie. When bronchitis threatened, I'd warm my hands at the fire and then smooth warmed camphorated oil gently over her wheezy chest. 'No' too hard noo,' she'd gasp. 'Just rub it weel in, but dinna scart me wi' yer claws.'

'Claws, Grannie!' I'd say indignantly. 'Ah hivnae got claws.' But I'd be careful, and then I'd put a layer of lovely pink Thermogene on top. This was an airy-fairy material which seemed to do Grannie a lot of good, but it was terribly wasteful and had to be burned when it had done its magic, for it couldn't be washed.

We knew Grannie was gey bad when she wanted Thermogene, for that was the last resort before we sent for the doctor. At three-and-six a visit this was delayed until the last possible moment, and often the camphorated oil and Thermogene saved us sending for him, for it did the trick, and Grannie would be breathing easily in no time at all.

For the wee tickly cough she sometimes got she liked Victory Vee lozenges. These fiery cough sweeties were reasonably safe from marauding small fingers, but we loved her other favourite cough-soother, acid drops. We were always coaxing her for one when we thought my mother was out of earshot.

For our own coughs, my mother pinned her faith on emulsion. To me it tasted like Brasso, but we had to swallow a spoonful every day in winter to prevent colds. I didn't demur, though, when it came to the spring tonic and her other standby, Parrish's Chemical Food. Sweet and sticky, and a lovely red colour, I could hardly credit such a pleasant-tasting beverage could possibly do me all the good my mother swore it would.

For that other scourge of winter, chilblains, everybody had a different cure. The Spartans among us declared that to run barefoot in the snow shocked the fiery chilblains into submission and, what was more, kept them at bay for the rest of the winter. Others thought a plaster of mustard and paraffin most efficacious, and gladly endured the smell of paraffin which clung to socks and bedclothes for ages.

One old woman in the next close declared there was nothing better than the inside of a banana skin laid coolly on the chilblain to draw out the heat and effect a miraculous cure. My mother preferred Snowfire, that nice inexpensive green block, shiny and greasy, which was also a certain cure for the hacks we got on knees and knuckles on dank wintry days. Oh the agony of my serge skirt slapping round my hacked knees to the point of rawness and bleeding, and then the blessed relief of that healing Snowfire. I shuddered with sympathy for the children who had hacks on their heels, for these were most difficult to close. Everybody agreed goose-fat was the best remedy for this painful condition, but as hardly anybody in the tenements had ever seen a goose, much less eaten one, ordinary lard had to do.

We all shared the nightmare of toothache, and agreed with Rabbie Burns, strong language and all, that it was 'the hell o' a' diseases'. Apart from the fact that it cost two-and-six to have a tooth extracted, we were all terrified of the dentist, and only the punishing agony of a tooth rotten beyond the solace of our home-made remedies would drive us to his chamber of horrors. I quite enjoyed oil of cloves, the flavour strongly reminding me of Grannie's delicious apple tarts, but Sloan's Liniment had a heat and bite when rubbed inside and outside my cheek which brought tears to my eyes.

Adults swore to the relief afforded by a tiny drop of whisky dropped into the throbbing cavity, and once, when my own toothache had reached the unendurable stage, I was permitted a tiny drop of the golden brew. Not nearly so nice as cloves or myrrh, in my opinion, but strangely effective.

If the toothache developed into a gumboil, a favourite cure was heated salt inside an old sock laid gently against the swollen cheek. This was the cure, too, for a sore throat, and it was quite a performance heating the salt on a shovel, then guiding it into the sock with the aid of a big spoon, making all possible speed before the salt cooled. It was slapped against the sufferer's throat, and yells of 'It's too *hoat!*' met with the invariable reply, 'It *has* to be hoat to do ye ony good.' A scarlet neck, stiffly held away from a chafing collar, was mute testimony next day that the victim had been right. It *had* been too hot.

It was seldom that the hot-salt-sock cure was required a

second night. When asked how the throat fared the reply usually came surprisingly swiftly, 'Ma throat's fine noo.' It seemed to me marvellous how one hot sock was such a powerful cure.

Hiccups, which my mother for some reason called 'hippocs', while they could be painful, were always regarded as something of a joke. A fright was considered the best cure, but as we always frightened each other anyway with our tales of Flannel Feet, and the Cowlairs Swifts, it was difficult to think up anything which could take a sufferer by surprise.

'Hold your nose,' we'd urge the sufferer, 'and drink a cup of water upside down.' The contortions which followed before it was realised that what was meant was simply drinking fom the opposite side of the glass had the amateur doctors in hysterics, sometimes to the point of taking hiccups themselves. Some set great store by pinching the ear-lobe while drinking water, but others favoured pinching the very tip of the nose.

When the nose itself gave trouble and blood poured forth dramatically there was only one cure—the wash-house key, ice-cold, pushed down the back of the patient's neck.

You could always borrow a wee rub of wintergreen from any of our tenement houses, for it was considered effective against all winter's aches and pains. We had read in books about iodine and camphor lockets for chest ailments and rheumatism, but this struck us as very fanciful, and we were more inclined to believe the testimony of the old folks, who swore to the effectiveness of a piece of raw potato carried in the pocket. Raw potato was also good against warts, as was the fasting spittle.

Rheumatism was an old people's disease, and anaemia a young one's trouble. Sometimes, when I was a bit anaemic after 'flu, I'd have to take Blaud's Pills. I found these so difficult to swallow that my mother was driven to try to break them on the kitchen table, using the poker as a cleaver. Those attempts dented our table for all time, and when the question of pills was raised as a cure for anything she would stare accusingly at the marks, and tell the story all over again of how thrawn I was at refusing to gulp down such a wee pill. But an uncle gave us a good laugh by coming to my defence with the suggestion that maybe I had a wee throat like a whale, which balked even at a tomato skin. 'She's certainly got a memory like an elephant,' retorted my mother, 'so maybe she's got a throat like a whale. Onywey, she's ruined my good table.'

For her own persistent affliction, blinding headaches, my mother found nothing better than a cloth dipped in vinegar, which I placed over her eyes as she stretched out on the bed. As the cloth dried, I'd dip it again and again in the saucer of vinegar, and soon she would drift off to sleep, soothed by this pungent bandage.

One old lady told me that when she was a wee girl her mother's cure for all the ills that God could send was the 'traycle' tin. This was a tin filled nearly to the top with black treacle, and it was put on top of the range to make it warm and runny. Into it went a big spoonful of Epsom salts, one of senna powder, one of Gregory's powder, and a pinch of sulphur. Then the lot was well stirred, round and round, and the whole family had a teaspoonful every night till the tin was empty. The taste was horrible, she told me, and the grit stuck to their teeth, but not a lad in the family ever suffered from pimples, and they all had clear and smooth skins, and required no other medicine throughout the year.

5

It was great to be back at school again. I could never understand why some of my chums hated it, for I enjoyed every moment, marching upstairs to the rollicking tunes pounded out on the piano by the youngest schoolteacher, wheeling off to our separate classrooms, and starting off the day with a hymn 'Jesus loves me', or 'Who is on the Lord's side?', or 'Dare to be a Daniel', roared out with enthusiasm.

Our school was a red sandstone building, new and modern in its day, with handsome heavy gates and matching railings, and a lovely big playground. A huge drill-hall filled the centre of the ground floor, and all the classrooms branched off this to house the younger schoolchildren. A gallery ran right round the upper floor, and the classrooms of the bigger children led off this gallery. At one end, high in the wall, was the big clock which kept perfect time. This clock was the pride and joy of the 'Jannie', as we called the school janitor. Not only did he keep it well oiled and correct to a second, but it was his duty to ring the bell underneath the clock to announce playtimes and lunchtimes.

When the morning seemed interminable, and one had to 'leave the room', it was a reassuring sight to see the janitor standing by the clock, poised in readiness for the exact minute to sound the bell, and to know that release was near.

I don't think I ever put my hand up to utter the parrot sentence 'Please may I leave the room?' to indicate urgent need to go out to the toilet, all the time I was at school. For one thing, I wouldn't have missed a second of my lessons, and for another I was curiously shy about letting anybody know that the lavatory was my goal. We had one boy in our class who loathed history lessons, and as soon as the teacher announced that we could put away our jotters and take out our history books his hand shot up. The entire class knew he was only going to race round the playground for the next half-hour, but the teacher never tumbled to it, and I expect he went through his whole school life without knowing a thing that happened before the first world war. We used to catch one another's eyes as he sauntered towards the door, and we'd press our lips together to keep from giggling, for we wouldn't give him away, but we were baffled that the teacher could have been so blind as not to notice that Billy never reappeared until he had heard us safely finish our chanting 'The Battle of Bannockburn was fought in 1314', 'The battle of Flodden was fought in 1513', and 'The battle of Waterloo was fought in 1815'. As the last echoes of long-forgotten battles died away, Billy slipped through the door and took his place in class once more, ready to continue his education.

The mid-morning playtime was, I suppose, really to allow us to make ourselves comfortable, but we wouldn't have dreamed of wasting valuable time on mere toilets. Those who had 'left the room' in school-time were already comfortable, and few of the others gave such matters a thought. Our minds were on the opportunity for a quick game of skipping ropes, or high and low water on the low school wall, or chases, or the forbidden unholy joy of sliding down the coal-bunkers. The rusty hinges were a terrible hazard to school bloomers, and Grannie used to be mystified as to how I could cause such ragged tears in mine if I was behaving myself as I ought. I never dared tell her of the coal-bunker games or she'd have warmed my ears for me.

Apart from those of us who threw ourselves energetically into the games, there were the handful whom I secretly despised, and called under my breath 'tumphies'. Their mothers were ranged outside the school gates, and they fed and nourished the 'tumphies' through the bars as though they were animals in a zoo. I shuddered at the mere idea of such mollycoddling and was glad my own mother was safely at work and couldn't be tempted to such outrages. These cosseted ones usually had scarves tied over their school caps, or their tammies, to give extra warmth, a fashion I wouldn't have been seen dead in, and I'd snort contemptuously as I saw little cans of tea or cocoa passed through the bars, followed by buttered rolls, or toast, or slices of cake.

It was due to Grannie that I was so disapproving of such goings-on, for when I had told her about the mothers outside the railings she had snorted, 'Spoilt, fair spoilt. It's a wonder their mothers havenae anything better tae dae than tae waste their time putting their weans off their dinners. Just making them soft, that's all.'

I was so sure Grannie was right that I wouldn't even take a play-piece with me and eat it during games, as most of my chums did. My appetite was undimmed by any mid-morning indulgence, and I flew home at lunchtime ravenous. Grannie knew I wouldn't loiter on the way, hunger lending speed to my legs, and she'd have the mince and tatties on the table, or the soup, good broth, followed by the beef the soup had been made with, and mashed tatties and turnip. Sometimes it was sausages, and sometimes it was tripe, but it was always good, and always eaten with enthusiasm. Nothing had crossed my lips since my early-morning roll at breakfast-time, and I was more than ready for whatever was put before me.

Because my hands and face weren't sticky or dirty with play-time pieces, my adored Miss Oliver selected me to take the attendance figures of the entire school each morning at eleven o'clock playtime, and again in the afternoon at the three o'clock playtime break. I felt bursting with importance as I raced round from class to class, a stiff-backed folder under one arm, and the teacher's beautifully sharpened pencil lent to me to mark down the numbers there were in each class. These attendance figures were chalked on a small blackboard outside each room, so that I needn't disturb anyone if I were a few minutes early or late and the teacher busy with her class. I would then swiftly add up all the numbers, and arrive at the total number of children at school that morning, and then again that afternoon, and absentees were checked against the figures when I took my folder to the staff-room for safe keeping in the file there. It was strange to see all the teachers there, drinking tea and nibbling at biscuits. Tea! Fancy having time to make tea at playtime. It always seemed far too short when we were tearing about at our games, for it to have been possible to have brought a kettle to the boil and infused tea, and poured it out, but they had managed it somehow. My eyes darted about, trying to solve this mystery, and then I spied a gas-ring roaring away at full pelt under a kettle, no doubt for washing up their dirty cups, and realised that of course that was why they could have tea so quickly. They didn't have to wait for water to heat over the coal in the range, as we did at home. Schools had tons of money and it would be nothing to them to pay for that expensive roaring gas which provided the boiling water for their tea.

I was never offered as much as a sip of their tea, and would have been horrified if I had been. Teachers were teachers, and pupils were pupils, and a wide gulf yawned between. I was uneasy to see them at such unguarded moments, drinking and eating, and was glad to be dismissed with an 'All right, Molly back to your room now.' I never followed those attendance figures to their conclusion, when they eventually reached the headmaster's desk, and the truants were reported to the 'School Board'. I was in great awe of male authority, and shuddered at the mere idea of 'plunking' school and having one of those dread creatures come to the house to demand what was keeping me from my education. But many others had no such scruples, and cheerfully accepted the wallopings they received from mothers or fathers who had had to face the 'School Board', as we called the truant officer, and try to explain why their boy or girl hadn't been at school.

Only dire necessity ever kept me at home, either my own illness or Grannie's, and then I would return with a wee note; 'Please excuse Molly, but she was required at home', or 'Please excuse Molly but she was in bed with a severe cold'. This was accepted without argument, because everybody knew that books and learning were meat and drink to me. Not so some of the others, poor things, who were known as regular defaulters, and whose notes were perused with a quizzical eye, and doubts cast as to who had actually written them. We all felt sorry for the boy or girl as the teacher's eye mercilessly scanned the note, for a lie on top of absenteeism could only end in the strap, and crossed hands at that to make it sting even more. Some of the teachers were suspected of dipping their leather tawse in whisky to make them bite with a fiery fury, but I could never imagine any teacher wasting expensive whisky in this way when the leather strap was quite painful enough without a thing being added to it. I only ever had the strap once, and I was deeply ashamed, so vexed indeed that I never breathed a word of it at home to let them know I had fallen from grace. The teacher had gone out during a drawing lesson, and left us to continue with our crayoned attempts to copy an orange. The girl next to me had a tiny glass tube filled with 'hundreds and thousands', those little coloured sugar dots no bigger than a pinhead, which had clogged together and refused to come out, however hard she sucked. Trying to help her, I hit the bottom of the tube sharply, and the whole lot shot out in a wet blob, soaked with her saliva, and landed right in the middle of her drawing, exactly at the point where the orange stalk had been. Under our horrified gaze, the coloured sugar began to run, and in a minute the orange looked as if it were affected by a horrible scabby disease. We dared not touch it in case we got it all over our clothes, and we knew the teacher would be furious with us for spoiling the precious sheet in our drawing book. Fear made us hysterical, and as we caught one another's eye, we burst into peals of laughter which we simply couldn't control. The girls in the back row crowded round to see what we were laughing at. We held our sides, and gasped out an explanation between bursts of giggles. It was infectious and soon the entire class was shouting with abandoned laughter.

The door opened, and the teacher walked in. 'What is the meaning of this?' she demanded. The rest of the class fell silent, but my neighbour and I were well beyond control now. Tears of laughter poured down our cheeks. We shook, and our voices squeaked as we tried to speak. The teacher walked slowly up to us, her eyes disbelieving that I, her pet, had actually been the cause of this unseemly noise. She looked at the drawing, tightened her lips, and bade us both come out to the front of the class. There was not a sound in the room now. Nobody had ever seen me get the strap, and I felt sick and bewildered that I could have got myself into this terrible situation. How would I stand up to it? I wondered. Suppose I shamed myself by bursting into tears in front of the whole class? The tears threatened to come even before the strap was drawn from the desk, and I opened my eyes as wide as possible to stop them from forming in a humiliating shower. Oh how I envied those who were able to swagger out and hold out their hands, with an arrogant wink to the rest of us. I prayed soundlessly, 'Oh God, please let me not cry. Please let me not cry in front of everybody.' The teacher was drawing the tawse through her hands and looking at me. 'I had expected better of you, Molly,' she said. 'I expected you, as top of the class, to know better.

What do you suppose would have happened if the inspector had been coming today, instead of tomorrow? He'd have thought I had a class of hyenas!' The rest of the class, sitting safely in their seats, ventured a little giggle at this witticism. She turned on them sharply. 'You were all just as bad, so be quiet, and let this be a lesson to you.' She raised the strap, I held out a shaking hand and shut my eyes. The strap fell gently on to my rigid palm. I had heard if you held your hand as stiffly as possible it didn't hurt so badly. I didn't feel anything. I was still praying. Quietly the teacher said, 'Go back to your seat now.' I opened my eyes and stared at her. Only one stroke of the strap. Sometimes she gave as many as six. I looked at my hand. There wasn't a mark on it, not so much as a pink flush where the strap had fallen, no hurt at all. Only my pride had been bruised and splintered. But my prayers had been answered. I hadn't cried.

When we had settled down to our drawings again the teacher began walking round behind the desks to see how we were getting on, and when she reached us she showed Margaret how to blot off the worst of the sticky mess and cover in the rest with shading, and in the end the inspector seemed to notice nothing when he came to inspect our work next day. When she looked at my work she laid a hand on my shoulder and pressed it comfortingly, and the hard knot in my stomach warmed and loosened, and the blackness of my disgrace lightened a little. And the tears which I had conquered so successfully now burst their dyke, but nobody could see them as I bent lower and lower over my page and filled in the shadows round the orange with delicate little strokes.

The inspector who examined our general work was bad enough, but the one I dreaded most was the music inspector. He had been in the war, and wounds had left him with one side of his face twisted, and the lower lid of his eye was pulled down in such a way that he looked as if he was permanently leering. For some reason he liked my husky voice, and after we had sung our class songs, 'I saw three ships a-sailing', 'She left her baby lying there', 'When I'm lonely dear white heart', he would tell us to sit down. Then, tapping his tuning fork against his other hand, he would say 'What about Molly Weir singing "Robin Adair" for us?' 'I've got a sore throat,' I would whisper. Terror had so gripped me that I indeed sounded as if

I were in the throes of a bout of laryngitis. But he knew perfectly well that it was sheer fright which was making me hoarse, and he ignored my excuses. 'We'll find the right key for you, eh?' he would say, striking the tuning fork against the desk, and making me forget my fears in the magic of this little instrument which could produce such a sweet note when it was laid gently upended on the desk as now. Sweetly the note sounded, he'd raise his hands, and I would keep my eyes firmly fixed on my music book, pretending I didn't know the words, so that I needn't look at him and be reminded that I was standing up all by myself in class singing a solo. He also liked me to sing 'Jock o' Hazeldene' and Grannie's favourite, 'The Rowan Tree'. The rest of the class were sympathetic, and used to commiserate with me afterwards. 'Aye, he's got it in fur you a' right, Molly,' they would say. 'Thank goodness it's no' us he asks to staun up an' sing. Jeez, it must be terrible.' And it was. Nobody, least of all me, regarded it as a compliment that a music inspector should request a solo—I regarded it as a punishment and I spent anguished hours wondering what I could possibly have done to make him torture me like this.

We never sang the class songs outside the classroom, but we had a fund of little songs which pleased us because of their funny words or comical rhymes. We would join hands in a circle in the playground and chant, giggling foolishly at the end,

> 'S-O, so, ma big toe,
> Fell in the sugar-bowl,
> And Ah didnae know.'

This was followed by:

> 'Sent fur the doctor, he widnae come,
> Sent fur the ambulance, pum, pum, pum.'

· One day we were so carried away with ourselves we sang the words louder and louder, and faster and faster, as we raced round in our circle, until a classroom window was thrown up and Mr. McAllister's furious face appeared. 'Be quiet, you big girls,' he yelled in a frenzy, 'or move to another playground.' We were stunned into complete silence that he had heard us yelling such idiotic words, and crept away to the other end of the sheds where we could intone, without bothering anybody,

'Come a riddle, come a riddle, come a roat, toat, toat,
A wee wee man, wi' a rid, rid coat.
A stave in his haun' an' a stane in his throat,
Come a riddle, come a riddle, come a roat, toat, toat.'

We had some that we sang far from school ears, because we knew the teachers frowned on our dialect, and we were never absolutely sure what they regarded as vulgar. So we kept for the back courts or Paddy Oar's park such ditties as:

'Ma Maw's a millionaire,
Blue eyes and curly hair,
Hokey, pokey, penny a lump,
That's the stuff tae make ye jump,
Ma Maw's a millionaire.'

And when we followed the watering cart, with its lovely spraying jets to lay the dust, we burst into:

'Ah'm gaun doon the toon,
Ah know wha's gaun wi' me,
Ah've a wee laud o' ma ain,
An' they ca' him Bonnie Jimmy.
He took me to a soirée,
He took me to a supper,
Him an' I fell oot,
An' ah dipped his nose in the butter.'

And there was a marvellous bit of rhyming selling which we all learnt by heart from a man who used to sell things at the corner of Vulcan Street, by the marble fountain, every Friday night:

'For you've all seen a cork in a bottle,
But you've never seen a bottle in a cork.
Anything with a hard, smooth surface.
A billiard ball, a button or a coin.'

We would repeat this until we could rattle it off like an auctioneer, vying with each other to get it as crisp and expert as the man on the soap box by the fountain. We hadn't the faintest idea what he was selling, but we were certainly sold on the hypnotic effect of his swiftly delivered patter. We used to stand on the fringe of the crowd, lips parted with expectation, and the moment he came to 'For you've all seen a cork in a bottle', we joined in the chorus with him, word for word, and the men standing round would give an ironic cheer, while the man on the soap box would shout: 'You weans should be in yer beds. Scram.'

When we watched rival schools playing football we enjoyed bursting into song, both schools taking it up, and yelling out the name of their own school at the appropriate line:

> 'Hyde Park, Hyde Park, as it used to be,
> The best wee school that ever ye did see.
> For when they score, you'll hear a mighty roar,
> Hurrah for good old Hyde Park.'

While we were shouting 'Hyde Park', the other school would be trying to drown us out with 'Albert', or 'Petershill', and the noise was deafening.

We felt unbelievably daring when school holidays approached and we'd rush around singing:

> 'Only one more day, and then we shall be free.
> No more English, no more French,
> No more sitting on a hard wooden bench,
> When the Jannie rings the bell,
> Out the gates we'll rush . . .

and, depending on who was within earshot, we'd finish 'pell-mell', nice and douce-like, or, if it was younger ones we wished to impress with our grown-up abandon, we'd substitute the words 'like hell'. 'Hell' was a terrible word to sing out loud in a song like that, and we shivered at our own daring. Our mothers would have cuffed our ears for us if they'd heard us, but we made very sure they never did.

We felt we were terribly lucky in having Paddy Oar's park immediately behind our school. We never knew who Paddy

Oar was or when it had been his park, but my mother had some vague idea that it had once been grazing fields which Paddy had let out to farmers as summer quarters for their animals. No cow or horse lent a rural air to the landscape even in our day, but the park was a gold-mine for our raw materials when we played at sand shops. During school holidays we would stream towards Paddy Oar's park as soon as we'd swallowed our breakfasts, and we'd spend the entire morning collecting bits of stone. We had brought old chisels or bits of tin for digging up specially coloured pieces, and we jealously kept our best finds to ourselves, so that we would have something exclusive to sell when the time came to open shop. We'd run panting back to our back courts, old aprons bulging with our prized materials, and after our dinner we settled down on the hard surfaces of the back courts to champ the stones into beautiful heaps of powdery stuff, some fine for flour and icing sugar and spices, others coarse for sugar, rice, barley and semolina. The special pieces were greatly coveted, for they had a deep rich colour just right for curry powders and ginger and cinnamon, and there was a lovely whitish stone which ground down perfectly to a fine rice flour.

We were as busy as bees, silent and absorbed in the preparation of our stock for our little shops. We would pile our wares in neat little heaps on the window-sills of the wash-houses, or the ledges of the kitchen windows of the houses at ground level. We would arrange a sheet of stiff cardboard so that it stuck out at right angles like a weighing scale, with a heavy stone to keep it in place, and a variety of little stones to act as weights ranged alongside. Then we flew about the earthy back courts, digging out old pieces of broken dishes, of which there seemed to be an endless supply, to form 'wally money'. The pieces with a tiny chip of gold still visible were 'sovereigns' and the others were graded in value according to size, from pennies to half-crowns. An old sweetie tin was our money till, and we drooled over our 'sovereigns' like any miser.

We drew lots to see who would start selling first, for, of course, the whole joy was in selling, but if you didn't buy, then you didn't sell, for your customers boycotted you. So the first 'in', as it were, would yell, 'Shop open, come and buy, ready-money buyers.' We had no idea what 'rea . . . dy-mo . . . ney buy . . . ers' meant, and that it had come down to us from the shopkeepers who refused to give customers 'tick' and demanded payment on the nail.

As soon as the first notes of 'Shop open' sounded, the other shopkeepers would leave wee sisters or brothers in charge of their stalls, with instructions to yell the alarm if the boys appeared and threatened to wreck the place. They would stroll over and critically survey the rival stall, make a few leisurely purchases which they promptly threw away, filled with envy of the shopkeeper and the fun she was having weighing out minute quantities of 'flour' or 'sugar', and the fussy altering of the weights which preceded 'I'm sorry, that's a ha'penny over, will I leave it on?' The saleswoman was longing, of course, to be told, 'No, that's too much, take it off', so that she could enjoy juggling with weights and scoop, but the purchaser was keen to start her own selling and usually said, with a lordly air, 'No leave it on, I've plenty of money in my purse', and she would hand over the correct amount of 'wally' money, so that at least there could be no prolonging the transaction with having to wait for change.

It didn't take long for the person next in line to get fed up with being a mere customer, and she'd rush back and set up the rival cry 'Shop open', but all too soon her turn was over, and with a sigh she'd join the ranks of the customers once more. I used to take my shop up to the house when the day's selling was over, and many a clout I got from Grannie when she found herself crunching horrible sand under her feet and taking it all over the kitchen floor on her slippers. 'Whit's a' this dirt?' she'd demand furiously as she scattered it over the floor, and I'd shriek with dismay and rush to rescue my dispersed treasure.

There was a special part of the park which had gorgeous sticky clay which we used for our clay shops. It was cold and wet and heavy to dig out, but we lugged back great dods of it, and, using flat pieces of wood begged from the fruit shops, who always had plenty of orange boxes, we battered it into various shapes. With what patience we designed boats, houses, saucers, blocks of butter, pieces of cheese, marzipan potatoes and pounds of margarine. The wash-house ledges weren't so desirable for clay shops, for the boys congregated on top of the roofs and pelted the shopkeepers with ferocious aim, with wet clay stolen from the stock. Not only did those boys rouse us to spitting fury, but they incensed the washerwomen too, for while they were up there they took the opportunity to stuff the chimneys with old rags and when the women lit the boiler fire next wash-day, smoke and soot would come pouring into the wash-house and spoil the good clean washing which was ready for the boiler.

With our clay models the salesmanship was different. We all created our own shapes, and we dispensed with wally money on this occasion, and went in for barter. It was a thrilling decision to have to weigh up the splendour of an offered miniature Clyde steamer for a submarine which one had designed with loving care.

And even when it wasn't providing stock for our shops Paddy Oar's park had yet another joy for winter fun. The slopes round the highest part, behind our school sheds, were satisfyingly steep, and formed into deep furrows, and with borrowed draining boards and old trays we would toboggan from what seemed incredible heights right down to the back school wall. How swift the descent was, and how long the toil upwards to begin all over again, but our legs were strong and sturdy and we accepted the hard slog uphill for the sake of the wild whoosh down again, when we seemed almost to be flying.

We saw no danger in this until one day a big girl in my class, heavier than the rest of us, couldn't stop her tray when she got to the bottom of the run, and banged her head right into the school wall with a thump that stopped the rest of us, who were toiling uphill, dead in our tracks. She lay at the bottom so still and silent that we thought she was killed. Her forehead was gashed open, and blood poured from it. We stared at her, frightened to move, then somebody ran for the janitor and he came and she was carried into his wee house in the playground. We'd never been inside his house, and in spite of the drama of the accident we were curious to notice that he had a range exactly like our own, with a cosy glowing fire burning, and a brass kettle on the mantelpiece. A doctor was sent for, and Dorothy had four stitches put in her forehead, and that was the end of our mountaineering. The headmaster came to the drill-hall next day, and lectured us about such dangerous play, and made us all solemnly promise that we would not attempt to take part in any sort of games at that particular part of the park. Och it was a shame, but the sight of that still figure, forehead dripping blood, had frightened us enough, and we kept our promise, and sadly put away our draining boards and trays. But we couldn't get over the fact that we hadn't even *known* it was dangerous until one of us had been hurt. How hard it was to know when you were being good and when you were being bad, even if you went to Sunday School and Church and everything.

6

As well as the big Church, where we went to Sunday School, and Bible Class, and had our church parades of Girl Guides and the Boys' Brigade, we had the excitement in summertime of tent missions coming to Springburn to convert us. We didn't know we were being converted from heathenish ways, we just enjoyed the sight of a huge tent being erected on the piece of waste ground at the end of Gourlay Street, and we begged to be allowed to help to hand out the little leaflets telling all that Jock Troup would be preaching and saving souls that night and all week from 7.30 p.m. As soon as our tea was swallowed, we raced back to get front seats, and the adults crowded in at our backs, greatly entertained to be having hell-fire preached at them inside a tent. Jock was great value, and we all imitated him afterwards, not in any spirit of derision, but in profound admiration. He could make the flames of hell so real, we felt them licking round our feet, and the prospect of heaven so alluring we often stood up to be saved several times during the week, just to see him fall on his knees in thankfulness at having plucked so many brands from the burning. His hymns were different from those in Sunday School and had a sort of music-hall ring to them which we all enjoyed.

One obviously designed to appeal to our Scottish sense of economy, went:

'Nothing to pay, no, nothing to pay,
Straight is the gate, and narrow the way,
Look unto Jesus, start right away,
From Springburn to glory, and nothing to pay.'

We particularly liked 'Springburn' coming into the hymn, not realising that he just substituted whatever district he hap-

69

pened to be visiting, and we felt he had composed this hymn specially for Springburn sinners.

Another rollicking hymn Jock honestly and freely confessed he had obtained from another hot gospeller, who had written it especially for us children, went like this:

> 'Zaccheus was a very little man,
> And a very little man was he,
> He climbed up into the sycamore tree
> For he wanted the Lord to see.
> And as the Saviour passed that way
> He looked up in the tree
> And said, "Zaccheus, you come down,
> For I'm coming to your house for tea." '

I thought that was a marvellous hymn, and it bore out my mother's wisdom in always having a wee something in the tins in case anybody came in unexpectedly, and could be offered a biscuit or a piece of shortbread and not just plain bread and margarine. Fancy if it had been the Saviour dropping in with a reformed sinner and you'd had nothing special to give them! That would have been just terrible. After I'd learnt that hymn I always made sure that our tins held at least four abernethy biscuits, just in case.

We attended Jock's services every night, and I used to come home and act them all over again to Grannie, and when she told me to be quiet she was fair deaved with my shouting, I would say, 'Well, Jock Troup said the streets of the New Jerusalem would be filled with the voices of little children,' and Grannie would say, holding her hand to her head, 'Weel if their voices are like yours, folk'll wish they had gaun some-place else for a bit o' peace.' 'All right then, Grannie Weir,' I would say huffily, 'the man's come all this way to show us how to be saved, but if you don't want to be saved, I'll just tell him tomorrow night and he'll come and pluck you from the burning himself.' 'My Goad,' Grannie would say, 'that wean's gaun to be a meenister, I'm mair shair o' it than ever,' and for some reason she seemed to be trying to stop herself laughing. How could she be so calm when Jock Troup told us we had but little time to repent, and she was far nearer to Judgment Day than I was!

After a whole week of Jock it was quite peaceful to awaken the next Sunday morning to the lovely sound of the Salvation Army silver band which played at the end of Gourlay Street before moving up Springburn Road to the Salvation Army Hall and its morning service. They were splendid musicians, and the silvery notes were welcomed by everyone within earshot as a most fitting way to start our Sundays. They just played tunes at that time of day, but later on in the evening they had an outdoor service and we all went along to hear them and to join in the singing. My auntie was a Salvationist and it was a proud day for her when she 'got the bonnet', which was only awarded after a qualifying period. We liked the way the officer who took the service shouted, with a high clear voice, so different from the soft tones of our minister. We didn't reason it was because he had to make himself heard above the traffic, but thought he was shouting straight up to heaven, so that God could hear what a good job he was making of it. After the outdoor service we marched up Springburn Road behind the band, and went into their hall, to listen to another short service, and discover how many sinners felt they now wanted to be saved. There was a long bench at the front, called the Penitents' Bench, where those wishing to be saved knelt and were received by the officer who had taken the service. I found this all very moving, and was saved twice, once for myself and once for Grannie, since she wouldn't budge outside the house to make sure of salvation in person.

But neither Jock Troup nor the Salvation Army had Sunday School picnics, and we felt Church Sunday Schools had a great advantage in this respect. Some of our chums went to every Sunday School in the district whenever the time drew near for the trips, as we called the picnics, and actually went to the Protestant, the Catholic and the Methodist churches just because one gave tattie scones, the next gave sausage rolls and the other gave pies. I thought this was a terrible thing to do, and felt that God must have been very confused wondering how to treat people of such fickle faith. At least all our religious tastes were Protestant, and we didn't go to the Tent Mission or the Salvation Army for anything but the sheer enjoyment, although I daresay if a trip had also been included we wouldn't have said no.

The trips were always on a Saturday, and the sun always

seemed to be shining. There were carts drawn by fine Clydesdale horses, and these were used to take the older people and the youngest children, whose legs weren't so strong as ours were. We all met at two o'clock in the street outside the Church, and with our tinnies tied round our necks with tape, and wearing our best summer clothes, we marched behind the Boys' Brigade band up to Springburn Park, or out to Auchinairn to a field kindly lent by one of the farmers or the gentry.

As soon as we arrived, we tore one end of our ticket off at the perforated edge, where it said 'Cakes' and handed it to one of the ladies who stood behind a huge hamper, and she gave us a poke of pastry. I loved those pokes we got at the trips, and I looked inside them right away. I just had to check what was inside, although I knew the contents never varied. Always exactly the same things, and I was always delighted. A round thick high sponge cake, with pieces of sugar on top and a strip of paper round the outside, which we called 'a sair heidie', because the paper reminded us of the hankies our mothers tied round their foreheads when they had a headache. Two squares of pastry with a layer of bashed fruit in between, with sometimes a few stones from fruit which had been incautiously cleaned, and this we called a fly cemetery. I always swopped this one, for I hated the name 'fly cemetery' and wouldn't have been surprised if there had indeed been some flies in among that funny-looking fruit. Strangely enough there was always somebody who actually liked fly cemeteries and there was no difficulty in getting another coffee bun in exchange. Mmmm, I loved a coffee bun. Sort of biscuity, dark brown and crumbly, and mysterious too, for it didn't taste of coffee and it didn't look like a bun, and I didn't know how it could have got its name. And a fern cake, with white icing on top, and a dark brown chololate fern traced over the white. I usually took this home for Grannie, so I couldn't blow up my poke and burst it as many of the others did when they'd eaten all their cakes. The other end of the entrance ticket had a perforated slip with the word 'Milk' written on it ('Tea' for adults) and it was a great novelty to have our tinnies filled with creamy milk straight from the churns which lined the refreshment corner of the field.

After the food we had the games and the races. What an excitement to see the men stretching the rope across the end of the measured distance, and we'd stand panting with nerves waiting for our age-group to be announced. 'The hundred yards will now be raced by the under tens.' We gave our ages to the men in charge of the start of the race, and the entrants who were younger than ten got a starting point nearer the winning tape, according to age, right down to the age of five. The five-year-olds were half-way to the post, but then their wee legs weren't as strong or as fleet as the older ones, and they needed this encouragment to get them to race at all. 'Noo watch me,' the man at our end of the 100 yards would say, 'and as soon as I drap ma hankie, off youse go.' Parents and school pals were ranged the whole length of the sidelines between starting and winning posts, cheering the contestants on. Every eye was on the starter's hankie, and the minute he dropped his hand, we were off, arms flailing and legs going like pistons, and hearts pounding as if they'd jump out of our chests. Och what a distance the finishing tape seemed to be, however hard one ran! It was easy to pass the wee five-year-olds who toddled happily at their own pace, lost interest, and started playing among the daisies, but completely impossible to catch up the fleetest of foot, who had breasted the tape almost before my legs, at any rate, had got into their stride. And then the winners proudly panted out their names and their ages, and were given their prizes. I never won that sort of race, but I came into my own at the 'fancy' races—the three-legged, where two of us tied inner legs together with a big hankie, and trotted up the field in harness. This needed a bit of manœuvering, and identical rhythm, and we used to trot about practising until we'd developed what we thought was an unbeatable style. There was generally a prize for me for that race. And the thread-the-needle race. I had eyes like a hawk, and always threaded Grannie's needle, so was experienced at sucking the end of the thread into a sharp fine point, ready to be jabbed through the eye of the needle at the proper moment. This speed with the needle helped to compensate for the lack of top speed in my legs, and I usually got a lucky bag for this race too.

But the races we all enjoyed best were those run by the fathers and mothers. It was hilarious to see mothers running up the measured distance, fat ones puffing and blowing, thin ones recovering their youthful zest as they raced out in fine style. Hair-pins fell out of buns, and blouses came adrift from skirts, and it was highly comical to see the mothers trying to stuff their blouses back to hide their camisoles, while racing along the slippery grass. I loved the sight of their rippling hair flying unbound in the breeze, and was delighted at how young they looked when they were pink-cheeked and dishevelled like this. There was much giggling and panting as they bound up their hair into douce buns again, but I couldn't help noticing they were not in the same hurry to do this as they had been to tidy up their blouses, and I had a notion they quite enjoyed the free feeling of their hair tumbling down their backs, and the admiring comments made by the men on the 'fine heids o' hair' they had.

The men were almost as funny when it came to their races. They took off their jackets and handed them to the women to look after them. They rolled up their trousers, revealing long socks above their sand-shoes, and sometimes long combinations. They adjusted their 'galluses', as we called their braces, to let their chests take in great gulps of air. They did impressive 'knees-bends' to loosen their muscles. Meantime the wives stood by, eyes amused or critical, holding the coats over their arms, while the children whooped and cheered on the sidelines. Somehow the sight of men running sent us off into peals of laughter, and I remember being so surprised during one race when Mr. McCarthy's galluses burst and his trousers threatened to tangle up his legs, his wife calling out: 'Wid ye look at Wullie McCarthy! I knew fine that button widnae haud, but wid he take time to let me sew it on for him! Not him!' The other women tut-tutted sympathetically while shouting with laughter at the sight of Mr. McCarthy trying to rescue his breeks, but what amazed me was that his wife had called him 'Wullie McCarthy', just as if he was a stranger. I had never heard women describe their husbands as anything other than 'ma man' or 'ma Hughie' or whatever their Christian name was, and it was the first time it had struck me that once upon a time misters and missuses had been separate human beings, with separate names; and always after this revelation I tormented the lives out of everybody by asking them: 'Whit was your name afore ye were Missus Brown?' I was fascinated by this knowledge that women had a different name before they married, and that there was a time in the distant past when their own husbands' names had been quite strange to them. I decided that I really didn't want to change my surname, and I thought maybe I would be an old maid, for I had learned you kept your own name forever if you stayed a 'miss'. Or maybe the minister would let me keep my own name if I asked him, if I decided, after all, I would like to be married.

The Sunday School trips put us in the mood for picnics, and the next Saturday saw us setting off for Springburn Park with borrowed lemonade bottles filled with water. We used to pretend we could detect the faint sweetness of long-vanished lemonade or Iron Brew, and wondered that anybody could have been so careless as to leave the precious drops which flavoured our picnic water. That water tasted so different drunk from a bottle, we could deceive ourselves it had a far better taste than the stuff straight from the tap, for it surely borrowed a wee bit of the magic of the lovely fizzy sweet stuff we all loved. Our bread and margarine, with sometimes a wee bit of corn mutton, tasted all the better too, washed down by this enriched water. We had all learned at Sunday School about the wedding party where the Saviour turned the water into wine, and who knew but that something special had happened to our bottled water for our picnics in the park. We spent hours of blissful play in the park, sustained by our simple picnic fare, and how good it all was after the back courts because we had real grass and warm sunshine. We all had empty jam-jars and wee 'nets' made out of old hankies fastened to pieces of thin wood. We fished for baggies, our name for baggie-minnows, and transferred them to our glass jam-jars, and felt drunk with success as we watched our catch swimming round and round in their glass-walled prison. We'd take them home, with slimy green stuff in the bottom of the jar, which was supposed to keep them alive, but which so disgusted our grannies or our mothers that they quietly poured the lot down the sink, ignoring our wailing cries. We were forbidden to paddle in the park pond, in case we'd 'catch our death', for who in our tenements had towels to spare for weans to take with them to dry themselves? Those who fell into the water, through over-enthusiasm, just had to run home to get a change of clothes and a walloping, and they ran home alone, for the park was a good twenty minutes' walk from our houses, and the rest of us weren't going to cut short our play because somebody else had been daft enough to fall in the pond. I remember one time my brother Tommy fell in, and

75

nothing would persuade him to go home and leave the exciting fishing contest, so he took off all his clothes and lay on the bank to dry himself in the sun. Grannie was scandalised when she heard the story, for, of course, his clothes were still damp when he came to be undressed to go to bed, and she was sure he would get pneumonia. She refused to be convinced that the sun had been 'rer and hoat', even if his jersey and trousers hadn't dried so quickly as his skin, and he was dosed with a big spoonful of emulsion that night, although it was high summer and not our usual season for staving off the ills which stalked us on dank winter days.

My mother was never a natural picnicker. She had a finicky preference for eating at a table, and a timidity about insects and wet ground. But sometimes we managed to coax her to take us on picnics, and we always wanted to go to Rouken Glen, because it was the longest tram ride from Springburn. She couldn't be bothered with the fag of taking three excitable children all that way every time, and occasionally she would fob us off with taking us out to Auchinairn. We'd troop out of the tramcar, take one look round, and shout accusingly in one voice: 'This is no' Rouken Glen.' 'How do you know?' my mother would counter defensively. 'Because we just do.' We'd stand mulishly and repeat annoyingly: 'This is just no' Rouken Glen.' 'Well, it's every bit as good,' my mother would parry. 'And if the rain comes on, we're far nearer home and we'll be home quicker.' We were furious at the weather coming into it, for we didn't examine the sky for rain-clouds. And then the sight of a very climbable tree would divert us, and soon we were shinning up it, playing Tarzan, or cowboys and Indians finding another even more exciting tree, with thick branches where we could actually sit down, and frightening the birds with our yells. We'd cut weeds for Mrs. McGregor's canary, and grasses and wild flowers for Grannie, who never came on picnics, however hard we tried to persuade her.

Once, after Grannie died, my mother took us on a picnic to Rouken Glen, and to our delight she provided no dull bread at all. The entire meal was made up of thin Scottish crumpets and potato scones, spread with fresh butter, which we all loved and which was a marvellous treat, washed down with water from the lemonade bottle. The 'toffs' had tea in the lovely Mansion House in Rouken Glen, and we peeped in the door to watch them sitting at their tables, spread with cakes and scones, and decided they must all be 'gaffers' and their families, to have so much money that they could afford to buy a real tea instead of bringing food from home. But we didn't envy them that day, for we hadn't even had to eat bread and margarine before our crumpets and tattie scones, and we had had real fresh butter. 'Aye, ah'll bet ye they didnae get *that* in the Mansion House,' we told each other happily. That was a perfect day out of doors with our mother. It was pleasing to see her sitting among the flowers, undistracted by any sort of work, and feel she was admiring our prowess as we climbed the trees and played races with one another in a wild corner of the park. She didn't have many days when she could afford to 'stand and stare'.

We didn't take a picnic when we went to the bluebell woods, for we only went there in high summer, and there was plenty of daylight for us to come home from Sunday School, change into our everyday clothes, have a jeely piece, and set off for the walk over Crowhill Road and out to Bishopbriggs, and on to the bluebell woods. We were always told by Grannie and my mother not to pull the flowers out by the roots—or there would be none for another year, and we did our best to be careful. We were full of glee and excitement, for nobody was allowed to pick the flowers in the Public Park, and this seemed a wonderful bounty from nature supplying us with all those thousands of bluebells which were there for the picking. Hours later we would come trailing towards the car terminus at Bishopbriggs, with arms full of wilting bluebells, heels blistered and sore, and queue up patiently for a tramcar, for it was too far to walk both ways from home and back, and we had kept a penny from our Saturday pocket money for the tram ride home. Many a precious bluebell was trampled underfoot as we battled to get on to those overflowing tramcars, and many more perished against our hot jerseys before we reached home. I remember once we found wild raspberries in a corner of the woods, and they were a gift straight from heaven, for it was one of my favourite fruits, and to get them for nothing, without committing the crime of pinching them from somebody's garden, seemed sensational.

For in spite of all our bible teaching, holidays in the country, which Grannie loved, were a terrible temptation to us. We were entranced to see fruit growing on bushes in country gardens, quite unprotected by any sort of fencing, and it didn't need much egging on on the part of the local children to help ourselves. They knew perfectly well we weren't supposed to do this, and no doubt were delighted to see how credulous city children could be. We must have been condemned by the garden-owners as city vandals when they saw us dart in and out of their gardens, mouths crammed with fruit, but maybe there was such an abundance that they didn't worry overmuch, for we only took what we could swallow, and we were so choked with guilt as we chewed, our terrified eyes never moving from the windows, that it was pilfering on a very tiny scale. I used to be sick with fright and guilt in case anybody would tell Grannie or my mother, but somehow we were never found out, and that made it seem worse because we *should* have had some sort of punishment for our sins. And yet maybe my punishment came at night when I had to leave the cosy lamplight of the kitchen and go through the garden to the wee hoosie at the far end to use the toilet, for the bushes were full of dark shadows and strange shapes, and my heart went skittering to my mouth at every rustle which shook the leaves. I was sure the devil was lurking there, ready to pounce and take me away with him to the bad fire. It was then that the fruits of conscience were tasted to the full, and oh how I regretted those mouthsful of stolen gooseberries or raspberries.

Grannie usually took us down to the country in advance, for my mother was generally working and she joined us only at week-ends. We used to dash up to the station on a Saturday afternoon to meet her train, and chanted from the advertisement stretching along the wall in front of us:

'They come as a boon and a blessing to men,
The Pickwick, the Owl, and the Waverley pen.'

We also memorised a horrible advert for Keating's powder:

'Big fleas have little fleas upon their backs to bite 'em,
The little fleas have lesser fleas, and so ad infinitum
—Kill the lot with Keating's Powder.'

We all knew about fleas, and it was something to be ashamed

of, and not talked about, and we were amazed at the cheek of those Keatings' people putting it up on a huge board for all the world to see. We didn't know what 'ad infinitum' meant, and anyway we caught ours by putting down a basin of cold water as we undressed, and the fleas headed straight for the water and drowning. Who needed Keating's powder?

There was an even stranger advertisement in the station, which puzzled me for years, which read:

'If it hurts you to laugh,
Don't read London Opinion.'

I thought that was a gey queer way to sell papers, warning people off them. Nobody I asked could work it out either, and I never ever saw anybody reading this paper, and I decided it served them right that nobody bought their old paper when it was advertised in such a daft way.

During one of those country holidays there was great excitement, for the little town had a visit from a member of the Royal Family. The streets were crammed with sightseers, but my brothers and I became tired of waiting for the royal personage and the procession of dignitaries to arrive, and we wandered to the back of the crowds and peeked over a bridge where a river sluggishly wound its way. Suddenly, to our horrified interest, we saw a huge water rat swimming from one bank to the other, and we became so engrossed in its progress that the royal person, procession and all, had passed by the time we turned round. I had a vague feeling that we had missed something important, but my brothers stoutly voted in favour of the rat. 'Faur better fun,' they assured me. 'You've missed nothing.'

On one holiday, when my mother had managed to accumulate a rare healthy divi from the Co-operative, she had the fanciful notion of taking rooms 'with attendance'. We were very curious as to what this meant, and she told us impressively that it meant that we would just have to do the shopping and the cooking ourselves, and the landlady would keep the rooms clean, and clear the table, and do all the dishes for us. No dishes to wash or dry—oh that was a great idea, we thought. But it didn't work out that way. My mother, never having been used to anyone working after her, became embarrassed at the thought of our landlady having everything to do, although she was being paid for it, and she made us volunteer to do the washing up, a job we hated. 'She's getting peyed fur it!' we would hiss rebelliously, as my mother pushed us out behind the landlady's retreating back and the tray of dirty dishes, with the instruction that we were to offer our services. My mother ignored our unwillingness, and shut the door on us. To our increased fury, the landlady generally accepted our muttered offer, and the boys would stand scowling with the tea towels, while I banged the dishes into the bowl of soapy water, and washed them as fast as I could. We longed to rush out, for we hated wasting a precious minute of the holiday, and then when the job was completed, and everything put away, we were ashamed at the landlady's praise of us and how well my mother had brought us up, to be such rare wee helps. 'Rare wee helps' indeed, when we had been press-ganged into doing those hated dishes. So we scuffed our feet, torn between shame at the undeserved praise, and annoyance that our mother's hard-won money was being taken for attendance that wasn't real attendance at all in our childish eyes. We felt the least that woman could have done was to have given us a rebate. My mother was quite serenely indifferent to our miserly reasonings, and was clearly enjoying the novelty of being somebody of substance in the eyes of our landlady, somebody with enough 'roughness' in her purse to be able to afford the delightful extra of 'attendance'.

7

M Y mother hated being out of work. Apart from the loss
to us of the pay packet, her restricted budget was felt
right down the line by everybody who was just that much
worse off than we were. The wee washerwoman who did our
washings for half a crown was the first to go, but because it was
unthinkable to deprive her of her entire livelihood, my mother
would rush round all the neighbours in our close, and ask if
they would let the washerwoman wash the stairs for them at
fourpence a landing. 'Och aye,' they agreed. 'It'll only be for a
wee while, for a smert wee wumman like you is sure to get another job soon, Jeanie, and we'll manage fourpence till she gets
daein' your washings again.' So that was one-and-fourpence to
help out the wee washerwoman during this lean period. But
the man who did the staircase window for fourpence had to be
refused for a while, and my mother took out the steps and did
this large grimy window herself, awaiting better times.

When at last she obtained the coveted job in Cowlairs we
were all in seventh heaven. She had gone along to the gates
every Friday, trying to catch the eye of the foreman to see if
she would get first chance painting the big wagons. At first
he was dubious, for she was very tiny and very slim, but she
was so eager, and so desperate, he decided to give her a chance.
It was only on a temporary basis, at first, to see how she would
manage such heavy work, but what she lacked in strength she
more than made up in energy, and for those first few weeks
while she was on probation we grew used to seeing her come
in from work, take her tea in a dream, and then push aside the
plates and drop her head on her arms on the table and fall
sound asleep. We'd stare at each other, and wonder if we
should disturb her by clearing the dishes and getting them
washed, or if we should just leave them and let her sleep, and

risk her wrath at all the washing up still lying about at bed-time.

And then one Friday night she came in, eyes shining, and not tired at all. 'I've been taken on,' she announced. 'It's permanent.'

After her spell of unemployment this prosperity went to her head, and my mother celebrated it by the wildest burst of extravagance we had ever known. She bought a piano on the pay-up! A piano! And on the pay-up! We caught our breaths in frightened admiration. What would Grannie have said, Grannie who frowned on buying anything unless she had the money in her hand, and who considered any form of hire purchase was the road to ruin. But my mother reasoned that if we waited until we had all the money which a piano cost we would never get one in this life, for there would always be something more pressing. Och, and anyway it would be marvellous to have a piano for parties, and she knew I had always longed to learn to play this instrument. It would give us some real music, and would help to drown the clatter of Tommy's drum-sticks on top of the rubber practice-pad. He was learning to be a drummer at the Boys' Brigade and drove us all frantic with his endless 'para-diddles' on the dresser-top, for our ears could find no tune at all in this noisy hammering.

My mother revelled in this purchase. She didn't waste a second on mere tone when she bought it. It was the beautiful black polished case which entranced her. The sideboard was pushed to the end of the room where it squeaked tightly against the sofa, and the piano was installed, magnificent and shining, along the wall opposite the fireplace. We all stood silent, drinking in its splendour, while my mother flicked off imaginary specks with a duster. She would work overtime, she told us, and what with that money and her good weekly wage she would never even feel the instalments. If only *one* of us could have sat down and played a tune of triumph at this splendid moment her cup would have been full. But she was determined to give me every chance to develop a talent, and she arranged for me to have music lessons at sixpence a week from a wee man who worked beside her. Somebody had told her he was a dab hand at the piano, and when she had approached him to see if he would consider teaching me he had said at once, 'Of coorse ah'll learn the wean; ah've still goat the books ah hid when ah wis a wee fulla, an' she'll easy pick up hoo tae use her fingers on the right keys.'

He was a widower, and lived alone, and his dank fusty single apartment fascinated me. The first thing I noticed was the smell. A compound of dungarees, tobacco and airlessness. I felt sure the window was never opened from one week's end to the next. A hook which wouldn't have disgraced a crane stuck out from the back of the door, and on this hung his wardrobe. Raincoat, heavy coat, jacket, bunnet, and sundry odds and ends. The room was crammed with furniture. Two big chairs with newspapers stuck down the arms, two kitchen chairs and a big table of heavy mahogany, like the ones normally used in our tenements for supporting coffins. Surely he didn't take his meals off that? But he did, as I had plenty of opportunity to discover during later lessons, for he walked about making his tea, peeling his tatties and frying his sausages while I stumbled through scales and fingering exercises. The frying pan was never off the hob, and it was clear to me he lived on nothing but 'fries'. Grannie would never have approved. I imagined I could hear her say, 'Dear to buy, hard on the stomach, and no' nearly as nourishing as guid stews, cooked long and slowly to draw oot every bit of good from the meat.' But of course Mr. Patterson would never have had time for all this, and him at his work all day. I had never met a widower before, and accepted this strangely smelly room as part of the aroma of a house without a woman. His dresser was covered with dishes, and books, and a draught-board, and dominoes, and at the end a fascinating object which I discovered was a pipe-rack. He arranged all his pipes on it for me to see the complete effect. I'd not seen such a thing before, and decided it was a lovely tidy idea to store all those pipes so neatly together, but they smelt to high heaven. I could never see my mother letting them sit so near the frying pan, but he didn't seem to mind. It dawned on me that men weren't nearly as fussy as women in these matters, for when I asked him how he cleaned them he said, 'I don't. The tobacco tastes faur better frae a weel-used pipe.' No wonder they smelt. Apart from the food we ate, there wasn't a thing in our house that wasn't cleaned at some time.

At the end of the lesson he would wipe his hands and sit down at the piano and thunder out 'Scots wha ha'e' and 'Bonnie Dundee' until the dishes danced on the dresser and the smelly pipes accompanied them in a gentle jig. I thought he was a marvellous player, and with all the noise he was making I didn't mind raising my voice in song, and the concert only ended when the sausages in the pan were in danger of burning or the potatoes boiling over. He told my mother I was 'a wee warmer', but he decided I had learnt enough and he couldn't conscientiously take my mother's hard-earned sixpence any longer when I knew how to run up a few scales and pick out carefully the tune of 'The Bluebells of Scotland'. 'The rest is nae bother,' he assured me. 'Ye'll easy pick oot a' the other tunes for yersel' noo ye know the ropes.'

But I never did. We had no money for sheet music, and this slight knowledge of reading music ruined any ability I might have had to play by ear, so I badgered my mother to try another teacher, the father of a school chum who charged seven-and-sixpence a quarter. That seemed a fortune, until we worked it out and found it was only three-halfpence a week more than Mr. Patterson. But this was a dull, dour man who took not the slightest interest in me. The room was cold and clean, with a flickering gas mantle which gave out a cheerless light, and there was a damp feeling as though the fireplace had never known the blaze of comforting coal. Mr. Torrance held open the door for me, sat me down at the piano in front of a sheet of music, retired behind his newspaper and never uttered a single word during the entire lesson. If I asked a question he just cleared his throat, raised his eyebrows, and either shook or nodded his head. I had dark suspicions he was only wasting my mother's good money, and felt there must surely be more to teaching than this. We'd be far better off spending the seven-and-sixpence on music books ourselves, and my mother would get the pleasure of hearing me actually learning! So one night I announced to the silent Mr. Torrance as he rose to show me to the door, 'Ah'm no' comin' back. Cheerio.' And that was the end of that. I don't know whether he was shocked, or disappointed, for his face registered nothing, but I knew a small sense of triumph that he wasn't going to escape into the room away from his family to enjoy a good read of the paper at my mother's expense any more. I might not be able to play the piano, but I wisnae daft, thought I, as I skipped home to the warmth of our own fireside, and to my mother's laughter when I told her what I had done.

So we bought a book of Harry Lauder's songs, and I sat down confidently, armed with my knowledge of all those scales which I had mastered, using all the right fingers, and found my progress went at a snail's pace. Far from enjoying hearing me learning, my mother wondered audibly when that wean was ever gaun tae play onything that sounded like a tune. I *longed* to be able to sit down and rattle off 'Will ye' no come back again', which she loved, or 'I Love a Lassie' from Lauder's repertoire, but although the tunes dirled in my head, my fingers just refused to echo this smart tempo. I could only manage dirges which gave plenty of time to read and find the notes.

'Gi'e Tommy a wee shot,' she would say, and Tommy, to my shame, would sit down, without benefit of instruction from any music maestro, and rattle off tune after tune by ear. All that money wasted on me, and every note of every tune had to be wrestled for, while he sat down and pounded notes by the dozen and a tune emerged. And he didn't know a crotchet from a semi-breve. It was maddening. But it made a welcome change from those drum tattoos, and it was grand to sing out a rousing chorus accompanied by our fine piano, even if mine weren't the fingers which drew the tune from the instrument.

But Tommy and I did manage one hilarious duet, me doing scales, and him battering away with his drum-sticks, at the end of one of our flittings. We hadn't moved house for at least a year, and my mother was getting restless. We knew this when we saw her begin to look round the house with a critical eye. The range wasn't drawing properly, and she knew fine that the factor would do nothing about renewing vital parts. The room windows let in a terrible draught—the frames were old, so nothing could be done. She was sure the woodwork on the kitchen sink was rotten.

Then one night after tea she announced casually that she had heard of a rare house in Millarbank Street, which wasn't only half-way to Cowlairs and would mean less walking for her, but it actually boasted a bathroom! The property had originally been intended for the higher-paid employees of the works, and had been good once upon a time, but had come down a wee bit socially, and the rents were reasonable. We were all getting too big for baths in the zinc bath in front of the fire, anyway, she told us. We hadn't noticed this but she said she had. To us this was just another excuse for flitting, which we cheerfully accepted.

This move was too far for us to be able to indulge in the economy of running round with most of our household stuff, so we had a horse and cart, kindly supplied to us by the coal-man. My mother rushed out and swept off the coal-dust from the cart before our furniture and effects were loaded, and the horse trotted off with a nice turn of speed, our stuff swaying perilously as it turned off Springburn Road, but kept in check by the boys who sat beside the driver, urging the horse to 'Gee up' while they held on to stools and chairs which threatened to crash to the ground.

We no longer had Grannie to examine the flues for dangerous soot, and my mother had rashly accepted the word of the out-going tenant that the chimney had recently been swept. It was a bitterly cold night, and as she got the room to rights she piled masses of flitting junk into the fireplace, for the double purpose of getting rid of it and heating the icy room. She heaped on old rotten linoleum she had found lining a press, old wallpaper, boxes, junk of every description, making a grand clearance while she was at it. There came an ominous rushing noise in the chimney, and we knew the worst had happened even before the hot soot began falling on the hearth.

'Heavens, the chimney's on fire,' my mother called out in anguished tones, as though we weren't all fully aware of the fact. She felt it was in the worst possible taste to introduce herself like this to her new neighbours. It would be a terrible start to life in our new house if we set the joists of the whole building on fire.

Suddenly I had an inspiration. As there were twelve families in the tenement, it was almost impossible to tell from the blazing chimney seen from the street which tenant was the offender, so I leaped into the front room, sat down at the piano, and raced up and down the scales like mad. My mother thought I had gone off my head until I explained my craftiness.

'You see,' I shouted above the din of the piano, 'if they hear us playing they'll never think it can be our chimney. Who would suspect us of fiddling while Rome burns?' We'd just heard about Nero in school.

My mother began to laugh helplessly, and Tommy, infected by the spirit of the thing, seized his drum-sticks and beat out a rhythmic accompaniment to my scales, while Willie and my mother threw salt on the fire to put the flames out. The strategy worked. We were never found out. As my mother said afterwards, 'That piano ferrly earned its keep, and a' thae piano lessons werenae wasted, efter all.'

The roaring fire in the chimney had done one good thing, though. It had heated the water, and for the first time in our lives we were able to turn on a hot-water tap and fill a basin with beautiful, piping hot water. I was all for taking a bath, for the sheer joy of lying down in a full bath in our very own house, but my mother decided against this. The bath needed painting, she said, and she'd read of a new paint which was guaranteed to be perfect for baths and to be unaffected by the temperature of even the hottest water. She decided green would be ideal, for it would look like the sea when the bath was filled, and she followed the makers' instructions to the letter, letting each coat dry thoroughly before applying the next. Then after three coats had been lovingly applied, the bath was filled with cold water so that the whole surface could harden. We hung breathlessly over the shimmering water, and pressed surreptitious finger-tips against the side to see if the paint was drying properly, and longed for the moment when the time would be ripe for the first bath. On a Saturday afternoon, when everyone was out, I decided if the paint was ever going to harden it must have done it by this time, and I let the cold water out, replaced the plug, and turned on the hot tap. I was determined to be the first to sample this wonderful new luxury. I carefully measured in a tablespoonful of Woolworth's bath salts—pink and scented—and sniffed rapturously as the perfumed steam rose and swirled about the room. Gently I lowered myself into the water, and lay back, rejoicing in the novelty of a bath at home, with no shouts from the cubicles next door, and no watchful attendant to curtail the length of time as I wallowed in sleepy bliss. I sat up and began to scrub myself with the loofah and found I couldn't move my bottom. I had stuck to the bath! I shot to my feet in alarm and found that my nether regions were thickly coated with green paint! Frantically I began to scrape it off with the blunt side of an old knife my mother had left on the ledge. Then I felt my feet sticking to the paint. I moved to another part of the bath, thinking it was maybe only in the centre that the paint hadn't dried. As I walked from one part to another, the paint lifted off in layers, each one acting like a sucker to pull off the one beneath. First green paint, then white

87

paint, right down to the rusty metal of the bath itself, stripped of all its top coatings. I was hysterical by this time, partly with terror at having ruined the bath and all my mother's good painting, and partly because the sight of paint festooning my feet like thick-soled sandals convinced me that nothing short of burning would ever get it off. I couldn't even get out of the bath, for in the excitement of getting into it, I hadn't put a towel down, and I daren't walk over the floor to look for turpentine or a sharper knife. At that moment my mother walked in, smelt the bath salts and threw open the bathroom door. She took one look at me, covered in paint, at her fine bath stripped of its lovely sea-green surface, cuffed me over the ear, and disappeared. 'Mother,' I yelled after her, 'come back. I couldnae help it. The paint just melted wi' the hoat water. It couldnae have been the right stuff ye used.' This infuriated her even more, for she prided herself on her knowledge of paint. Didn't she use paint every working day, and weren't the gaffers expert at giving advice on the right quality to use for a bath? By this time she was scraping paint off my feet, and rubbing vigorously with an old piece of towel dipped in turpentine. It sent me off into paroxysms of laughter, for apart from being agony, it was also tickly. She began to laugh herself. 'Och I'm glad it was you, and no' me,' she said at last. 'I'd never have got it off in time for the dance the night if I'd had the first bath.' Then she sighed. 'And right enough, if it hasnae dried in a hale week, it couldnae have been the right stuff for baths.' Oh how I admired her generosity in admitting it, for I knew she was heart-sick at the rusty mess which her grand bath had become, and I promised to help her to rub it all down with sandpaper, and take a shot at applying the next lot of paint, and this time we'd go up to the drysalters and get expert advice, and not *dream* of putting hot water near new paint for *weeks* after the last coat had dried. By that time, surely, the fire in the soles of my feet would have cooled, and the blisters on my bottom healed. But I'd let one of the boys have the first bath next time, just in case.

When we first moved into this house we had noticed, as a sort of bonus, that it was above a fish-and-chip shop. This, we thought, was great. We wouldn't have far to go for our favourite treat of shop chips, and the occasional luxury of fish for special occasions. We hadn't the least suspicion that there might be hazards in living above such pungent smells. As the weather grew warmer, everything in the house smelt of fat. The blue smoke from boiling vats of dripping drifted upstairs and filled our rooms. Worse was to come. The fat which was so nice to sniff when passing a chip-shop door on a cold night was now nauseating us, for it clung to our jerseys, our coats and our bedclothes, and filled our noses as we dressed and undressed, or pulled the blankets up round our chins in bed. And we discovered, to our horror, that this penetrating fat was a perfect Pied Piper to every mouse for miles. When we turned out the gas at night the patter of their scurryings was as insistent as Tommy's drum-sticks. My mother was terrified of them. She began to jump at every shadow. One morning, as she put her foot into her slipper when she jumped out of bed, a startled mouse leaped out before she could squash it. Her screams wakened the whole stair. That was the end, and we knew it. She went shuddering off to work, vowing she wouldn't stay another night in this infested building. It was impossible to keep that vow, of course, but by the end of the week she had found another house, in Keppochhill Road, two stairs up. There was no bathroom, but there were no fumes from fish and chips, and no attraction for mice. There was, though, an inside toilet. On balance, we decided this amenity was the best possible exchange for a rusty old bath, for it wasn't absolutely necessary to have a bath too often, whereas the toilet was in use all the time. Oh and what a luxury not to have to share with any other family. A whole toilet for the four of us. Dreams of comfort could envisage nothing finer.

This move was one of the most enjoyable of all the Weir flittings, but the fish and chips for the party afterwards did not come from the shop below the house we were so thankfully leaving. We decided to patronise the newest shop off Keppochhill Road, whose white tiles, and the immaculate overalls of the lady behind the counter, ensured absolute cleanliness. The quantities were tiny, compared with other slapdash shops, but we could be sure the fat hadn't been shared by a colony of mice. Maybe it was the grandeur of having a bath and a piano at the same time, but we seemed to be getting pernickity in our ways, or giving more thought to cause and effect, for up till that time we'd never concerned ourselves with the possibility of mice thriving where chip fat was plentiful. Certainly other folk didn't seem so finicky, for there was no shortage of takers for the houses situated above all the fish-and-ship chops in Springburn. And the family who took the place we left were delighted to get it, rusty bath and all, especially when we could assure them, hand on heart, that there wasn't a bit of dirty soot in the chimney.

Mind you, we couldn't really be surprised at mice enjoying chips, for I was sure it was the chips they went for, and not the fat. Even Bruce, the little Highland collie Tommy had brought home from one of his long walks into the country, loved our fish-and-chip shops. In fact, when he ran away for a few days, leaving us all heartbroken, the first places we looked were the fish-and-chip shops. When the ones in our immediate neighbourhood yielded nothing we scoured back courts as far down as the Moss-House on our way to the next cluster of chip shops there, and in the other direction we went as far as the Low Road, nearly to Bishopbriggs. Nothing. Oh and how empty the house seemed without him. We had grown used to being greeted with a rushing, welcoming licking, and an eager wagging tail every time we opened the door. I had spent hours training him to be obedient. I refused to pick him up, even when he ran after every passer-by in the street as a puppy, for he had to learn to follow me when I called, and to use his own legs to get about, just as I had learned. How proud I was when he came to heel at a word from me. Even my mother missed him, although he nearly drove her mad by eating any food she thoughtlessly left within his reach.

Then one night I was sent to deliver a message to an auntie who lived about a mile from us. It started to rain when I left her house, and she insisted on treating me to a penny ride on the tramcar, so I wouldn't get soaked. As I sat on the top deck, enjoying this unaccustomed treat in the middle of the week, my gaze fell on the open doorway of a chip shop a full three stops before the fare stage for our house. There, standing with his paws on the counter, an ingratiating tongue lolling, was our Bruce! In one bound I was at the top of the stairs. I clattered down, and threw myself off the platform recklessly, although the tram was fairly tearing along between the stops. I was terrified Bruce would take off again and we would never find him. I had only a passing swift regret for the lost three tram stops for which I'd paid and not enjoyed.

I panted into the shop. 'Bruce Weir,' I thundered as severely as my relieved heart would allow, 'where have you been?' The girl laughed when she heard me. 'My,' she said, 'I've never heard onybody crying their dug wi' a second name. Whit's up? Wis he lost?' 'For four whole days,' I said tremulously, relief at the sight of Bruce standing there, safe and sound, threatening to dissolve in tears. 'Four days,' she said wonderingly. 'Jings, nae wunner he was dyin' fur a chip!' I allowed him to eat just one, and then ordered him out of the shop. He slunk out ahead of me, with guilty backward glances, a furtive sort of lope quite different from his usual eager gait. When we reached home Tommy walloped him so that he would know it was wrong to run away, and that he must never do it again. I held his collar while Tommy smacked his bottom, and I couldn't see for tears, because while he was being punished, Bruce was licking my hand. I supposed he had to be punished for his own good, but I couldn't bear this humble acceptance and loving forgiveness. I would far rather he had bitten both of us.

8

WHEN I was a wee girl in Glasgow, Hallowe'en was celebrated by all of us with keenest enjoyment. The weather always seemed clear and frosty, the skies filled with stars, and there was the exhilaration of dressing up in strange garments, with the added tension and nervousness of a performance about to begin. I usually wore Grannie's old hat, when it had got beyond the stage when a bunch of cherries or a spray of flowers could rejuvenate it, and I sat it on top of my head at a rakish angle, over my blackened face. A long skirt of my mother's, and Grannie's tartan shawl completed the disguise, but I wasn't able to round off the effect with my mother's high-heeled shoes because I couldn't even hobble in them, so my long-legged boots and black woollen stockings just had to be worn, even though they were completely out of character. This was a terrible disappointment, for I longed to prance about in elegant high heels, but for running out and in closes and up and down dozens of stairs sure footing was vital, and boots it had to be.

There was much giggling and mutual admiration when we all met after tea, and set out on the rounds of all the neighbours' houses. Sometimes, greatly daring, we went beyond our own district, and we shivered with excitement and a little dread at the thought of knocking at such strange doors. We were very critical of the brasses, and surprised to find that in some posh closes the name-plates weren't a patch on the glittering gold polish our own mothers managed. We each carried a little bag, home-made from an old petticoat or blouse, with a draw-string top, to hold the expected apples and nuts and sweets we hoped we would collect, and we prepared our acts as we raced along from close to close. We never expected to be handed our Hallowe'en gifts just for knocking on a door and chanting,

'Please gi'e us wur Hallowe'en!' We knew we were expected to do a turn to entertain our benefactors.

We would be invited into the house, and the family would sit round in lively anticipation as we went into our performances. I usually sang the latest popular song, and I particularly liked one requiring the use of my hostess's flue-brush, which I stuck over my shoulder and used as a bayonet. Very dashing I thought this, and so did my audience! There were recitations and ballads, and we generally finished with all of us doing a Highland Fling. We received our applause with flushed and happy faces, and we opened our draw-string bags to receive the apples, and the nuts, with maybe a piece of puff candy or some home-made tablet. Tablet was a great treat and so tempting that it was devoured on the spot, and seldom rested in the in the bag for a second. A turnip lantern lit our way and we went bobbing through the darkness like glow-worms. The preparation of those magic lanterns was a great ploy. We hollowed out swede turnips skilfully, made two slits for the eyes and a perpendicular line for the nose. A curved slit made a smiling mouth. A little hollow in the bottom held our candle, and the complete effect was golden and delightful. I may say everybody in our district ate mashed swedes for days afterwards, using up the discarded insides of our lanterns.

A party was a great excitement at Hallowe'en, and everyone went in fancy dress. Home-made, of course, for these were unsophisticated as well as hard-up days, and only 'toffs' would have known about hiring clothes. Angels and fairies, their wings fashioned from cardboard boxes coaxed from the Co-operative, and covered with coloured crinkled paper, were ten a penny, for the girls. The boys favoured pirates and cowboys, which were easily fashioned from old hats, and their father's leather belts, and toy guns. All this helped to break down the shyness we would have felt in ordinary clothes, although Hallowe'en fun was so different from any other form of merriment there was never a minute of sitting still wondering what you were expected to do. After the tea, with its salmon sandwiches if we were lucky, or corn mutton if money was tight, followed by the jellies, the games started. The big zinc bath was pulled from under the bed and filled with cold water, then rosy-cheeked apples were tumbled in in a colourful shower. A chair was placed with its back to the bath, the apples and water given a vigorous stir to send them bobbing as wildly as possible and make a difficult target, and we would each kneel, one at a time, on the chair, head sticking out over the top edge just as though we were about to be guillotined. A fork was held between clenched teeth, and we'd gaze at the bobbing fruit below us, waiting for the moment when the biggest and reddest apple was exactly placed for our aim, then *plonk*, down went the fork, usually to slither off between the bouncing apples. There would be howls of glee from the on-lookers, and gulping disappointment from the unlucky contestant as he or she climbed down from the chair to go to the end of the queue again. Not till everybody had speared an apple would the next game start, and, of course, it became harder and harder to succeed as the numbers of apples grew fewer and fewer with each win, and the final apple had the whole room shouting opposite advice. 'Drap yer fork noo. *Noo*, Wullie. Ach missed it', 'Gi'e the watter a steer, it's easier when it's movin' ', or 'Don't steer it noo, gi'e 'im a chance seein' there's only wan'. And from the faint-hearted, or those who wanted to go on to another game, 'Ach just gi'e 'im it, and let's get on wi' the party.'

There was a lovely game, unpopular with parents but be-loved by us children, where a huge home-baked soda scone was covered in treacle and suspended on a string from the centre gas bracket, or hung from a string stretched across the room. It was sent spinning by the leader, and then, with hands clasped behind our backs, we would leap into the air and try to snatch a bite. What a glorious mess we were in at the end of this caper, hair, eyes, cheeks and neck covered in treacle. Mothers and aunties and uncles urged us instantly towards the kitchen sink, 'Go and dight yer faces noo, we don't want treacle a' ower the hoose,' and what a splashing there was under the cold tap, and a battle for the solitary towel as we removed the mess.

And, of course, we loved the trinkets which were buried in a mound of creamy mashed potatoes. Even the poorest family could afford tatties, so everybody could enjoy this traditional bit of fun. The quantities of potato we consumed in search of our favourite ring or threepenny piece must have saved many an anxious hostess from worrying how she was to fill us up.

The older girls were full of romantic notions concerning apples. They'd try to take off the peel in one continuous strand, which they threw over their left shoulder, and whichever initial it formed was supposed to be that of the lad they would marry. Oh the teasing and the blushing if by chance the initial formed was that of their current heart-throb. The boys pretended they had no interest in this performance, but there was plenty of jeering and pushing when the initial fitted, and a casual pairing off when the game had finished. Especially if the next game was the one where an apple was placed on the top edge of a door, with a chair placed on either side, a boy on one chair and a girl on the other. They each ate towards the core, and the winners were the couple who reached the core—and a kiss—in the shortest possible time.

We children thought the swinging apple game was far better, and it was funnier too. There were up to six contestants at a time required for this game, which made it rare and noisy and exciting. They had to stand in line, in front of six apples suspended on cords from a string stretched across the room. The apples were set swinging, and the point of the game was that, without using hands to help, the contestants had to bit the fruit right down to the core. The winner, of course, was the one who finished first. The apple could be manœuvred on to one shoulder only *once* during the game to assist the eating, but otherwise everybody leaped and bit like hungry birds, and a most comical sight it was for the onlookers. It was especially funny when the grown-ups took their turn, and we held our sides with laughter when specs slithered down perspiring noses, when braces parted from buttons, and when false teeth were dislodged on hitting an apple too suddenly. We could have played this game all night, but all at once the apples were finished, and it was time to go home, this time without lanterns to light our way, for, of course, we didn't take them to parties, only when we went out chanting 'Please gi'e us wur Hallowe'en'.

What a long time it seemed between Hallowe'en and Christmas. The nights were dark, but they didn't keep us in, and we flew out and in the closes following our usual games of High-Spee-Wigh, and Buckety-Buck-Buck, and the boys had their own back courts and we had ours, for we wouldn't have dreamed of mixing. The boys had another game, which was fiercely condemned by the grown-ups and was always guaranteed either to irritate or frighten the victims half out of their wits. This was called 'clockwork'. A button or a lead washer was threaded on to a long piece of black cotton or thin string, on the pulley principle. The terminal point was fixed with a pin to the wooden sash of the kitchen window, and then the boys stole through the back court, carefully paying out the string. Silently they climbed on top of the wash-house, to give them the necessary height and keep them out of sight, and for the next hour they rocked with laughter as they tormented the occupants of the chosen house. They'd give the thread a little jerk, the button or washer would run down, knock against the window-pane, tap, tap, before being eased back. Inside the house, where folk sat quietly reading or talking, for there was no radio to make a noise, the tap on the window was like ghostly fingers. 'Who's that?' a voice would call out. 'It's somebody at the door,' a dull-of-hearing grannie might answer. 'It's no' the door, it's the windae.' 'My Goad, wha would be at the window at this time o' night?' The curtains would be parted, and a face would peer out into the darkness. The boys, convulsed with giggles from their hiding place behind the chimneys on the wash-house, would wait till everything was quiet again, and start off their tapping once more. You would have thought the neighbours would have suspected 'clockwork' instantly when they heard a tapping at the window, but we were all brought up on a diet of ghosts and Flannel Feet, and the first thing anybody thought of was the supernatural or some unnamed horror. It was bad enough when this game was played on the people who occupied the houses in the close, for their windows were at ground level and it might just have been a friend knocking, but when some daring boys climbed the rhone-pipe and fastened the string and button contraption to a house one storey from the ground, they even had the added success of a few screams from the mothers, who were convinced it must be a descendant of Jack the Ripper at the very least. But when the tapping went on, and nobody launched himself over the window-sill into the room, the truth dawned. Windows would be thrown up, and groping hands would seek the string and the pin fastening it there, and a furious tug from the irritated occupant of the house ended the game for that night. Sometimes a ground-floor husband, who no doubt had played the game many times as a wee boy, would steal through the back close and slip through the shadows to the wash-house.

With a roar, he would vault among the boys, and send them scattering in terror as he tried to cuff as many ears as possible in the dark. This successful turning of the tables generally put the husband in a great good humour, but so scared the boys that clockwork got a very long rest, and other livelier games took over, with no risks of a thumping involved.

Our mothers were always warning us about the dangers of jumping off the wash-house dykes, or playing near the broken railings which divided the back courts, but these were our playing fields and we accepted the cut knees and bruised heads as part of the added spice. Once, when I was very small, I had a passionate urge to climb right to the top of the railings, and as I clung with fingers and toes to the rusty iron, I turned round and urged a chum to 'Push me up, ach goan, juist a wee push and I can hing on to the top bar'. As I turned my head, she obligingly pushed, my head fell back and the spikes went right through the skin. I jumped down, put a hand to my curls, and drew it away dripping with blood. With shaking legs I ran up the two double flights of stairs to the house, where my mother was just changing out of her dungarees. She took one look at me, and moved the kettle over the fire to get hot. The news went round the stair like wildfire, and in two minutes our kitchen was like a first-aid station. 'Have you got sherp shears, Jeanie?' demanded one. 'You'll hiv tae cut away her hair.' 'Oh don't cut ma hair,' I wailed, 'I don't want to be baldy.' 'Ye'll no' be baldy,' said Mrs. Sampson soothingly. 'It'll grow in again, but ye don't want it a' stickin' tae the bluid, dae ye?' Mrs. Sampson had a bandage and Mrs. Dalrymple had some sticking plaster. My mother had now filled the white enamel basin with warm water, and was urged to add salt to clean the wound. Nobody had cotton wool, so she used an old clean hankie to dab off the blood, and carefully she snipped away at my curls. It stung like fury, but she had gripped me between her knees and I couldn't move. 'Get a' the roost washed off, Jeanie,' the women urged, 'or it'll fester.' Oblivious to my cries, my mother washed and rubbed until I was sure she was right through to the bone. Plaster was applied, then, for good measure, some boracic lint, then a bandage, and then I got a skelp across the legs for having given everybody such a fright. There were no cuddles for weans in our tenements when they played at such dangerously daft games.

Even more serious was the fall suffered by one of Tommy's chums who lived in the next close. He was a quiet, very thin boy, who never seemed to get enough to eat. His father always seemed to be out of work, and once when my auntie went to visit them when the mother was ill she saw the father mixing flour and water and frying it in the pan, pretending this paste mixture was pancakes. Auntie had cried when she told us, but we thought it was quite clever of him thinking of such a thing, for we weren't used to menfolks taking the slightest interest in cooking. It must have been this sort of diet, though, which made the boy Alan so pimply and listless, and yet when the boys went exploring over the roof-tops of a workshop at the Railways one summer night it was Alan who got the devil into him and accepted the dare to jump from one wooden roof-frame to the next without touching the glass. He hadn't the energy for such leaps, and the next moment had crashed through the glass to the floor beneath. Luckily, a policeman had seen them, and when he heard the crashing glass, phoned immediately for an ambulance. He took little notice of the other terrified boys, and sat by Alan until the ambulance arrived to take him to hospital.

Few of us got any sleep that night. It seemed terrible that a summer game could end in such disaster. Our mothers told us that Alan had had to have dozens of stitches in his cuts, and his blood was so poor, if he were to raise his arms above his head, he could die! Raised arms would draw the blood away from his heart, it seemed. 'But how'll they stoap him fae pittin' his arms above his heid, Mother?' I asked. I always put my arms on top of my head when I went to sleep, and I didn't see how Alan would know what he was doing if he were sound asleep. 'Oh a nurse will sit beside him to make sure he disnae,' my mother said. We all prayed for him when we went to bed, and I lay and tried to pretend I was the one who mustn't move my arms or I would die, and I found it was torture to stop them creeping up to the top of my head. Oh I was so glad it wasn't me in that hospital. Oh this proved that our mothers knew best. Oh how good we would be if only Alan got better. It was touch and go for a week, for his constitution wasn't good. All the years of poor feeding had taken their toll, but he was a bonnie fighter when it came to it, and maybe our prayers helped, for he confounded the doctors and got better. We had a marvellous party when he came home. We didn't have it in his house, for five of them lived in a single-end with hardly a stick of furniture, so we had it in the back court, on pay-day. We had bottles of Iron Brew, and, when that was finished, wee pokes of health salts to make fizzy drinks, and Torrance's pies (one between two), and biscuits. And we drew chalk stumps on the wall connecting our wash-house and the one in the next back court, and played cricket, using an old tennis ball and a bat Alan's father had made from an old piece of orange box, and it was great fun seeing all the mothers down in the back court with us. Alan looked quite different. The food in the hospital must have been a wonderful surprise to his stomach, for he had filled out, and his thin cheeks were rounded and pink, and, best of all, he hadn't a single pimple. When I asked him if it was terrible not having been able to put his arms above his head, he stared at me. 'I never pit ma erms above ma heid in bed,' he said. 'I coorie doon and put them roon' ma shoulders to keep warm.' I decided the doctors must have been daft not to have asked him that, instead of making a poor nurse sit up all night making sure he didn't do something he wouldn't have thought of doing anyway, I thought if ever I had to go to hospital I would tell them everything I did and didn't do, so nobody's time would be wasted.

Alan's mother, with her sad face, red nose and pimply complexion, looked absolutely bewildered with all the excitement over her son's recovery, and I felt she must have something else to look forward to, so on an impulse I asked her to come along to our very next Guide concert. 'You don't have to take off yer coat,' I assured her, thinking I was being tactful, for I knew she didn't have a good dress for Sundays which she could reveal at a concert, but she needn't feel self-conscious in her brown tweed coat. 'I'm allowed to take somebody in for nothing,' I told her happily, 'because I'm producing one of the wee plays, and I'm helping to make the cakes.' This wasn't really true, but I knew I could easily make some tablet and sell it and raise the threepence to buy her a ticket. 'Whit about yer mother?' she asked me. 'Does she no' want to go?' 'Och naw,' I said. 'She's been umpteen times and she's going to a dance anyway that night.' That part was true, and Mrs. Dalrymple's eyes brightened as I described the lovely tea she would get, with home-made cakes and scones which we would bring round in the interval. These concerts were very popular with the mothers, and we did everything ourselves. They were held in the church hall, and the church officer rigged up a real curtain for the occasion, which we thought was very professional. For weeks beforehand we rehearsed our little plays and sketches, and I rejoiced in the heady power of producing several of them, ordering my cast about ruthlessly, and even replacing them if they hadn't learnt their words well enough. The captain and the lieutenant subcontracted the cooking chores. One batch of us was detailed to make scones, another to make pancakes, a third lot to make apple tarts or sponge cakes, and the money for the ingredients came out of the funds. On the night of the concert we streamed from our closes bearing large plates of home-baking, which we laid triumphantly in the church kitchen where a few mothers had been roped in to help set out trays of cups and saucers, fill sugar bowls and cream jugs, and see that the tea urn was working all right. This was put on at a wee peep of gas as soon as the concert started, so that the water would be boiling at the precise moment the curtain closed at the end of the first half of the concert. Having attended to the domestic side of the affair, we flew backstage to change into our acting clothes, and shivered with nervous delight as we heard chairs scraping and our audience filling the hall. They were out to enjoy themselves, were uncritical and easy to please, and they greeted our sketches and recitations and songs with enthusiastic applause, and we believed them when they told us we were 'as guid as a pantomime'.

At the end of the first half, eyes shining with delight that we'd all remembered our words, and drunk with power at our ability to send them all off into hilarious laughter, we raced to the kitchen for the plates of scones and cakes, and became waitresses handing out all the melting home-baking to our audience, who had now pushed their chairs round the walls of the hall to give us plenty of room to attend to them. The mothers came from the kitchen with teapots, for we weren't to be entrusted with hot tea in case we'd skail it over good coats, and soon everybody was sipping and munching to their hearts' content. 'Hiv wan o' thae scones,' they'd recommend a neighbour. 'Wan fae Jessie's plate, fur Mrs. Grant makes a scone as light as an angel's wing.' Pursed lips from a mother indicated she too had made scones, and was furious at somebody else's being preferred. We'd been well warned by our officers not to indicate the bakers of any of our proferred goodies, but old customers among our audience easily recognised tried and trusted pastry and were not to be fobbed off with just anything stuck under their noses. One fat lady sent me into hysterics when she tried to pop a piece of apple tart into her mouth, and it disintegrated and scattered over her ample chest. Rescuing the pieces, she said with a wink, 'Missing the rosebud every time.' This description of her large laughing mouth struck me as being so funny that I couldn't wait to get home and tell my mother about it. Every time I saw that big fat woman in the street afterwards I daringly called her 'Rosebud' under my breath, and enjoyed the incongruous description all over again.

Wee Mrs. Dalrymple was enchanted with everything. As my mother would have said, she fairly 'came oot her shell', and laughed and clapped, and drank tea, and devoured everything that was offered to her, whether it be entertainment or food. I nearly burst with pleasure when at the end, as I was on my way to the kitchen to help stack away the dishes and collect my scone plate, she caught my arm and said, 'My, that's the best night I've had for years, hen. Wait till I get hame and tell Erchie a' aboot it, he'll hardly believe whit rer wee turns youse a' are.' Her face was so flushed, her nose didn't look red at all, and the pimples were invisible, and I was amazed to discover she was quite nice-looking. What a transformation for threepence!

I wasn't sure whether I liked the concerts in the winter or the evening picnics in the summer best, for the Guides taught us to indulge in the exciting luxury of cooked food after an evening walking or trekking in the country. No dry or soggy sandwiches for us then. We'd saved up for weeks and bought little flat frying pans with folding handles which served both as cooking utensil and plate. We were shown how to make a fire from the paper we'd taken with us, and twigs we gathered on our walk. Stones were cunningly positioned to provide protection and a strategic draught, and we'd crouch over damp twigs and paper until a glow told us the fire had caught, and then it was turn and turn about to make cheese dreams or sausages. Another fire was started a little way off and this was for our tea, and what a lovely smoky taste it had. I was charmed with how easily an ordinary cheese sandwich could be transformed into a delicious gooey delight by the simple process of turning it over and over in hot dripping or margarine until it was crisp and brown on the outside and running with soft melting cheese in the centre. Not that we often managed to achieve such perfection, for we were all thrusting our frying pans over the rim of the spluttering fire at the same time as the girl who was supposed to be having sole use of it, and we were far too impatient to wait for a golden outside and a soft centre. A prodding finger would tell us our sandwich was warm and we'd shout, 'Oh, mine's ready', and the sight of our rolling eyes and munching jaws would be too much for the steadier types, and soon they were eating their half-cooked sandwiches too. I only really learned what it ought to look and taste like when I made some one night for my mother's tea at home, and after that I took time to wait and achieve proper results on our Guide picnics. Nobody had to tell us about litter, for we burned all our papers in the fires to help the cooking, and we ate every single bit of food we brought. If one couldn't finish what she had cooked there were plenty of eager takers to snap up the leftovers. In fact, some of the girls brought nothing, and, as I primly quoted from the Bible to them, depended on 'the crumbs from the rich man's table'. 'Ach you and your bible,' they'd retort, 'there's aye plenty left, and onywey we helped to blaw into the fire tae get it gaun.' That was true enough, but still I felt if other folk could take the trouble to provide a sandwich, however small, so could they. I was a great one for fairness, and scornful of lazy ways, and anyway Grannie had taught me to despise mooching.

It was strange how the language of the Bible always sprang so readily to my lips. I loved its rolling phrases, and used to race along to school chanting, 'Tell it not in Gath, publish it not in the streets of Askelon, lest the daughters of the Philistines rejoice, lest the daughters of the uncircumcised triumph.' And as I turned the corner, I wailed, 'Ye daughters of Israel, weep over Saul, who clothed you in scarlet, and other delights, who put on ornaments of gold upon your apparel.' What marvellous sounds they were. And yet when we went into the playground I could also chant with the others,

'The Lord said unto Moses,
The Jews have a' big noses.'

And when we played a running game I could sing with the rest, 'Matthew, Mark, Luke, John, hold the cuddy till I get on.'

I saw no difference between this doggerel and the back-court chant of

> 'Dan, Dan the funny wee man,
> Washed his face in the fryin' pan.
> Combed his hair wi' the leg o' the chair.
> Dan, Dan the funny wee man.'

They were just daft rhyming sounds, but ah, the language of the Holy Bible was quite different and stirred me to the heart. There was a special prize given at our Sunday School, and seeing my interest in the Bible's teachings and my ability to memorise, the superintendent gave another girl and me special coaching up at his house every Friday night for the six weeks before the examination. We'd trot away up Balgray Hill after our tea, and I drank in the splendour of the fine red sandstone terrace house, with its stained-glass windows in the hall. Stained glass! I'd never seen that anywhere else but in Church, but maybe he got it specially because he was a church superintendent and they'd had a few bits left over when they'd put in our stained-glass window in the Church. We wiped our feet carefully on the bass mat inside the front door, and tiptoed through the tiled lobby to the big room at the back. There our teacher sat at a desk spread with papers of old examinations and proceeded to question us on our bible knowledge. He seemed smaller in his own house somehow, and different wearing his working jacket and not the black one he usually wore on Sundays. But he soon stopped my mesmerised staring by thrusting an examination paper into my hands and bidding me sit down and answer the written paper now. He recommended we study the book of Luke for the main part of the exam and I committed the entire book to memory, striding up and down our kitchen every night at home until I had got it all off by heart. That was that, I thought, they wouldn't catch me out now, for I knew it word for word. What a boon this was later on in my school exams when bible knowledge was one of the subjects, and I could choose the New Testament. With St. Luke's help I flew through the paper, and made sure of good marks for at least one subject. And the dedicated little superintendent's coaching paid off too for I was dazed and honoured to be presented with the special John Brown prize with the best marks for all the churches in Springburn. My goodness, maybe my grannie was right, maybe I was going to be a minister! I was sorry for my fellow-student, though, who had taken the special coaching with me each Friday. 'Ach I didnae want tae go to thae lessons,' she said stoutly. 'Ma daddy made me go, but ah knew I wisnae in the hunt.' I hoped she meant it, for I was beginning to realise that when one wins, another has to lose, for this was the first time I had been taught in a class of two people, when I could see the loser had worked too but had not met success. When a youngster was immodestly boastful of triumphs, and somebody else criticised this, we used to say in the tenements, 'Ach well, if ye don't blaw yer ain trumpet, naebody else will blaw it fur ye.' But I knew this was no time for blowing trumpets, and I kept very quiet about my John Brown prize, and put the special bible on the shelf without showing it to anybody. I was surprised to find all these mixed feelings in myself. Was it possible I was learning sense, as Grannie had always predicted I might some day?

9

I HADN'T much sense, though, the day the teacher finished up an English lesson by instructing us to see for ourselves how widespread was the habit of bad spelling, by taking a look at the big signboard on the rag store opposite the school. The rag store was the mecca of all who were short of a few pennies to tide them over till pay-day, but were without anything which would be acceptable to the pawnshop. Old fenders were lugged round and put on the big scale, and the heavy weights adjusted to find an exact balance so that justice could be seen to be done. Prices were chalked on a board inside the shop. Woollens tuppence a pound, iron a penny a pound. We watched like hawks to make sure we weren't being done, for we regarded the old man as our natural enemy, who would short-change us if he could get away with it. It seemed to take a mountain of old woollens to make up a pound, and, of course, only jerseys or skirts or trousers torn beyond redemption found their way there. Great gaping sacks of old clothes were ranged all round the tiny shop, and there was a mound of old fire-irons, ashpan fronts, pokers, kettles with the bottoms burnt out, which compounded to make a curious smell which made us catch our breath when we came out of the fresh air. Grannie or my mother seldom had anything for me to take there, for everything in our house was either unpicked and used again, or washed and hemmed and turned into dusters or polishing cloths. But often my chums' mothers were pleased to exchange their old bundles for welcome coppers to buy chips or Lorne sausage for their tea, and I went with a chum and thoroughly enjoyed my peep inside this ragged emporium. We had paid no attention to the big hand-printed sign above the door, for we knew exactly what went on inside the shop and that the old man wanted our rags and our old iron. Fancy the teacher reading the sign though, and what could she have found? We could hardly wait for four o'clock, and raced across to the rag store, wondering what we had missed. It was as good as playing guesses in the sweetie-shop windows. There were so many spelling mistakes, we sat down on our school-bags or our cases, whipped out our jotters and pencils and started writing them all down. 'Will bye anithing.' Giggles from all of us. 'Oh there's another one,' and we laughed triumphantly, 'only one l in woollens.' 'Och, look how he's spelt cardigan, with a "k".' 'And trousers with two oo's.' This was great fun, we thought. Wondering what all the commotion was about, the old man came out, looked at our convulsed faces and the signboard above his shop. 'Whit ur youse daein'?' he demanded. 'Whit's up?' In perfect truth and innocence I piped up, 'We're writing down all your spelling errors—the teacher told us.' The teacher no doubt had merely intended we silently note the inaccuracies and take a lesson from them that we must be more careful in our own writings. She certainly couldn't have intended this open assessment of the old man's poor spelling.

After I'd spoken there was silence. He didn't chase us away, as we'd thought, for we'd half-risen from the pavement ready for flight. Instead his face slowly crimsoned, and he turned back and went into the shop without a word. I felt sick. I suddenly realised how terrible this was, giving somebody such a showing up in front of everybody. And maybe he hadn't had a good teacher like ours to teach him his spelling when he was a wee boy. How could I have *done* such a hurtful thing, and me with the John Brown prize for bible knowledge. 'Tell it not in Gath,' I cried to myself as I ran home. 'Publish it not in the streets of Askelon.' For a long time I couldn't face that old man, but one day when I went in with a chum to help her carry a clothes-basket full of rags I gave him a wee gollywog Grannie had made before she died, for good luck. He took it and pinned it on his skimpy cardigan, and I knew I was forgiven.

But who could have dreamed a wee lassie like me could hurt a grown man, and who could have thought anything I said could bring a shamed blush to the cheeks of somebody I'd always thought of as an old skinflint. Oh when would I ever learn!

It was around this time that I plunged into the mysterious

world of domestic science at school. I, who was a natural swot, who loved books and learning, now found myself in a strange practical world where I had no great natural aptitude (apart from cooking) and where my tiny build was a positive handicap. We marched round Springburn Road to Petershill School because Hyde Park, our own school, had no domestic equipment. This was a great novelty in itself, and I was prepared to enjoy everything. For laundry lessons we went down to a dark, damp, steamy basement. Little tubs were filled with soapy water and we were shown how to scrub the garments we'd been asked to bring. A soiled pillow-case one week, a dirty jersey the next, some tea-towels another week, socks, and so on. Mothers were highly amused at this tiny washing, but we took it all very seriously. Hot stoves were ranged along one wall, and their fierce heat soon dried our washings, while we listened to the teacher tell us how we must scrub some materials gently, and that we must never rub woollens, and how socks and handkerchiefs had to be washed separately. Little flat-irons were neatly ranged against the hot stoves and were heating while we absorbed all this information. We'd never realised there was so much to getting clothes clean. Our mothers just went to the wash-house, and seemed to manage everything quite naturally. We felt quite sure they'd never get through their work if they were as finicky as this teacher.

Then came the ironing. Our linen was laid smoothly on the ironing board, and damped with tiny sprinkles of water if it was too dry. The iron had to be picked up just so, and given a tiny spark of the cold water from the cup, to make sure it was the right heat. If it bounced off in a fiery spark, that was perfect. We must on *no* account use spit! But there was only one cup and we grew tired of waiting our turn. Everybody we knew used spit, and so we did too, and many a burnt wrist we got in consequence, for we jerked the iron back to apply the saliva surreptitiously and if the wrist was too small, as mine was, the weight of the iron tipped it back just that fraction too much and it stung the wrist with a fiery tongue. Then it was a rush back to the stove to get rid of the iron, and a war-dance of agony till the burn stopped stinging. We soon learnt, though, that the pain stopped if we plunged the burnt place in water at once, but, of course, if the teacher saw us racing for the sink and the cold tap she knew what had happened and we were sent to the end of the queue, and had to miss our rightful turn at the ironing board. What with the heat of the stoves, the steam, the weight of the irons, the burns, I felt I was in hell. One day the teacher said to me with a sigh, after inspecting a half-washed tea-towel, 'I'm afraid you'll never make a washer-woman, Molly.' I looked round this inferno and muttered, 'I've no intention of being a washer-woman.' I waited for the heavens to fall, but she actually laughed. It was much better after that, but I only got through this course with the skin of my teeth, with exam marks that made me grit my teeth in despair.

The cookery classes had been started earlier and were great fun, and no trouble to me, thanks to Grannie's good teaching. And then it was my turn to be amazed at how difficult some of the girls found these lessons. Where they were neat and quick and enviably professional with washing tub and iron, and I was all thumbs, the moment it came to weighing out ingredients and rubbing fat into flour, or beating fat and sugar, they were in agonies of indecision. They'd race round behind the big scrubbed tables and show each other their mixing bowls, while the teacher was busy. 'Is that a' right?' they would ask. 'Ah don't know whit she means when she says it should be like fine breadcrumbs', or 'Oh gosh, I'll *never* get this bloomin' margarine and sugar to look like cream'. And I, who was a dead loss with the smoothing iron, would have my cake, or scones, in the oven, and was able to spare a hand to get their baking ready for the oven.

But when it came to the sewing machine I was back once more to bewilderment and misery. I hadn't even dreamed I could be so thowless, for I loved the ordinary sewing classes. With enjoyment and great care I did tiny gathers on a little piece of flannel, and the result was like a dainty Lilliputian bedspread. Buttonholes on linen looked flatteringly professional. My hems, which took hours, showed not the faintest stitch through to the right side of the material. I did cross-stitch, and I even managed blanket-stitch and honeycombing, and I had actually looked forward with keenest anticipation to the day when I would reach the stage when I'd be introduced to the joys of the sewing machine. Fancy being able to whizz along seams in seconds, where hand-sewing would take hours. I was dazzled at the prospect, and could see myself making all my mother's curtains, and running up wee pieces of gingham into summer dresses for myself. Maybe even managing a blouse for my mother. At last after the Easter holidays wee Mrs. McKenzie took the cover off the old-fashioned machine, told us to gather round while she explained the various parts to us, and our eyes sparkled with joy at having the luck to learn to be dressmakers in the school's time. In my innocence I had imagined all I needed to know was how to get the material to hold still while my feet pumped the treadle, and the magic union of thread and material would follow. I was soon to learn otherwise. There were terrible hurdles to be overcome first. There was a shuttle which had to be threaded, and before even *that* could be done a wheel had to be loosened, another little gadget brought down to hold the shuttle, and the final snapped off thread brought through a slanting slot which, as far as I was concerned, gripped the thread in a steely jaw and refused to release it. Then came the battle to insert the shuttle, and bring the thread out of a little central hole. This completely baffled me. The other girls could sit down, hold top thread gently but firmly in steady fingers, give a quiet pressure on the treadle, and up popped the thread for them, like magic, without the faintest sign of a tangle. Never for me. With a sigh Mrs. McKenzie would show me over and over again, while the others got on with the finishing touches to their garments.

Threading the needle was just as bad. My tummy turned somersaults of mingled eagerness and dread as the moment approached for me to step forward, perch nervously on the chair, and try to copy the teacher's instructions. Heart pounding, I'd put the reel on top of the little spindle upside down. Gently Mrs. McKenzie would turn it right way up, while the rest of the class sniggered into their sewing. I'd attempt to wind the spool without first slackening the wheel at the side. Snap would go the thread. Red-faced, my eyes smarting with tears of shame, I'd correct this mistake, only to overfill the spool and have the extra thread whirl round like a dervish, while my feet, which ought to have stopped by this time, still threshed round with wild abandon.

I begged Mrs. McKenzie to allow me to do all my sewing by hand, but it was no good. She was being paid to teach me to familiarise myself with the use of the sewing machine, and teach me she would or die in the attempt. Well, she never died, indeed if anybody was going to die it looked more like being me, for the nervous tension of every sewing lesson was now enough to bring on a heart attack. I never did learn to familiarise myself to anybody's satisfaction, least of all my mother's.

We had a drop-head sewing machine at home which was my mother's pride and joy, and which stood like an ornament in a corner of the kitchen. My mother had bought it second-hand, because nearly everybody in the tenements felt this item was an essential part of household equipment. Think of the money that could be saved by turning sheets sides to middle, by giving a new lease of life to pillow-cases, or turning ones past repair into hankies. Of the curtains which could be run up from sale material. Oh a machine was a godsend to anybody. But somehow it didn't work out that way in our house. In fact I basely thought I must have inherited my ineptitude from my mother, for she was always on the point of going to use it for one of those many marvellous savings, but somehow she never did. I began to feel she was as frightened of a sewing machine as I was. She'd encourage a neighbour to try it, and to show her how to do this splendid bit of renewing of worn sheets.

So warm was her admiration, as feet flew up and down on the treadle, and sheets gained new life before her very eyes, that the neighbour carried on and completed the job, basking in the warmth of my mother's genuine praise. While all this was going on, I'd stand by, sucking in my cheeks in concentration, trying to watch every single movement of the expert.

When the neighbour left, an old piece of material was coaxed out of my mother, and I'd sit down at the machine, sure that *this* time I had the measure of it. I would place material carefully under the lever, just as the neighbour had done, I would check the size of stitch, tautness of thread in needle, make sure the side-wheel was properly tightened, and balance my feet on the treadle in readiness for the tattoo to follow. In about thirty seconds the needle was back-firing, then plunging up and down on the same spot. Panic filled my breast and my feet forgot their rhythm. The wheel flew backwards and the thread broke. Seething with fury and frustration, I'd leap to my feet, kick the machine for a stubborn brute, and head for Springburn Park and the road leading to the Campsies.

Only a good long walk could calm me down. Those attempts to familiarise myself with that unconquerable machine were the starting gun for many a marathon hike towards the hills, and maybe even the basis of my reputation as one of the best walkers for miles around.

And I never did get making my mother's curtains. On the one occasion when she had rashly entrusted a piece of precious curtain material to me I'd had to unpick every single stitch because the stuff had somehow got itself puckered and wouldn't lie flat. We both stared at the rows of wee holes bizarrely flanking the re-sewn seam, and my mother declared she could never hold her head up again if folk saw such a mess at her windows. Ruining my wee bits of cloth was one thing. Sabotaging her treasured window-drapes was quite another and she wasn't having it, not even to spare my feelings. I couldn't blame her. I sighed gustily, and I had to agree in my heart with my school-mates who told me, 'Aye, ye can maybe pass exams, hen, but you're rotten at the sewin' machine.'

And then thankfully we went on to embroidery, both with silks and beads, and this was much more to my taste. We had the excitement of ironing transfers on to our garments, and following the design of little flowers and scrolls with all the traditional stitches passed on to us by clever Mrs. McKenzie. My mother picked up a bit of brown serge at a sale, which I made into a dress at school, and I decided to embroider a scroll design round the neck in tiny brown beads. The other girls thought I was mad, risking ruining a dress in this way, for our other transfers had been stamped on to pillow-cases, or hankies, or nightgowns. But Mrs. McKenzie approved this flight of fancy, which she flatteringly said was how dress designers worked to achieve originality, and she helped me to iron the transfer on to the serge without scorching the material. I think she felt I needed some encouragement after my disastrous attempts with the sewing machine. I was allowed to take my dress home to work on this bead embroidery, for there wouldn't have been time to do it in class if it was to be ready for the school concert, and I curled up in the big chair every night after I'd done my homework, fascinated to see the flowers and curves take substance as each bead was carefully stitched into place. The neighbours followed the progress of this embroidery with keen interest. With their practical approach, they'd never heard of anybody putting beads on clothes, which would make both washing and pressing difficult, but we all enjoyed a touch of luxury, especially when it cost nothing but a packet of beads at sixpence, and they were forecasting a future for me as a finisher in some swanky dressmaking establishment. They were sure the toffs would love to have beads on all their clothes and would be glad to let me work for them. I was so surprised and flattered by all this praise that I instantly saw myself top embroideress in a posh dressmaker's, then I realised how long it was taking me to get round that wee neckline. 'Naebody could afford to pay good wages to somebody who took hours and hours and hours to do one neckline,' I thought. Anyway, could I be bothered to sit still for all that length of time, just sewing? Reluctantly I put the dream aside. There were far too many exciting things to be done to spend my life sitting sewing.

And then, suddenly it seemed, I was within three months of leaving school. Exams followed fast upon one another, and the whole tempo of schooldays changed, for now we were having all our teachers' good work put to the test, and writing down answers which would decide what sort of leaving certificate we would have to present to future employers. The girls in the Co-operative again gave me special pen-nibs to flatter my handwriting, and I used an old ivory pen-handle, a treasured favourite, which I thought brought me good luck. I cleaned my ruler to make sure there wasn't a speck of grease on it, and a rare wee pencil-sharpener brought all my pencils to a fine neat sharpness. The teachers provided clean sheets of blotting paper. The answers were to be unlocked from head, heart and memory. There wasn't a sound to be heard in the room but the scratching of pens and the rustling of leaves as we turned over our papers to finish our questions. It was a strange feeling, just seeing the teacher sitting quietly behind her desk, nothing written on the blackboard, and not a word to say to us after the opening advice to read through the question, make sure we understood it, and answer to the best of our ability. She was only to be consulted in emergency, if a question wasn't entirely clear. The only respite from study during this time of concentration and decision were the hours spent finishing the dresses we were all making for the prize-giving on our very last day. My mother had bought a little remnant of pale green sponge-cloth for a few shillings, and this was not only to be my exam entry for the dressmaking class, but was also to be worn on my very last day as a schoolgirl. Mrs. McKenzie helped us to cut out our dresses, and supervised every move, and as a great favour I was allowed to make the whole thing by hand, as I was terrified to trust the pale purity of this material to the devilish whims of the sewing machine. This concession was granted, because I promised on my part that I'd make and embroider the white collar which was to finish the neckline, instead of buying one at the wee shop up Springburn Road for 6½d. Mrs. McKenzie said that as I wanted to spurn the machine, I should go the whole way and make the entire dress by hand, collar and all, and prove that all I needed was patience and sewing cotton. And anyway, she was always keen to see us master the art of embroidery.

The dress pattern was of the simplest. High round neckline, short sleeves, skirt gathered with little stitches on to a longish bodice, and the white collar was made from a left-over piece of material from another girl's blouse. Round the edge of this collar I worked little blanket stitches in pale green, the exact shade of the dress, and as a final touch I worked small clusters of French knots in the corner of each front scalloped edge.

The night before prize-giving we had a concert for our parents, and for this I wore the brown serge with the beads round the neck. Fancy having *two* new dresses at once! I kept running to the wardrobe and looking at them, hardly able to believe that they were mine, and that I had made them all myself. I thought it was truly marvellous of the school to let us sew like this, for I never regarded sewing lessons as lessons at all, but just a sort of playtime between the serious stuff of learning. A great chum Maggie called round to collect me for this concert. She had grown to alarming proportions during the previous year, and her mother had decided that for the school concert she must wear what we called 'stiff stays', and what the shops called whalebone corsets. She was only fourteen with a large sad face, and lank greasy dark hair, but she was clever in class, and she held for me the fascination of having a father who kept a fruit barrow, and who always had a barrel of rotting apples in the lobby, to which the family could help themselves. These were apples 'touched' with the weather and so not perfect enough to sell, but good enough for the children to munch for nothing. I found this fruity smell entrancing and a great change from the usual house smells of soap and dungarees. I didn't much like the apples themselves, for they were usually cookers and far too sour for my taste, but Maggie munched them with noisy enjoyment, finishing them right down to the smallest core before she would throw the stump away. She ought to have been slim as a willow, and have had a complexion of milk and roses with all this fruit, but alas her face was sallow and heavy, and her figure definitely in need of something. I was horrified, though, to find that it was to be stiff stays for her at such a tender age. 'But, Maggie,' I said, shocked when she told me, 'How will ye breathe?' After the freedom of a Liberty bodice I felt such constriction would be like a strait-jacket. 'I don't know,' she said mournfully, 'especially when it comes to the high notes of yon songs we're to sing.'

When she arrived to collect me we all stared at her curiously, as she perched herself stiffly on the edge of the chair. I'd told my mother and my brothers of Maggie's stiff stays as I couldn't keep such interesting news to myself. Poor Maggie. She couldn't bend, and she might have been wearing armour-plate below her blue taffetas, she looked so rigid. We didn't say a word, of course, for we didn't want her to know that we were all aware of her corsets, and then to my fury and embarrassment Tommy, who had been sitting chortling over a piece of paper and pencil since she came in, thrust the paper under my nose and there, large as life, he had drawn a congested Maggie seated perilously on a collapsing chair, and underneath in large letters he'd written: 'Maggie Gourlay in her stiff steys!' I burst out laughing before I could stop myself, and delighted with this success, he stuck it under Willie's nose, then my mother's, and there was poor Maggie looking from one struggling laughing face to the other, murmuring 'Whit is it? Can ah get seein' it?' 'Naw naw, Maggie,' said my mother at last. 'It's juist a daft family thing ah'd be affrontit to let onybody else see.' I seized the paper and threw it on the fire, ashamed of our laughter, and gave Tommy a skite on the ear in passing for his cheek. It would have been awful if, on top of the misery of her armour-plating, Maggie had realised she had been the subject of that unexpected cartoon.

When we got outside I tentatively touched her back with an exploratory finger to see how the stays felt. It was like touching a brick wall. 'Oh, Maggie,' I cried, 'I hope I never get fat! I hope I never have to wear these things. I'd *die*. It must be like being suffocated.' 'Och I expect I'll get used to them,' said Maggie gloomily, 'But right enough, they're murder. You'll have to sing twice as lood when we come to the high notes, for I know fine ah'll never get them oot.' But the funny thing was when we got to the concert, the teachers complimented her so heartily on her trim figure, so nicely encased in whalebone, that she forgot her discomfort and sang as blithely and bonnily as any lintie. It was splendid to hear her, and to be reassured so convincingly that she could breathe after all. I was so happy for her, and I wanted to make up to her for our family laughter and that comical drawing, so I went and collected the tea and the cakes for both of us, and left Maggie purring to the praise of the mothers who told her she had a rer wee wasp-waist noo, and was a fine figure of a wumman. I got back in time too to hear them say that they'd never heard 'The Eriskay Love Lilt' and 'The Tangle o' the Isles' sung better. Maggie's cup was full. For those were the songs our class had sung on its own, and Maggie had taken a solo verse in each. So her stiff stays hadn't handicapped her the least little bit. She drank her tea and ate her cakes with zest, and told me all about the job her father had found for her and which she was starting the week after she left school. Her dad knew the fruit and flower trade, even though he only had a barrow himself, and Maggie was going to work in a posh florist's shop, and would learn to make bouquets, and wreaths, and deliver flowers and plants to the big houses out Great Western Road. We both thought this was a marvellous job, for we both loved flowers, and had once been so carried away by our passion for the scented delicacy of pansies in the Public Park that we had picked two purple ones each, and had hidden them in the elastic of our school bloomers before we ran home to put them in water. The poor, crumpled things had refused to revive in water, and we had learnt our bitter lesson that not only could we not enjoy them, but neither could anyone else. Oh just fancy having all the flowers in season to play with, and to be taught such an artistic trade.

I, to my amazement, was going to college. My mother had hoped for a job for me behind one of the impressive mahogany desks in the Co-operative offices. This was the summit of her ambition for me. To her, the Co-operative had the all-embracing security of a merciful God. It provided the food we ate. It provided us, through its rare dividends, with savings for holidays, for blankets, and all special occasions. It gave jobs to my brothers, delivering milk, and actually gave them woollen gloves in the winter to stop the cold of the can handles biting through to their fingers. And surely, she thought, if only they could be persuaded to give me a job as a clerkess, we would be set up for life. She actually persuaded Tommy to start there as a message boy and go on to being a grocer behind the counter. When at last the light dawned, and he realised he was the squarest of square pegs in a round hole, and that he wanted to write and explore the world, she nearly broke her heart, certain that he would die a pauper, but not before he had lived to regret giving up such a splendid job. If he'd abdicated from the throne of England she couldn't have been more shocked or grieved. However, as I have told elsewhere,* my head teacher had other ideas, and somehow she got my mother's permission to let me try for a scholarship to a business college, pleading that this year without earning would be well spent and would be the rock on which I could build my future. My mother and I bleakly knew that the fees weren't the only obstacle—where could we find the money to dress me suitably to fit into such a background? The other girls would be from moneyed homes and we never had a spare sixpence. But my teacher's eloquence won the day, and my mother reluctantly gave up her dreams of seeing me take my place among the lucky ones to be privileged to sit behind one of those prized mahogany desks in the offices of the Co-operative.

So my schooldays weren't finished, after all. After the prize-giving there would be a year, a whole year, of college. It was the very stuff of fairy tales, for I'd never known anyone outside story books who had gone to such a place.

But first there was the prize-giving and my last day at my own school, which I had known and loved forever it seemed.

*See *Shoes were for Sunday*.

THE sun shone down from a cloudless blue sky on my very last day as a pupil at Hyde Park School. We had gone home at lunchtime to change into our best clothes for the prize-giving, and I felt I had never looked so clean or, to use my mother's words, as if 'I had just stepped out a bandbox'. My hair had been washed for the concert, of course, and was shining and clean, and I had pushed the waves up with my hand, as my mother did with her own red hair, to make them fall deep and furrowed over my ears. My pale green sponge-cloth home-made dress was so impossibly elegant that I held my hands stiffly away from my sides, in case the smallest trace of human moisture should sully its perfection. My mother had allowed me to wear my Sunday shoes for this special occasion, and I gazed happily at my feet encased in what the box described as 'champagne fine leather'. We'd never seen or tasted champagne, so took the shop's word for it that it looked like my shoes. Oh how dainty this impractical light leather seemed to me over my white socks, and such an exciting change from my long-legged black lacing boots and hand-knitted black stockings. I stood in line, still as any mouse, savouring the bliss of shoes on my feet on a Friday. The pebbles which I'd have normally used as miniature peevers to while away the time were ignored today, in case I'd scuff my toes and damage the splendour of my Sunday feet. I would have to walk up in front of the whole school to receive my prizes, and I wanted to be worthy of the honours I was receiving. For not only was I getting my leaving certificate, and books for English and bible knowledge and arithmetic, but I was also getting a silver watch from all the teachers because I was dux of the school. A silver watch! For me! I couldn't believe it. It was the first time such a thing had been done at our school, and they told me it was to mark the special privilege of my having been accepted at college, and because my work had shown such promise. They had actually asked if they could keep my school essays and had said something daft about the writing demonstrating to future pupils how imagination could bloom in unlikely surroundings. Of course they could keep them, I said. I'd never expected to have them back anyway. What did I want with them now that they were finished. I had loved writing them and used to go into a hypnotic dream over them, but they were only composition, after all, and I didn't see anything special about them. So while everybody else had their work returned to them, the school kept mine.

My mother was agog to hear all about it when I came home later that afternoon. What had the headmaster said? Did my teacher like my dress? She hoped I had been told how many turns to wind the wee knob at the top of the watch, so I wouldn't burst the main spring. This was a terrible risk, it seemed, and it was vital to know exactly how many turns to give. And I must *never* turn the hands backwards, if it stopped, for that would be the end of my watch. I nearly disgraced myself in her eyes, though, when I told her about the concert which had followed the prize-giving, when we had all been given sweets from a huge box handed round by the teachers, and then had been asked to recite or sing our favourite pieces. We had returned to our separate classrooms for this treat, and when we had exhausted our repertoire there were still about fifteen minutes to go before the teacher could decently dismiss us, so to fill in the time she had asked what we would like to do. For my first command performance I responded enthusiastically to the class yells of 'Molly Weir doing Malvolio's speech from *Twelfth Night*', followed by 'Molly Weir doing the snake dance'. My mother declared that Shakespeare, even if she didn't understand a word of it, was all right, but to do a snake dance in front of the class *and* the teacher was in the worst possible taste. 'Well, they wanted me tae dae it,' I protested feebly. I had felt in my bones I shouldn't have done it, but I'd been carried away by the shouts of my class-mates. My mother shuddered and cast her eyes heavenwards. 'Whit must have the teacher have thought o' you, and efter them gi'en ye a silver watch.' I had copied this dance from the performance of one of the adored film stars of the penny matinées; she was a slinky siren clothed in floating veils, who writhed and waved her sinuous arms under the hero's nose, and inflamed him to nose-flaring passion. It must have looked quite different performed by a wee panting school lassie in home-made apple-green sponge-cloth dress, waving her sinuous arms under the nose of a small elderly schoolteacher, whose gold glasses pinched her little button nose. But my mother's condemnation made me feel ashamed, and robbed the prizes slightly of their fine taste. Was I never going to learn to be a lady? I wondered. It was very difficult to know when I was behaving badly, for the teacher had been startled at first, which had alarmed me, but then she had laughed till her eyes all misted up and she had had to take off her gold-rimmed glasses to wipe them. She hadn't seemed annoyed, but maybe they weren't tears of laughter at all. Maybe I had disappointed her, just as I had my mother, this little teacher who was my good angel and to whom I owed the chance of going to college and getting a good start in life. I would never know, but oh I would work, how I would work when I went to that college, and I'd make her proud of me, for surely at the end of a year studying alongside the children of the gentry I'd know the difference between the beauty of Shakespeare and the vulgarity of a penny matinée dance. Oh I hoped so. I hoped so very much indeed.

How strange it felt not to have any school to attend on Monday. My mother was out working, of course, so my first taste of being a lady of leisure was looking after the house. I did the shopping and the cooking, but my mother emphasised I wasn't to do much housework, for she was sure I would breenge about and knock things down in my zeal. I could be trusted to set the fire, for I'd seen Grannie do this hundreds of times, and I could make the beds and sweep the floor, but I was to leave everything else until she came home at night. Our wee washer-woman was with us again, so the washing was taken care of, and we just had to do the ironing at night, and the brasses on a Friday or a Saturday. My mother scrubbed the floor, and I liked going down to the back court with her while the floor dried, and shaking the mats, and brushing them against the tenement wall. But I didn't think I liked this domestic life as a full-time job. It was too quiet with no

Grannie to tell me what to do, and the fun vanished when you were doing housework all by yourself. I began to understand why those young housewives who moved into our tenements enjoyed our admiring glances and comments as we perched on their window-ledges in the close and watched them at their household tasks. How lonely it must have been for them, transplanted from the cameraderie of the shop or the factory to the emptiness of a room and kitchen.

Ah but it wouldn't be for long as far as I was concerned, I told myself, for we were all going on holiday with my mother when she had her ten days off at the Fair, and then in August I would go to college. As I peeled potatoes for our dinner, I tried to imagine myself at this strange place. Would I be able to do the lessons? I would have to travel on a tramcar down into the town every single day, once in the morning, and again home at dinner-time. I'd walk back after my dinner to save the fares, and I'd walk home at five o'clock, for there was no hurry then and my legs were strong and willing. I could work out the time-table, but try as I might, I simply couldn't *see* the setting. Och well, there was plenty of time to think about it before August. But first there was the holiday. We pored over the advertisements in the 'holiday' column of the newspaper. We wanted the seaside. My mother said she preferred the country. Then we spied an address in Perth. We looked it up on the map, to make sure my mother was right when she told us it wasn't too far from Crieff, Grannie's birthplace, and it looked a splendid choice. The best of both worlds, really, for although it wasn't a seaside place, it had a grand river, and two Inches—what a funny name Inches—what could it mean? Best of all it was cheap. It sounded just fine for us. 'Room and kitchen with two beds, convenient for station and river. All linen supplied.' This last was a great boon, for it meant we could travel nice and light. No need for a hamper. This was far better than attendance, especially when we knew from bitter experience that my mother would never have taken advantage of attendance anyway.

It was a lovely holiday. A special sort of holiday. My mother was with us right from the start of the holiday for the very first time, and she came everywhere with us. I was in a sort of limbo, poised on the brink of the adventure of college, a prospect which half delighted and half terrified me, and

for hours. When I asked her where she was going, she answered vaguely, 'Doon the toon.' There was a conspiracy of silence about the names of the shops where my mother bought my clothes now. She didn't want me to know that she had a marvellous source of second-hand clothes at a wee shop near the Barrows, and delicacy forbade me to hint that I had guessed as much. There was a woman, I know, with whom she had an understanding, who kept a stall near the market, and this good soul kept aside specially good items bought from one of the big houses beyond Botanic Gardens. I had good cause to bless the well-lined girl who must have grown like Jack's magic beanstalk to be finished with her lovely clothes so quickly, for I couldn't believe anyone could have shown such a wanton lack of fondness for such expensive garments merely out of a desire for change. They looked so new that it was easy for me to pretend to my mother that I believed they came straight from an ordinary shop, and weren't the cast-offs of some 'toff's' daughter. What did it matter to me, anyway? The quality was staggering, and the cost out of my mother's hard-earned wages only a few shillings. Thanks to this unknown rich girl, so providentially one or two sizes bigger than me, I had a beautifully cut navy gaberdine raincoat for autumn days, and a heavy navy-blue reefer coat with matching navy velour hat for the coldest of wintry days, and those, with her navy gym slip, and my own jerseys and school blouses, which mercifully still fitted me, would see me through my year. 'Aye,' said my mother happily, when we'd tried on everything for fit, 'ye can haud up yer heid onywhere. Noo pit them away, and if ye can juist manage no' tae kick the toes oot yer boots, we'll dae fine.'

On the Sunday night before my first day at college I laid out my clothes for the morning. The weather was warm, so we decided my brown and white check gingham would be neat and cool, and my brown sand-shoes and white socks would be a douce respectable match. Books had already been listed and provided out of the scholarship, and I packed these in my school-case.

I could hardly sleep for sick excitement and when morning came I couldn't even swallow the roll I'd halved with my mother. How strange it felt to be waiting for a tramcar at half past eight in the morning. I'd never queued up for a tram with people setting off for work, and I hadn't realised how many folk slept in, and came dashing out of closes signalling furiously to the tram-driver to slow down so that they could jump on and not have the frustration of waiting for another car to come along. When my car came I clattered upstairs as usual, but at this time of the day it was packed mostly with men, and they were smoking, and I could feel my eyes begin to water with the heat and the smoke-haze. Oh goodness, I'd have to travel downstairs in future, for I didn't like this. That first morning I took the car right round to Bath Street, and walked along to the front entrance of the college, but later on I was brave enough and knowledgeable enough to come off at West Nile Street and cut through the lane, which saved a good two or three minutes while the tram was held up at the lights. I felt terribly self-conscious as I walked in those doors and up to the first landing, where the details of the classes were posted. I was far too early, and there was hardly anyone else there, so I stood and read the notice-board, trying hard to look as if I belonged. 'Secretarial Course'—ah that was mine! 'Shorthand, typing, arithmetic, bookkeeping, English, French, amanuensis, business methods, preparation for Royal Society of Arts examinations.' My stomach turned over at the strangeness of the subjects. English, French and arithmetic I knew, but what of the others? To take my mind off all this newness which I'd have to absorb, I turned to the other list. 'Civil Service Course'. What a rotten name. Civil Service. It sounded a bit like Domestic Service. I didn't think I would fancy that. I was glad nobody had thought of giving me a scholarship for *that*. Suddenly I was aware that the landing had filled with movement, and when I turned round I was surrounded by men and women. Not boys and girls. Men and women. How tall they were, and how old! Oh help, I'd never be able to study with such grown-up people. And what would they think of somebody as wee and as young as me daring to suppose I was in the same class as them? They were more like schoolteachers than pupils.

It was worse when I got into my first class, for I found that when I sat on my seat I couldn't reach the desk, so I had to sit on my feet, and there was an amused giggle from everyone, including the teacher, when I asked if I was allowed to do this. I didn't speak to a soul, apart from that teacher, on my first day. We changed rooms for each subject, and this was entirely new to me. We'd never done that at Hyde Park, apart from going away to another school for the domestic science subjects during our final years. What a clatter there was as we charged along corridors to the next class, and I was amazed that we weren't told to be quiet. Our Miss McKenzie would never have tolerated such a row. Maybe the teachers were frightened to tell those big men and women to hold their tongues. That must be it. I was dazed with the noise which ricocheted off the narrow corridor walls and went echoing up to the high ceilings. We seemed to do nothing but rush from class to class that first morning, and register with each teacher. I was glad to get out into the air at lunchtime, and join the queues waiting for the cars which would take us home for our dinner break. Hardly anybody ate in town in those days, and the cars were packed to bursting point. 'Full up inside,' sang the conductor as I leaped on to the step of the first red tram which came along. Oh well, I'd just have to thole all that smoke again. But to my surprise the air on the top deck was quite clear. Nobody, it seemed, was going to waste money smoking at this time of day, or maybe they didn't want to spoil the taste of their good dinner. Oh this was great. I could travel home on the top deck, after all, and have a good look out of the window. The shops were shutting for their dinner hour, and I was interested to see the assistants or the owners all dressed for the street, locking the doors after they'd pulled down the blinds. I hadn't realised how wee some of them were, having only seen them behind their counters, and some of the fierce ones looked quite ordinary with their hats on. One baldy-headed old man who kept a second-hand bookshop looked startlingly important with a dark Homburg on his head and a silver-knobbed cane in his hand. Mind you, we'd always suspected he was different from the rest of us, for he put hilarious notices in his windows when he went on holiday. One year it was 'Escaped—till 14th August' and another year it was 'Gone from the haunts of men— till 15th September'.

By the time we reached the Cally, the men were teeming out of the big railway workshop exits, and they marched alongside the tramcars, like an escorting army. I'd never realised how they filled the pavements as far as the eye could see, until this moment when I was able to look down on their heads from my seat aloft. Black faces above dark dungarees moved like a dark tide, with here and there a flash of amazingly white teeth as somebody laughed in response to a mate's comment. How quiet and purposeful they seemed, and although I had never heard the words then, I was conscious I was looking at the living embodiment of the dignity of labour. My mother had no time for conversation, for she was only in for her dinner too, and she was dishing out the broth for the four of us when I arrived. My brothers were also hurrying, for nobody had time to dally when the lunch period lasted only an hour. We had the boiling beef the soup had been cooked with, plus some potatoes my mother had heated through with the soup, and a bit of turnip to mash with them, and then it was time to clear the table, wash the dishes, and scatter to our various jobs. 'You go on,' said my mother to me, 'You'll need a' yer time if you're to walk back to the toon.' So the boys helped her with the dishes, and off I went, on foot this time, to complete this bewildering day. Some of the Cally men had already drifted back to the work gates, and were sitting on their hunkers against the low wall opposite, chatting, or reading their newspapers. They wouldn't budge till the horn blew, I knew, but they liked to be within strolling distance so that they were ready to start work when the second horn went.

The shopkeepers, too, were opening up their shops, and pulling up their blinds, in readiness for the afternoon's business. I realised I would be able to follow this pattern every day, now I was to be walking and travelling at regular times myself, and a sort of simmering excitement began to bubble up inside me that I was becoming a part of the busy life of Glasgow, and would be able to observe all sorts of exciting things on my way to and from college. I wasn't terribly sure whether or not I was going to enjoy being a student, but I was certainly going to enjoy two tram rides a day, and two rare walks to and from the town through interesting, teeming streets.

When I got home at half past five that first day I quickly changed into my old serge skirt and my weekday jumper, and ran down to the back court to tell my chums all about the vast difference between a college and school. They were in the middle of a game of 'statues', when a pose was struck and frozen at the command of the leader. This was one of my favourite games, and I especially loved to call out the commands As I ran to join them, the leader waved me away. 'Ye canny jine in, we've got enough.' My stomach lurched even more wretchedly than it had done on arriving at the college. I felt the hostility. I was different from them now. I was a college girl. It was as though a gulf had suddenly yawned wide between us. I didn't know what to do. These were my chums. I didn't want to be different from them. Suddenly I remembered Grannie's voice when I'd been left out of a back-court concert given by the big girls, and I'd stood dejectedly beside them, miserable at not being allowed to join in the songs and dances. She'd thrown up the window and called me up-stairs, and when I got into the kitchen she had said, 'Whaur's yer pride? Dinna staun' there and let them see you're hurt. You're faur better than ony o' them onywey.' I'd been so astounded by her support, for normally I was never encouraged to believe I was any better than anyone at play-acting, that I'd forgotten my misery, and hugged to myself the fact that Grannie thought I was good.

Now I looked at my chums, and I realised I mustn't say a word about college. I had just wanted to share the strange-ness with them, but it might look like crowing. So I just called out with what I hoped sounded like a cheery indifference, 'Och it disnae maitter, I've to get the tea ready onywey,' and I skipped through the back court and up the stairs to the house. It was all right after that. I never brought home tales of student life, and when they did ask me anything I made it sound just like the schooldays we had all shared at Hyde Park, so we were friends again, but I felt I was leading a double life, where the inhabitants of one half were completely uninterested in the activities of the other half.

After about a week or so I settled down to the new routine, and began to enjoy myself. Everything was a challenge, and of all the subjects embraced in this secretarial course, shorthand was my true love. I honestly can't explain just *why* shorthand should have held such an attraction for me, but from the age of nine the very word 'shorthand' fascinated me. Perhaps it was because even then I knew I wanted to write, and as my thoughts and words always tumbled out at lightning speed, it seemed to me marvellous that a system had been devised where I could write everything down with the minimum of delay.

I can remember at this early age tricking my chums one day by announcing proudly, 'I can write backhand.' I knew with childish cunning that they would think I meant 'shorthand', for I was always talking about this magic writing, and when they clamoured round me eagerly. I began writing carefully on the wall with chalk. They looked at my writing, which differed from the normal only in that it sloped backwards instead of forwards, and they fell upon me with disgust and disappointment, so that I had to run as fast as my laughter would allow to avoid a hefty bumping.

One night, not long afterwards, I was coming home in the tramcar from an annual visit to the Kelvin Hall Carnival, and I was sitting with my chums in the wide-open portion at the back of the tram where we could all crowd together in comfort. Somebody had dropped a leaflet from the current business exhibition, and I dived and rescued it from under a passenger's feet. I had spied the enticing word 'shorthand'. The leaflet gave the first elementary lesson in shorthand, and I began tracing the outlines with my finger and memorising the rules there and then. A gentleman who had been watching me leaned forward, 'Don't worry about that sort of shorthand,' he said, 'You wait till you're older and try learning Pitman's. It's understood all over the country and most business offices prefer it.'

I, of course, didn't know one form of shorthand from another but I was always willing to take advice. I threw away the leaflet, and made a mental note that if ever I had the luck to be able to study this subject it would be Pitmans for me.

And now I had my chance. I was starry-eyed as I opened the manual and was given the first lesson in the subject which was to be a much-loved asset for the rest of my life. From the first moment, I took to it like a duck to water. It had a logic which appealed to me, and which made understanding very simple. The flowing nature of the outlines were absolutely designed for speed, and the system of inserting vowels made reading back no problem. I found, though, that mere love of a subject wasn't enough. It also needed complete concentration to master every intricacy of the system, but this was no obstacle when the exercise was as attractive as shorthand was to me.

I was like a race-horse who'd been waiting for years to have a shot at the Derby.

I carried my shorthand manual with me everywhere, except to church, I studied it in the bus, in the trams, queuing for the pictures and while waiting to have my hair trimmed. There was no more gazing out of the windows on the trams. My nose was buried in my manual. Grammalogues and phraseograms filled pages and pages of my notebooks, until they practically wrote themselves.

I was possessed. I'm sure of it. When people talked to me, I'd develop a glazed look in my eye, for I'd be writing down every word of the conversation in shorthand, in my head. At dances I drove partners mad by tracing the conversation on their backs with my fingers. 'Is that you writing shorthand again,' they'd demand irritably. It was. It took *years* to break that habit.

After six months' study I'd won a bronze medal for having made the most rapid advancement of any student of my year. I couldn't understand why they felt they had to give me a medal, on top of the boon of teaching me something I was passionately eager to learn. It seemed to me a daft way to throw away their money, but of course I accepted it and my mother was very proud, and hoped I'd stop working ower thae books so much and go oot and enjoy masel' a bit for a change.

11

I STILL hardly knew a soul at the college, for as well as being frighteningly grown-up, those big students spoke 'pan-loaf', and my ear was sharp enough to detect a vast difference between their accents and mine. It wasn't necessary to speak very much, anyway, apart from reading back our dictation in the shorthand class, and that didn't come at the beginning, and I was so busy drinking in all my new lessons, so that I shouldn't waste a minute in making Miss McKenzie's belief in me come true, that I didn't really see my fellow-students as individuals.

One day our shorthand teacher asked if any of us would like to visit a Business Efficiency Exhibition at the Kelvin Hall, as he had one or two free tickets. I peeped cautiously round the class, for if it had been Hyde Park and something had been going for nothing a forest of hands would have shot up. To my amazement, not a hand was raised. Fancy none of those big folk wanting to go to the Kelvin Hall. Well, I'd given them their chance. Up shot my hand. 'You'd like to go, Molly?' the teacher enquired. I nodded and whispered, 'Yes, sir.' 'One or two tickets?' he enquired. Oh! I could take somebody. 'Two, please, sir,' I said huskily. I felt this was generosity beyond belief. My tickets were for the following Friday, and my chum and I walked down after our tea. I'd already walked down to college after my dinner that day and home again at five o'clock, but we were so used to having no money for such luxuries as fares that another walk to the town didn't give us a thought. Our legs were strong and it was marvellous to have free tickets for an exhibition. We'd have walked to the Campsie Hills and back for such a treat.

Lizzie, the chum I took with me, was fascinated to have a peep at this amazing world of typewriters, shorthand machines

—yes, they actually had a machine with shorthand characters on it—comptometers, even dictaphones which did away with the use of shorthand altogether, for the boss spoke into a wee gadget, and the typist wore earphones and listened to his voice as she typed. I thought this must be terribly confusing, and I wasn't too keen on anything which ruled out the use of my beloved shorthand. We played with envelope-addressing machines, and we shot a pile of envelopes through an automatic stamping fitment. When we came to the typewriters, I showed Lizzie how fast I could type 'Now is the time for all good men to come to the aid of the party', which Lizzie thought was a daft thing to type, and then I typed out her name and address and she thought this was wonderful. She'd never seen her name in print before, and was most impressed, especially as I had lengthened it to Elizabeth. In fact, she was so pleased that, without realising it, I had re-christened her, for from that moment onwards she insisted on everyone calling her Elizabeth, and skelped her brothers on the ear when they forgot. On the way out, a man handed me a little printed slip. We took everything that was given to us for nothing when I was a wee girl, and we read every leaflet that came our way, for we felt that it was only right if folk went to the trouble to write something and give it to us, then we must show some appreciation and read what they had to say. This leaflet told us that there was to be an essay competition open to all the business colleges in Glasgow and district, and three prizes would be given for the three best compositions describing the attractions of the exhibition. Closing date was the following Friday.

I had masses of homework to do, for each teacher piled on the work irrespective of the demands of the others, and the only night in the week I went out now was a Saturday, while the only day I didn't work was a Sunday. But I loved writing, and it seemed forever since I had written an essay. So I sat down at the kitchen table the minute I got home and started to write. I was still writing at 1 a.m. when my mother came in from one of her much-loved dances at the Highlander's Institute. 'You're no daein' mair hame lessons?' she said, aghast to find me up at that hour. 'Och it's fur a competition,' I said, 'but I don't think it's good enough. Ah'm no' gaun tae send it in.' 'You'll send it in,' said my mother decisively, 'efter burnin' ma gas till this time o' the mornin', and your face as white as a dish-cloot.' So we found an envelope and addressed it, and folded up my sheets of writing, for posting next day. And then we had a cosy cup of tea together, and I ate the gorgeous marzipan walnut she'd brought me home from the dance. They always seemed to get delicious food at those dances which were such a relaxation for my mother after her hard work in the Railways. Petty foors, they were called, which was a gey funny name for such lovely sweeties. (It was only after some time at French lessons I realised I was giving the Glasgow pronunciation of *petits fours*.) There were sometimes little toffee biscuits, luscious black grapes coated in transparent brittle toffee, slices of oranges treated the same way, *glacé* pineapple, wee bits of fudge, and even tiny chocolate biscuits. My mother would save one or two for me, for I always wakened when she came home, and she would have them wrapped in some tissue paper to keep them from making the inside of her evening purse sticky. They didn't have such luxury items at every dance, just the special ones at Christmas, or Hallowe'en, or St. Andrew's Night, and they were a wonderful treat for me.

I'd almost forgotten the essay competition, in spite of my misgivings at having posted it, in case the college would get a bad name if my work wasn't judged very good, when I came out of class one day and found a crowd clustered round the noticeboard. The names of the winners were posted up, and at the top was my name, sole winner from my college. 'Who's Molly Weir?' I heard them ask each other. 'I don't know do you?' 'Oh, wait a minute. It's not that wee thing who sits up on her feet to reach her desk, is it?' 'Yes, I believe it is. I didn't even know she'd entered. I never heard her consult the teacher about it.' As if I would! If they were surprised, it was nothing to the astonishment of my English teacher, and the college principal. 'You entered for this competition without asking for any help, Molly?' said my teacher. 'Without mentioning it to anybody?' 'I didn't know I had to,' I whispered back, nearly in tears, for it suddenly occurred to me that maybe I should have asked permission before going in for the competition, seeing I had had to put down the name of the college. 'Oh you didn't *have* to,' laughed the teacher, 'but I should have thought you might have wished for some help from me.'

I stared back at him. Surely that would have been cheating? Getting somebody to help me with work which was supposed to be all my own? I would never have dreamt of doing such a thing, but I didn't know how to say it without sounding ungrateful, so I didn't say anything. The college principal was delighted. 'Well done, well done,' he beamed. 'We'll have to keep an eye on you, young lady. It's a great honour for the college.' The blood rushed to my face. He had called me a young lady! Oh if Grannie could only have heard him.

And suddenly after that I seemed to know everybody and everybody seemed to know me. They laughed at my eagerness to study, and called me 'the mighty atom', and I listened to the way they spoke and tried, without getting pan-loaf, to tone down my broad accents a little. My mother helped, for somebody had heard me describe lovely brittle toffee as 'glessie toaffie', and had said to her, 'I'm surprised that yon college your Molly gangs tae hisnae taught her to speak a bit better than that.' Actually we all had two languages, one broad and comfortable that we children spoke to each other, and another which we used in school. I'd been sharing my 'glessie toaffie' with a chum when this neighbour had overheard us giggling about it. 'Oh, Molly knows how to speak when she needs to,' my mother had said loyally. 'The weans a' speak like that to one another.' Fancy my mother knowing that we did, and fancy her also knowing that I could speak properly if I wished. I'd been shy of doing this at home, afraid that they would think I was going all uppity because I was at college and I didn't want to emphasise any difference they might have noticed. And yet it was very difficult to speak correctly not only to the teachers but to all the other students in an acceptable accent, and change back to the broader vowels of Springburn at home. So, with my mother's encouragement, and a nervous ear for jeering always on the alert, I began to speak 'teacher's language' everywhere, and to my surprise, after a few laconic 'Swallied a dictionary?' queries, nobody seemed to take a bit of notice.

My prize for the essay was a fountain pen, and it was presented to me by the Lord Provost, no less, in a vast assembly hall off Sauchiehall Street. To my surprise, my mother decided to come with me. She usually kept away from prize-givings or any public appearances where she might have to speak to officials, but she couldn't resist a peep at the Lord Provost, and she wanted to see me march up and receive my fountain pen dressed in my navy-blue reefer coat and velour hat. It was a golden opportunity for her to check that I was as well turned out as other college students, and have a look at the fashionable outfits worn by their mothers. 'Aye,' she nodded sagely as she took the scene in, 'you can see they're a' gentry.' Her green eyes sparkled with pleasure when she noted that my navy reefer equalled the quiet quality of the clothes worn by most of the girls, but she was a bit disappointed that the Lord Provost only wore an ordinary dark suit and there wasn't a sign of a gold chain. Still, he had shaken hands with me, and had commented on my extreme youth, and she felt we ought to celebrate this honour by having coffee and cakes in M. & A. Brown's, the tearoom, when we came out. We never had coffee at home. This was a treat specially reserved for enjoyment in tearooms, and my mother radiated rich enjoyment as she ordered 'Two cups of white coffee, please, and some cakes'. She took the waitress into her confidence, to my embarrassment, and insisted on my showing her my newly presented fountain pen. 'My, a gold nib and everything,' said the elderly waitress admiringly, 'and ye goat it fae the Lord Provost, did ye, hen? That wis rer.' She brought us double sponge cakes filled with cream, liqueurs and meringues, and gave us an agonising choice, for we could only afford one cake each, so I chose a double sponge and my mother chose a meringue, and we halved them, so we each got a taste of both cakes. The waitress flashed chummy smiles at us as she served the other tables, for she knew as well as we did that this was a very special occasion for us, and that we didn't have coffee and cakes in a posh tearoom on many Saturdays of the year.

As we walked over Sauchiehall Street, gazing our fill at all the shop windows, my mother kept patting herself on the back. 'Aye, if it hidnae been for me, you widnae have posted that composition,' she kept saying. 'Noo maybe you'll believe what I say and you'll listen to me when I tell you you should get oot mair and enjoy yersel'. It's no good for you sittin' in like that every night. I'm sure nane o' thae other lassies dae it.' My mother was so certain by this time that I had found the secret of successfully passing examinations that she thought

I was being unnecessarily cautious in going over and over my lessons every night. What with her confidence in me, and Miss McKenzie's faith, I was in a fever every time I looked at that pile of books whose secrets had to be mastered. How could she encourage me to go out to enjoy myself with so much work waiting to be done?

In fact the only week night I went out during that whole year of the scholarship was the following Friday, when an old school chum knocked at the door to see if I'd go with her to a Scout Concert being held in the church up Springburn Road. Her mother had bought two tickets, for Ada and her sister. but the sister had gone down with a heavy cold, and Mrs. Paterson thought I might enjoy a night out, as my mother had told her I never put a foot over the door at night from one Saturday to the next. 'Go on,' urged my mother. 'It's Friday and you've nae college tomorrow, so you can dae yer lessons before your dinner.'

I hesitated. I had dedicated myself to study, but it was Friday, as my mother said, and I was well ahead with my shorthand exercises, my arithmetic paper was finished, I'd polished off the bookkeeping homework and the wee bit of French, so all that was left was a précis for the English teacher and I knew I could easily do that in the morning if I really felt I might allow myself to go out. But was I weakening my character, yielding so easily to temptation? 'Och come oan, Molly,' said Ada, 'I don't want to go masel', and ye get tea and cakes, and the ticket would just be wasted noo.' That settled it. I couldn't let Mrs. Paterson's ticket go to waste, so I went.

The church hall was ablaze with lights, which fairly dazzled me. I had forgotten people still went out enjoying themselves. It seemed almost bewildering to be with so many pleasure-seekers, and I could feel my head swimming with the buzz of conversations going on all round me as friends greeted each other, and I sat quite dazed by all this commotion after months of quiet concentration on my books in the comparative calm of our room and kitchen. I was glad when the noise simmered down and the concert started, and the strange, disorientated feeling vanished as I watched the Scouts drilling, and competing with one another in raising a tent as fast as possible, and listened to musical items which struck me as being very expert. There was an interval half-way through, and we were given a bag of cakes, and tea in cups, not tinnies. I'd never been to an adult affair like this before, and hadn't realised it was only at children's concerts the tea or milk had to go into tinnies provided by ourselves. What a rich church this was, though, for the cakes were from Torrance the bakers, and there was even a sausage roll as well as four delicious pastries. I kept a cake for my mother, a wee chocolate one, which I knew she liked. After the interval there were comedy sketches, and a comic who led us all in singing the choruses, and it was all thrilling and marvellous and I was enjoying myself 'up to the nines', as my mother would say. And then suddenly it felt all wrong to be sitting there among that audience who maybe had no responsibilities to work hard, as I had. I felt miles away from my books. When the concert ended, I told Ada that it had been great, but if she got any more free tickets, would she please not offer one to me, for while one night off wouldn't do much harm, two might lead me down the slippery slope to slothfulness, and it would be sheer treachery to the people who had got me my scholarship. She was a big girl, Ada, who was studying to be a nurse and she laughed at me, but kindly. 'All right, Molly,' she said, 'I won't tempt you again. But you're a gift to the comics, for you've got a rare hearty laugh when you let yourself go, and forget how wicked you are in skipping your homework.' I felt a great rush of affection for this understanding, kindly girl. Poor Ada, at the end of all her years of study, she had to give up nursing, for she possessed every quality except one. She could build up no immunity to germs, and fell a victim to every germ and virus, and, worse than that, she was a carrier. It was a cruel shame, for all her dreams were of curing the sick and caring for them in every way. But she was a good loser, and turned to nursery-school work instead, and the hospitals' loss was surely the children's gain.

Sundays were a great oasis in the working week, and I felt no sense of guilt in not opening a single college book the entire day. How enjoyable it felt to be getting ready for the church in my best clothes and my polished shoes. It made Sunday *feel* special to be so differently dressed. It induced a feeling of leisure, and people seemed to put on quite a different personality. The pavements between our house and the church took on a different look too, as though the very paving stones knew they were being lightly trodden on by the fine Sunday boots of the men and the patent or kid shoes of the women and children, and the rhythm was different from that made by the tramp of working feet or the busy skipping weekday steps of hurrying schoolchildren. Everybody strolled, the better to take in what everyone else was wearing. Not so much as a new pair of gloves went unobserved as we made our way from close to church, but not a word of this was spoken until after the service when we all gathered in groups on the pavement outside. We were supposed to be thinking of higher things on our way to church, and it would have been considered in very bad taste to mention fashion at that moment. I remember the older sister of one of my chums being severely upbraided by her parents because she had thoughtlessly confided that she had been thinking of the carpet for her new house while she was singing the hymns in church. She was shortly to be married and hadn't been able to keep her mind from straying, but she was told in no uncertain tones that she had taken all the good of the service away by furnishing her house in the Lord's time. Her mother and father felt no good could come of such behaviour and if that was the way she was starting out her married life, well she mustn't be surprised if God, in His own good time, didn't remember it and hold it against her. Even her sister said to me it wasn't much good Phemie taking her body to church when her mind wasn't also in attendance! Secretly I felt if I were getting married and getting a brand-new house and spanking new furniture and curtains I'd have found it just as hard to stop mentally placing all my beautiful things in their place, even in the Lord's House.

We were released from this pious attitude, though, the minute we streamed down the church steps, and formed our little groups according to age and inclination. We who were in the Guides and taught at Sunday School swooped on each other, and admired our new hats, or freshly pressed coats, or new umbrellas. Long umbrellas had come in again, and as one of the chums had a job in a shop specialising in these elegant accessories, we were all saving every penny to take advantage of her offer to get one for each of us 'wholesale'. The lucky ones who had already got theirs were the envy of the rest of us who were still struggling. We admired every detail of each handle, how neatly it fitted over the arm, how fine the quality. The silk tassel came in for its share of attention—how perfectly it took up the tone of the silk cover. We shared the owners' fervent hopes that it wouldn't rain too soon, for how would they ever restore the slim folds to their original perfection.

Meanwhile the mothers were complimenting each other on their own outfits and how well the weans were turned out. 'My, you've goat her just lovely,' one would say to another, eyeing a child in new summer or winter outfit. The men looked very impressive out of dungarees, in dark coats or suits, with hats having snap brims for the younger ones and heavier Homburgs for the older men, plus a bowler here and there worn by the dashing lads who had had the good fortune to land a job in an office in the city. The boys were very aware of their manhood and of the fine figures they cut in their Sunday best, and a few shy smiles were exhanged with the girls who stole glances at them under their eyelashes, before all went their separate ways for their dinner.

All our romantic attachments were formed with these boys whom we met through the church. Our religious observance, which played so large a part in our lives, became more thrilling and exciting when we could peep across at the lads under cover of our hymn-singing, and later we might join up with them for a few delicious moments on our demure walks over Crowhill Road after evening service.

One of these boys appointed himself to be my permanent escort. Not only did he race after me on my way home between church and Sunday School, he also accompanied me on my walks to and from college and back and forth to the office. He adapted his tastes and time-tables to mine and after he met me seldom spent money on fares.

From such small economies were our life-savings begun, for although we didn't realise it then, we were forming the habit of saving, a habit which never afterwards deserted us.

We saved against every hazard life had to offer, and our clothes were specially guarded against premature shabbiness, or 'Tashing', as we called it. I always changed out of my good clothes into my school pinny or my dressing gown the minute I got home from morning service for it would have been awful to have spotted my Sunday garments with soup or gravy, or even dish-water while I was doing the dishes. Then it was on with my finery again, and away to Sunday School, and my class of wee boys. They too wore their decentest clothes, often shabby and sometimes darned and patched, but their boots shone, and their hair was slicked down in wet spikes with cold water from the tap. Their faces shone from recent washing, and they settled down with much pushing and jostling to sit beside favourite chums, then to listen with great attention to the stories of the Bible. They collected the little coloured text-cards, which they had to memorise, like football cards, and if any were left over due to an absentee there was always an eager claimant ready to deliver the card to the missing pupil. They had so few presents in their lives that even a text-card was a covetable item, and they chanted off the message as though it were a popular song. They each had a ha'penny for the collection bag, which they proudly produced at the right moment, and they vied with one another to answer questions at the end of story-time. They called me 'miss' when they answered, just as though I were a real school-teacher, but they clearly knew that I wasn't one, for they always insisted on telling me the latest episode of the 'following-up' film, in their own words, if they decided the bible story hadn't been exciting enough to provide colourful answers from them. I enjoyed my elevation to the teaching profession, and the boys were happy in the warm companionship and ritual of Sunday School, and if it wasn't exactly a quiet reverent class, somehow it all added up to a satisfying hour in each other's company.

After Sunday School there was time for a walk up to Spring-burn Park before tea would be ready, and we admired all the flower-beds, and strolled through the hot-houses, and in high summer listened to the music from a brass band from the bandstand. We wandered up to the flagstaff, and gazed with passionate envy at people rich enough to possess cameras, who posed their families artistically against railings or leaning against bridges, to make a collection of snapshots for the family album. We thought it would have been marvellous to have had a record of ourselves in our best hats, carrying our splendid new umbrellas, to keep such elegant moments forever. To cushion our disappointment, we would say to one another, 'Och they'll no' likely come oot anyway, it's no' sunny enough', and we'd run home for our tea, for there was still the evening service to attend. I loved the evening service in our church, which had a small enough congregation to let us sit in any seat we fancied and not to be confined to our own pew, and my chums and I always sped upstairs to the gallery. The altered angle of the pulpit and the choir and the stained-glass window made it all so different we could hardly believe we were in the same church. Even our voices sounded different when we sang the hymns, and the lighting at eye-level dazzled us and made it all seem like a dream. I had a hard job not to be like Phemie, the bride-to-be, whose mind wandered, but just when I found myself beginning to think of my lessons, and start tracing the sermon in shorthand outlines on the ledge in front of me, it was the final hymn and there was time for a last stroll out Bishopbriggs before bedtime.

Sometimes, though, the evening was devoted to family visiting, especially if we had a relative home from abroad. This was especially exciting if it involved a tram journey, for Glasgow Sunday trams would be packed to bursting point with couples coping with excited vociferous children, clutching their toys, and maybe a wee present for their auntie or their grannie. Go-carts were manœuvred good-temperedly by conductors, and the air was lively with young voices, as children were handed down to parents at each stop the car made. It looked and felt like a holiday, as sons and daughters went to pay their filial respects.

And much much later that night, returning from visiting our own relatives, the tram would again be filled, but this time with silent, exhausted young parents, their white-faced weary children lying with heavy heads against drooping shoulders. There would be a whimper as a stop was reached, and a sleeping child had to be roused, and a go-cart handed down, and then once more a heavy weary silence which almost lulled the rest of us off to sleep. I was always struck with the contrast of the two journeys, and of the toll an evening's visiting could take out of people. And I never ceased to marvel at the heavy stupor of a child in deep slumber, or the pale exhaustion of parents. Sunday, the rich interval in the working life, was almost over, and maybe our tiredness came from knowing that the next day was Monday.

Our Sunday clothes were hung on the hook at the back of the kitchen door to air, before being transferred to the wardrobe in the lobby, where they would stay until the next Sunday and never see the light of a working day. Many of our neighbours, in fact, knowing such clothes wouldn't be needed from one week-end to the next, pawned them on a Monday morning and redeemed them at the end of the week, and so had use of the extra money the clothes earned. This meant they didn't even need a wardrobe, but my mother shuddered at the idea of living 'on the steps of the pawn' as she described it, and would have scrubbed pavements before she would have entrusted our hard-won best clothes to the care of a pawnbroker. The men in the tenements seemed to remain in ignorance that their Sunday best provided many a wee extra titbit for their teas during the week, for when a death occurred and the funeral required their dark Sunday clothes before Sunday the wives who patronised the pawn flew round the closes in a panic, trying to borrow money 'right, left and centre', as my mother said, to redeem the clothes before their husbands could discover the truth. 'Aye,' my mother would say, as she handed over a precious two shillings to help a distraught wife build up the necessary sum, 'there would be murder if your Jimmy found oot his suit was in the pawn every week.' 'Oh I know, Jeanie, I know,' would come back the answer. 'Oh it's awfu' good o' you. I'll pey ye back on Friday. Noo if I can just get another two bob from your neebor, I'll be a'right. He'll no' look for his suit till he comes hame fae his work the night, and I'll have it oot hingin' on the back o' the door by then.' The women seemed to thrive on such dramas, and the threat of an unexpected funeral didn't stop them making their usual trip to the pawnshop the following Monday morning. The funny thing was that nobody ever acknowledged that they themselves pawned clothes, until death struck and the urgent need for cash revealed all. They followed the most elaborate pretence in getting the Sunday clothes to the pawn on Mondays. Some went first thing after breakfast, the clothes concealed in the middle of a bundle of washing, as though the bearer were on her way to the public wash-house. Another would hide a suit in a big carrier bag, under the 'empties' being taken back to the licensed grocers, and this trip of course, was at a very innocent time of day when people would be doing their ordinary shopping, and the bottles lulled all suspicion, or so the owner thought. Yet another would use a go-cart, with the suit carefully hidden under the baby's feet. They all knew each other's routine, and they staggered their visits to the pawnbroker, so they never actually saw one another while the business was being transacted, and they could all pretend quite happily that it never happened at all. But everybody knew. And nobody said a word. Live and let live was the tenement motto, and if that was the way some folk liked to live, well naebody was hurt by it, and the women enjoyed a conspiracy, even a conspiracy of silence, especially if it meant the men remained 'nane the wiser' of what actually went on.

12

AFTER the refreshing break of the week-end I was ready once more to plunge into the working week of lessons, walking back and forth to college, and homework at night. Because of my high speeds in shorthand and typing, I was now having separate lessons after the others had finished, for I was already writing shorthand at one hundred and forty words per minute, and being coached for even higher speeds so that I could demonstrate high-speed writing for the college in public. My typing speed too was well beyond the class norm, and I was breezing along at speeds varying from sixty to seventy-five words a minute, depending on the subject-matter. I thought it a great privilege to be allowed to use the college typewriters to practise on, and I moved from one make of machine to another, graduating to the lightest weights so that nothing would put a brake on my flying fingers.

Because of this special coaching, I grew to know the assistant head of the teaching staff very well indeed, because he was the only one whose tongue could get round dictation fast enough to equal my speedy fingers. At Christmas, as he knew my mother was a widow and had little money to give us children many extras, he and his wife invited me to have high tea with them. They lived in a very posh district on the other side of Glasgow, and my mother saw to it that my shoes were polished until you could have seen your face in them, that my skirt and jumper were pressed neatly, and my navy velour hat as perfect as brush could make it. I was going home first to change, after college, so all my clothes were laid out neatly, ready to be put on the minute I reached home. I didn't know anything about taking presents to my host, but fate took a hand and atoned for my ignorance. I had to change tramcars in the centre of the city, and as I sped across the road from one tram to the other. I noticed a beautiful spray of mimosa lying practically under the wheels of the oncoming tram. Somebody had obviously dropped it as they crossed the road from Malcolm Campbell's big shop on the corner. I've always loved flowers, and I couldn't bear the thought of those lovely things being crushed, and anyway it would have been a terrible waste. I swooped down, practically under the wheels of the moving tramcar, and rescued the precious blossom, marvelling at the little furry velvety pom-poms against the dark stem. What could I do with it, though? It was far too big to put in my button-hole and there was no paper round it. Och well, even if it seemed a bit daft, I would just ask my hostess if she would put it in water, for I couldn't bear to have it die. This was December, and although I didn't know it, mimosa was prohibitively expensive and would have graced only the wealthiest tables in Glasgow. I reached the address, and was nervously preparing my speech about putting the flowers in water for me, when the stained-glass door opened. Before I had time to take in a thing, or even open my mouth, my hostess fell on me with such cries of rapturous astonishment at my good taste, at my extravagance, as she buried her nose in the yellow pom-poms, that I simply hadn't the heart to explain that I had found the spray. How could I confess that spending money on flowers, apart from a shilling bunch at the Fair after our holiday, was something quite outside my experience. Wisely I kept silent, and sent up a prayer to heaven for so inexpensively teaching me the social graces.

My mother had to hear every detail of the visit. She wanted to know if they had a cakestand, and if they went in for a white tablecloth or a coloured one. When she heard that the cloth was not only white, but had white lace embroidery, *and* matching napkins, she decided they must surely have a first-class washer-woman and plenty of money, for such a cloth would have to be washed by hand every time it was used. She was very interested to know I was the only visitor, and that this childless couple had entertained me by playing gramophone records. I had heard a woman called Gally-coorchy, it sounded like, singing like a canary. It was years before I realised I had been listening to a very famous record by a world-famous Italian soprano, whose coloratura was internationally renowned. My mother approved my having refused sherry

144

on the grounds that I was a Rechabite, although my host and hostess seemed to think it was quite a joke. When I told her about the mimosa my mother said, 'Och whit a loss for whoever dropped it. I'm pleased you never let on you found it in the street, although mind you, they must have wondered whaur ye got the money to buy such a thing.' And then she laughed. 'By jings, it must have very nearly peyed fur your tea!'

One of the things I learned over tea was that as well as certificates for the end-of-year examinations the college gave money prizes for every subject which gained over ninety per cent in marks. I learned that the strange subject 'amanuensis' also carried this prize, and this was simply taking dictation in shorthand, and typing it out in a given time. What a bonus this seemed to me. For surely if you could take down shorthand at speed, and type at speed, this was putting icing on the cake to give you yet another prize for combining both and calling it amanuensis? My host and teacher laughed and said it didn't always work out that way, for sometimes students became so nervous they couldn't type back their notes, although they could maybe write them out in longhand if they could take their time to do this. It was the typing from shorthand which foxed them. Yes, I could see that now, for we'd only typed from the printed page to teach our fingers to touch type, and had never tried to translate our shorthand notes straight on to the machine. Oh, but I'd have a try at it, especially for a two-guinea prize. I wanted to use any prize money to come back to college for night classes, for apart from now realising I had still so much to learn about everything, I knew I couldn't sit my shorthand teacher's exam till I was eighteen, and I'd have to continue studying to keep my work up to scratch for that frightening examination.

There was no time to go out to play even when the nights grew lighter, for this commercial course ended up in a perfect frenzy of examinations. The results for each subject were posted up on the board in the hall within a few days of each examination. I was terrified to look at the arithmetic passes, for although this was one of my best subjects, the paper had seemed so straightforward I was sure I must have missed the trickery behind the questions. I'd perched up on my feet as usual at the desk, read through the questions, found nothing particularly worrying and had finished the paper in just about half the allotted time. I looked up enquiringly at the teacher, and he looked back in surprise at me. 'Is there something you don't understand?' he asked. I shook my head. I went through the paper and the answers again. I couldn't see a thing to add. If I started looking too intently for tricks, I might feel I ought to change everything. I couldn't risk it. Early or no, I'd hand it in. The teacher and the class looked up as I walked to the front of the class, and handed in the paper. 'You're sure you are finished Molly?' he asked. 'You've read it through again?' I nodded, and left the class, and those big men and women sitting writing stared after me as I shut the door quietly, sure I must be out of my mind not to use up the time available for checking and correcting. However, the results sent my heart skittering into my throat. The first prize of one guinea was mine. Arithmetic—ninety-eight per cent. After that I trusted my own judgment. I was always nervous before each paper, of course, but once I started writing, or typing, I forgot my fears and concentrated on proving that I hadn't wasted my time during all those months of study. Shorthand brought two guineas, typing two, and that comically named amanuensis another two. Altogether the cash prizes came to eleven guineas, a fortune, and there was a further shorthand medal, for the long test piece at one hundred and forty words per minute, and a solid gold medal for being best student of my year. Oh I hadn't let Miss McKenzie down. Nor the scholarship people. But it was agony to have to walk forward in front of all those big students and take my prizes and my certificates. Instead of the principal reading them all out at once, each was announced and awarded separately and I had to go forward again and again, and I became so self-conscious I could hardly see for embarrassment. The principal was in highly waggish mood, and when my arms were piled high with certificates he called out, 'Some gallant will have to escort Miss Weir home. I'm sure she will have plenty of volunteers.' That was what he thought! I was only a baby to most of them, and my brown and white check gingham dress, made by my mother from a remnant, must have looked very unalluring to those grown-up young men. Anyway, not a gallant moved a muscle in my direction. It was just as well, for I wouldn't have known what to say to them if they had. I ran like the wind when the prize-giving was over, because my mother, who was on the night-shift that week, was meeting me outside the college. We were going to celebrate by having coffee and a cake in Craig's, but to my surprise she took me into Watt Brothers first. I thought we had only been window-shopping on the way to Craig's, but she had been noting my enthusiasm for a dark red knitted suit, and she insisted we went in so that I could try it on. 'But, Mother, it's far too dear. And I don't *need* it. Wait till I get a job.' She brushed my objections aside. She was determined to celebrate my release from study (she thought I'd finished!) and the winning of all those prizes. She must have been saving for ages and she hadn't told me. I was so thrilled and touched that she should have thought of such a thing, especially with me earning nothing while all my chums were out working. I tried on the suit. It was lovely. We bought it, and I treasured and wore it for years.

I was now equipped and ready to be somebody's secretary, but in spite of my speeds and qualifications, nobody was at all interested in me. The college sent me for many interviews, and I was absolutely furious to be turned down again and again because I was judged too young or too wee. 'But I can *do* the work,' I'd argue rebelliously. 'Just give me a test.' A smile and a shake of the head. 'I'm sorry, we wanted somebody older, who could take responsibility.' I ground my teeth in a rage. I'd been taking responsibility since the day I was born, but how to make those snooty employers realise it? And after all the work I'd put in during all the previous year, and me with a gold medal in my drawer to prove it. It was being brought home to me the hard way that the most difficult prize of all to win was that of a pay packet. I felt so ashamed, and I could hardly bear the puzzled disappointment in my mother's face as I'd come back yet again from an interview, without a job.

And then one day I came home dizzy with triumph. My mother knew the moment she looked at my face that I'd landed a job. With a lawyer too—a most respected profession. I was engaged as a typist at the breathtaking sum of fifteen shillings a week, a shilling for every year of my age. My mother could now sit back and take it easy, I told her, her daughter was entering the world of commerce.

It was a very old-fashioned office, but it was my first sight of the business world, and I loved every single article with a passionate loyalty. There was a high desk, where the other female member of the staff and I coped with the books. Two small tables held our typewriters, and a tiny grate had a coal fire to warm our toes. There was a long mahogany counter where clients enquired for the lawyer, and the end of this was partitioned off from the public gaze. I used to disappear behind this screened-off portion when somebody came in whose solemn appearance gave me a fit of the giggles. I was too young to disguise my feelings, but too polite to let them see me laughing. I began to realise why those other employers had judged me too young to take responsibility. No wonder they couldn't trust me when I couldn't trust myself to keep a straight face when somebody talked too pan-loaf or raised a solemn hat two feet in the air when I approached the counter.

The ribbon in the office machine was indelible, so that letters could be copied in an ancient press with the aid of damp sheets and a heavy weight. Our old-fashioned employer was a splendid character, but he didn't believe in carbons, and I'm sure this copying press went back to the days of Dickens. I'd been used to modern ribbons in the machines at college, where if a mistake was made one just rubbed it out, but with this new horror of a ribbon it was impossible to erase an error. A horrible stain, a real give-away, just spread all over the letter and it had to be re-typed. On top of this, the ancient keyboard was different from the ones I'd trained on, and I made such a mess of the first letters I typed that I was sure I would be sacked. I was appalled at the amount of paper I wasted, but the other girl was quite unconcerned, and kept telling me not to worry, and anyway there was no hurry, for it didn't matter how long I took to get the letters done. The old boy wasn't used to speed! This to me, with a drawer full of certificates for speed and efficiency! The waste she took for granted, but it was a knife in my heart, and I felt Grannie would never have approved this easy-going attitude on the part of my colleague.

I was ashamed of my slowness and I felt I'd never master this strange machine with its dreadful ribbon. Instead of screwing up spoilt sheets and throwing them in the basket, I'd use the backs to practise my altered fingering, and then suddenly I found myself using the heavy old monster quite effortlessly, and that was a happy day indeed. With that worry removed, I was in seventh heaven and enjoyed every moment of my working day.

Although I was so young, I was sent out to collect rents in a very rough district. As I had neither a shawl nor a baby, I was the object of much attention, and it soon became evident to the whole district that I was from the factor's office. The only tenant who frightened me was a man who was slightly unbalanced, and who was convinced the entries weren't being properly made in his rent-book and that he would be thrown into the street any day for defaulting. Everybody dreaded being put out by the factor, and I knew this was a real fear. I had to explain every time I went into his kitchen that the rent-book was absolutely up to date, and I ticked off each entry while he gazed at me with wild, uncomprehending eyes. Poor soul, these rent days were a source of terror for him, and as for me I was always glad to get out of his wee, spotlessly clean kitchen.

But I was a great success with the other tenants, because I was so sympathetic to their requests for repairs. Coming from a tenement myself, and knowing how often my mother denounced the meanness of the factor when there were plumbing or joinery repairs to be done in our house, I sent off the repair cards to our workmen as soon as I got back to the office.

My employer was aghast at the money which was now being spent on keeping the property in good shape, but he couldn't deny I was right when I said, 'But the repairs *had* to be done, sir. The pipes were leaking', or, 'The window-ledges let in rain'. What good was it trying to explain to me that money couldn't be spent so freely on this work? I had brought money back for rents, and it was only right that the people paying these rents should have good homes to live in. My boss shook his head and retired to his room, despairing of making me see his point of view, so I had my way, and the tenants declared I was a wee warmer, and they'd never kent a better collector. It was a pleasure to see me each month, so it wis, and they didnae grudge a penny o' their rents nooadays.

I learned what a true gentleman was in working for this

dear old lawyer. He was always polite, always courteous and he trusted us implicitly. In the bottom compartment of the petty cash box one day I found about a dozen golden sovereigns, which he hadn't even known were there. I used to love to play with them, for they were bright and shiny like jewellery. One day when he found me making a long golden bridge with them he was astonished to discover that they were his, but he just left them with me, for he saw that I liked playing with them, and he knew I would as soon have thought of them as my own as I would have thought of carrying the typewriter home. We both took honesty for granted, and not even worth mentioning.

In another office along the corridor an elderly lady worked for her father. Well, she seemed elderly to me, with her old-fashioned mousey hair done up in a bun, her long thin hands and feet, and her black blouse and skirt. She always tut-tutted over my thinness, and was sure I burned up whatever food I ate long before it could build any flesh on me. She used to bring me slabs of home-made cake on Monday mornings, the left-overs of her week-end entertaining. When I'd ask her if she didn't want to keep it in the tins at home for a wee 'roughness' in case visitors called, she made a face and said it would be stale by that time. Stale! I'd never heard anybody describing *cake* as stale, for it would certainly never have lasted long enough in our tenements for such a thing to happen. This cake was a great treat in the office, though, especially when she also often found time to bring a little brown pot of tea with her, and we had quite a party behind the glass partition. There was no recognised mid-morning break when I was in an office, so we had to be very quiet about our orgies, and we hid everything behind a ledger if the boss appeared. I don't suppose for a moment he would have minded, for we on our part never worried about staying a bit later without payment if it were necessary, but the feeling that we were indulging in a forbidden picnic added to our enjoyment, and the spice of danger made us feel very wicked.

The boss went away for the entire summer with wife and family, leaving the other girl and me in charge of the office. The law courts were in recess, I think, and I was worried because we had nothing to do. I was desperately anxious to earn my fifteen shillings, but the older girl just laughed and produced her knitting, so we sat up on the window-ledges to catch the sunshine, knitting and chatting, or reading all day long, and answering the telephone when it gave the occasional ring. The older girl had window flirtations with a fellow in an office a few yards up the street, on the opposite side, and giggled and blushed when he would wave across to her. Sometimes they even spoke to each other on the telephone, but it went no further. I couldn't see how she could possibly be interested in this vague face, for it wasn't easy to see what he really looked like at that distance, and I privately thought they were both a bit soft in the head. Still, she helped me with my knitting pattern, and she was a nice girl otherwise, and if she wanted to make a fool of herself waving across the width of the street to a man, then it was none of my business. It wasn't as if we were neglecting our work.

When she went on holiday I was left in sole charge. As my brother wasn't working just then, I invited him to come and share my caretaker's duties. He was delighted to accept, and we used to stroll down to the office every day, both in plimsolls and bare legs, with a shilling between us for our lunch. By walking to and from the office, we added another sixpence to our spending money. This was no hardship, for we liked walking, and were at an age where everything on the road was interesting.

My brother was very impressed with the office, and spent hours playing with the machine for copying the letters, whirling the press at terrific speed and pretending his victim was lying underneath, ready to be crushed to death.

Then there was the fun of the internal telephone, where I stayed in the outer office and he went into the boss's room, and we spoke to each other after much feverish turning of the handle to make the bell ring. We were helpless with laughter during this escapade and couldn't talk for giggles, and of course being so young we couldn't think of a thing to say once we could control ourselves. When we grew tired of this we ventured one day to use the outside telephone to ring up an older friend who worked in an office in town, and he was furious and told us never to do it again or we would get him the sack.

Somewhat subdued, we wondered what we could do next, for the day seemed endless when we could only go outside for lunch. Suddenly my brother decided to climb up on top of the safe. It was covered in dust, and his plimsolls made most satisfactory prints all over the top. This was too enticing, and in a minute I was up beside him, and we played at jumping off the safe on to the floor, in a lovely flying motion. What the people below must have thought, I never stopped to think.

Just as we were in the throes of this fascinating game, whooping with laughter as we leaped from safe to floor, a startled face appeared round the door of the office and a gloved hand went to a mouth open with dismay. There was an instant of terrified silence which I couldn't break and then the lady enquired in amazed tones, 'What are you children doing here?'

Children! The very idea. I was restored to my dignity as caretaker and typist immediately.

'I am in charge of the office,' I said as coldly as my breathlessness would allow. 'Mr. Gardner is on holiday. Can I help you?'

Her eyes went from me to my brother, who was trying to hide behind the safe. 'And who is this?' the lady asked.

'He's my brother.' I explained. 'He's come to keep me company.'

'Oh! I see. Then I suggest you keep each other company a little more quietly. When will Mr. Gardner be back?'

I gave her the date and took her name, and she went. My brother and I were left, appalled, wondering if I would be sacked the moment my boss returned from holiday.

I don't know whether she ever told him and he forgave the whole episode on account of my youth, or whether she maintained a discreet silence, but I kept my job. My lovely job and my wonderful fifteen shillings a week.

Sometimes on a Saturday morning the boss's wife would call with her little boy, and I had to keep him amused. He loved the typewriters, and I used to make rows and rows of little soldiers for him, using the % sign, and then using the backspacing stop to superimpose a / over the shoulder as a gun, plus a 7 sign underneath, and a few other signs to make it all look real. We filled sheets of paper with those troops, and the wee boy carried them carefully home with him in an envelope. I was always fascinated with the boss's elegant wife, who had a high, carrying voice. 'Darling,' she would call out, 'can you let me have some money—I seem to be a bit short and I want to go to the shops.' I noted that he never once refused her, and just smiled with the greatest good nature and gave her what she asked. I could just see the tenement husbands if their wives dared to ask for cash so lightheartedly. They wouldn't have parted with as much as a curdy, for what was left in their pockets after handing over the housekeeping was strictly their own, and not to be shared. The rich must live very differently, I decided, when the husband kept the money, and the wives just asked for whatever they wanted, and were sure of getting it without an argument. I wondered if our tenement wives would like that, though, for they seemed to enjoy handling money, and wouldn't have trusted their husbands not to spend the rent money or the money for the store book on drink.

But oh how glad Mr. Gardner must have been that he was so good and generous and kind to this lovely lady, because one day, not long after they'd returned from their holiday, I heard him speaking to the doctor on the telephone while I was taking notes. Mrs. Gardner had a very sore throat, and the doctor was worried because she had a soaring temperature. He thought they ought to have a nurse in, and he was going to send a swab for analysis to the hospital. Mr. Gardner put down the telephone, stared into space, and then with an effort came back to the notes and finished his dictation. 'I'm going home,' he called out to us a few minutes later. 'I'll sign the letters in the morning. There's nothing urgent that can't wait till then.'

Next day he didn't come in. He rang us to say his wife was worse, and we were not to make any appointments for him for the rest of the week. My colleague and I were quite distracted. We couldn't work. My mother tried to reassure me when I told her of Mrs. Gardner's illness at lunchtime. 'Oh they'll have the best of doctors, and they'll do everything for her,' she said. 'She'll aye have the best of food and that stands onybody in good stead at a time like this.' I knew my mother was very wise and I tried to believe her, but a sick feeling in my stomach told me that this was a very serious illness, and yet I wanted so much to have confidence that a rich lovely lady like that couldn't die of a sore throat. But she did. Infection from a tooth had added to the quinsy throat, and there was an unsuspected T.B. gland which also flared up—or at least that was what we understood—and she was dead in forty-eight hours. I sat at my dinner at home, the tears pouring down my face, unable to eat a bite. That wee boy, for whom I'd made the typed soldiers, left without a mother. That fine man left without a wife. Not all his money had been able to save her. I laid my head on the table and cried more bitterly than I had been able to do when I lost my own grannie. I was grieving for all of us in that office, which would never be the same again.

I watched Mr. Gardner when he came back after the funeral, and he now looked a really old man. His shoulders sagged, his eyes were blank, and he lapsed into long silences in the midst of dictation. It was terrible. I was too young to be able to say a word in sympathy and left it to my older colleague, and I could only whisper in reply if he asked me a question, because I was frightened I would burst into tears.

I don't know how long it would have taken us all to get over this shock had it not been for the young client who got herself into the most terrible mess with an unwise marriage. She'd secretly married a chauffeur, and later found out what a mistake she had made, for she came from a very wealthy family and had been educated abroad, with every advantage money could buy. Then, of course, she'd met somebody from her own background, of whom her parents thoroughly approved, and with whom she'd fallen really in love. How could Mr. Gardner get her out of it? We were all plunged into this business up to our ears. The new young fiancé had to be told, for his co-operation was essential. He seemed to be able to forgive the girl quite easily, for she had only been seventeen when she'd married the chauffeur. Anyway, what with her having married without consent, and having been so young, Mr. Gardner managed to have the marriage ended, and the whole thing was accomplished in complete secrecy, without the girl's parents knowing a thing. We were all sworn to keep quiet, of course, as we signed papers and witnessed this, that and the other document untangling the mess. This had Ethel M. Dell beaten into a cocked hat, for it was real, and it was happening in our very own office. I was so sorry I couldn't tell my mother, or anybody at all, for I had given my solemn word. I don't know what they did about the marriage certificate, but it all ended with the girl getting married to the man approved by her parents, and they never knew to the end of their lives that their only daughter had been married and divorced before she had married the man they so approved as their son-in-law. Oh what an exciting chapter that was in our old-fashioned office. It was marvellous to be able to say, inside my head, 'And they lived happily ever after', and know we had helped to write those words. It all came at just the right time too to get us over our grief for poor Mrs. Gardner, and although we still missed her and spoke of her a great deal, the worst was over. Only when the little boy came to the office on a Saturday with a nannie did the ache start again, but it grew less and less, and by the time I decided I ought to try for a better-paid job I could think of her without tears.

13

ACTUALLY it was Mr. Gardner who put the idea into my head that it was time to move on. I'd never have dreamt of seeming disloyal by suggesting I would leave him. But he called me in one day and said that now I had had a year of good training in his office, with its demands of absolute accuracy, and its discipline with legal documents, I could do better for myself in a larger office. He could give me a tip-top reference, he told me, and he would be sorry to see me go, but with experience now added to those top speeds, it was a shame to keep me when he couldn't afford to pay me any more money. He told me, truly, that a year in a law office was the finest training anyone could have, and that if he hadn't given me a great deal of cash he had been able to give me an excellent start, and a good foundation on which to build.

My mother and I were quite happy with our fifteen shillings a week, but we were always willing to take advice, especially from a man who showed such interest in my welfare and whom we trusted completely. I didn't think of going back to college for help in finding this new job, but we all pored over the 'situations vacant' at home, and I sent off applications in my best handwriting, and promised that if accepted I would endeavour to serve their interests to the best of my ability. I was very pleased with such flowing phrases, and amazed that I didn't have a reply from every single advertiser. I had several, though, and turned down the ones in tiny offices, however tempting the salary offered, for my boss had impressed on me that I needed the competition of a larger establishment now. Eventually I settled on one with a very grand title, and which I vaguely thought had something to do with insurance. Compared with our Dickensian setting, with shelves filled with big tin deed boxes, all cosy and old-fashioned, this new office was the epitome of sparkling modernity. Huge plate-glass windows, overlooking Renfield Street, let in every fleeting ray of sunshine. The desks were light oak, the chairs were padded, and the typewriters were all brand new. Best of all, it seemed to me, there were about twenty people in the office, whose ages varied from mine at sixteen to quite middle-aged men and women. The boss was foreign, and quite quite different from Mr. Gardner, who, although kind and thoughtful, had only seemed vaguely aware of us as females. This one darted about staring intently into our eyes and, to my surprise, insisted on all of us using Christian names. By Mr. Gardner, young as I was, I had been addressed as Miss Weir. To this restless new boss I was Molly. It didn't seem right somehow. I didn't like him very much, but I liked the office, and I thoroughly enjoyed all the chatter and the romances of the older typists, especially the one who wore her engagement ring on a ribbon round her neck because her people would have thrown her out if she had dared to hint that she was getting married. I found this very thrilling, and quite up to the standards of the stories in *My Weekly*. Another girl had been persuaded to 'go steady' with a young man whose name was McGinty, but she told me that every time she visited his mother's house her heart turned over when she looked at the name on the name-plate, for she knew that she would never never marry a man with a name like that and find herself called Mrs. McGinty for the rest of her life. As my feelings were not involved, I urged her to give him up, for there was absolutely no use encouraging him if she didn't intend to marry him. But, she told me, 'I *like* him so much. It's just his name I can't stand.' And then a terrible thing happened. He was involved in a serious accident with his motor-bike and they sent to our office for May, the girl whose confidences I'd shared, to go to his bedside. He asked her to marry him, and there at the hospital bedside she said 'Yes'. When she told me this I could hardly breathe for emotion, it was such a drama. It was the very stuff of story-books. 'But, May,' I said, 'I thought you would never never be called Mrs. McGinty, what if he gets better?' She shook her head and her eyes filled with tears. 'He won't,' she said, 'I never will be Mrs. McGinty. The hospital told me there was no hope, and that's the only reason I said yes.' The hospital spoke the truth, but for a long time afterwards I worried and fretted over what she would have done if the young man *had* recovered. Strangely enough, she didn't marry anyone, and I often thought it would have been far nicer to have had McGinty on the letter box than to have had no letter box at all, or the door, or her very own wee house.

We mostly shared these tales while we were working late. We had to work for a whole week till 9.30, once every three months. It seemed to have something to do with interests and dividends or some figures having to be made up at such intervals, and we were paid two shillings per night, which was supposed to be our tea money. I'd never have dreamed of wasting whole two shillings on such a thing, for my mother and I decided it was a marvellous opportunity to do a solid bit of saving. Just fancy ten shillings for the bank in one short week, when normally it would have taken us months to put by such a sum. I brought a piece from home, and I was given a few chips from the other girls, who sent me up to the Savoy fish-and-chip shop at the corner of Renfrew Street for the fish or pie suppers they loved for their tea. We used to order them in advance, for we knew exactly when we would be working late, and that it would go on for the whole week, and I sped like the wind up Hope Street, collected my delicious-smelling parcel and raced back to the office before it could get cold. It was great fun eating our meal in the office like this, but the hours seemed to crawl so slowly afterwards that I often couldn't believe it was only half past seven when I'd look up at the big clock. Nobody bothered to sympathise that it was a very long day from 9 a.m. till 9.30 p.m. for a sixteen-year-old. The work had to be done, and I was glad of the chance to earn an extra ten shillings, and would have rebelled at the very idea that it was too much work for me.

The boss had a canary in a cage, and it was my job to clean out the cage regularly, and to see that the little songster had fresh seed and water every morning. One of the older girls had shown me how to do this the first day I arrived and she seemed glad to be rid of this task, but I quite enjoyed it, and it made an interesting start to the day, attending to this bonnie whistler. Another funny job we had to do in this office was to make up siphons of soda water for the boss. It was the first time I'd seen such a thing done, and I was fascinated. There was a siphon with a sort of wire netting all over it, which they told me was to prevent it exploding in a million pieces if anything went wrong, and we fitted a little metallic bullet into a slot, pressed down the trigger, and fired it into the water-filled decanter, instantly transforming it into fizzy soda water. I thought the whole performance was magic, but I was always a wee bit nervous of firing the bullet myself, and contented myself with standing by, waiting for the moment when water became fizz. My mother would have loved one of those, for she enjoyed, above all things, a wee drink of 'sody watter and milk' when she had a headache, or an upset stomach, but those special siphons were terribly expensive and far beyond our reach. But my mother liked hearing about such things, and thought it must be a marvellous convenience not to have to run down to the shops every time you needed a bottle of soda water.

One night the boss decided to stay on late at the office, with a client who'd come from abroad and seemed to have a lot to discuss which could only be done that evening. When he rang to tell his wife this, she said that somebody would have to be sent out to their home then, to deliver the meat he was bringing home for dinner. People were coming for a meal and it was too late for her now to go to the shops. It was about five o'clock, so I was told to get my hat and coat on and take the parcel. I was quite pleased to get away half an hour before the usual time, and I looked forward to the novelty of exploring unknown territory on the other side of Glasgow, and having my fares paid into the bargain. How strange it seemed to be taking a tramcar away out 'the other way' from Springburn, right beyond the Plaza, to the wilds of Clarkston eventually. The fog was drifting down when I handed over the parcel, and the boss's wife graciously handed me another—a box of chocolate truffles. Unopened. An entire half-pound. For me!

I hugged them to my jersey and raced for the homeward tram, pelted upstairs, darted along the top deck and made for my favourite seat right out at the front in the wee compartment above the driver's head. The fog had slowed everything down, and our driver was obviously impatient at proceeding in fits and starts, and when he could see a clear run he whirled the levers and sent the tram rocking like a roller-coaster along squealing yards of track. He was indulging in one of these wild bursts of speed when the fog obliterated everything in one of those blankets of patchy blackness which had irritated him all the way. It cleared just as suddenly, to reveal a tramcar only a yard or so ahead of us on the track, but too late for him to apply his brakes with any effect. It's the only time I hated my ringside view on a tramcar. I watched with horror the faces staring back at me from the back compartment of the other car, saw them rise to run back to avoid the worst of the impact, rose to my feet with a piercing shriek, and then bounced unharmed into the air as we crashed into each other with a sickening splintering of glass. Amazingly, nobody was injured, but both trams took a battering and we had to sit for nearly an hour while the police were contacted and all details noted. To calm my nerves—and my hunger—I ate every single chocolate truffle. I, who hoarded even a four-penny bar of chocolate to make it spin out as long as possible, devoured an entire half-pound box, getting sicker by the minute but unable to stop this orgy. I was white as a sheet when I tottered into the house, hours past my usual time. My mother was equally white, but her pallor came from fright, for she thought I'd been run over at the very least, if not abducted! We never knew a soul who had come to the slightest harm from attack, or who was in the least danger of being kidnapped, but this didn't stop my mother fearing the worst if we were late in coming home.

I didn't dare tell her about all the chocolates I'd eaten, for even in her relief from anxiety she'd have condemned such greed and extravagance. She was sure I must be starving, and rushed to get my tea ready. I took one look at the warmed-up pie she had kept for me, heaved convulsively and left the table at top speed. She put it down to the shock of the tram crash. But to this day I've never been able to eat a chocolate truffle with any enthusiasm.

Next day they were agog to hear all about my tram adventure when I got to the office, but some of the older ones were a bit critical of the boss for sending me away out to the other side of Glasgow in the fog. 'Well, what do you expect,' Mr. Mac, the oldest man said, 'moneylenders have to have hides like rhinoceros or they'd never be in this business.' I stopped as if I'd been shot. Moneylenders! Who was a moneylender? Not the boss, surely? I surely wasn't working for a moneylender! It was an insurance company—that's what it said in the letter headings. I rushed and seized a letter sheet, and carefully read the wording. There, it did say insurance, but what was this other word, 'Investors', could that mean moneylending? Suddenly I remembered my lawyer boss's face when I'd told him where I was going to work. He had wrinkled his nose and said, 'I could have wished it was some other type of business.' I hadn't known what he meant and just thought he would have preferred me to choose another, bigger, law office where I could carry on getting experience with more advanced documents. He must have guessed what investors meant. This was terrible. All the story-books I'd read condemned moneylenders. From *My Weekly* to Somerset Maugham I'd learned to what depths of despair the hero or heroine could be plunged, once they got into the clutches of moneylenders, and here was I, a member of the Church and a Sunday School teacher, actually helping one to make his fortune! I stared round the office, and wondered if they all knew. And if they did, how could they go on working there?

I didn't tell my mother of my discovery, in case she would feel too shocked by such a revelation, but I announced I was going to look for another job, maybe back to a smaller office again, which, after all, was nice and cosy and gave me a lot of responsibility. In a big office all the duties were apportioned according to age, but in a small office you had a chance of doing any mortal thing that needed doing, and this was far more interesting. This made such good sense to my mother, who knew my busy lively nature, that she didn't stop me studying the 'situations vacant' columns once more, and in a matter of weeks I had shaken the dust of the money-lenders' office off my shoes, and could hold up my head once more.

This new office promised to test my speeds all right, for there were three bosses from whom I had to take dictation, and an office girl whose business it was to do the filing, attend to the mail and look after the petty cash. The first morning I was bursting with curiosity to clap eyes on my very first office girl, for as I was the only typist, she was junior to me. I was far too early, and when the door opened, I nearly fell off my stool. In walked a female who looked far older than I did, who was head and shoulders above me in height, and who was dressed like a fashion model. She had

sleek black hair, and a pale face, and actually wore make-up!
How would I ever be able to send such an elegant creature for
stamps? Or tell her to get on with the filing? With a brief
'Good morning', she started to open the mail, still wearing
her coat. And what a posh coat to wear to work. A dark
coppery-red fine tweed, with a natty shoulder cape, and a
little matching cap. Shoes of fine kid exactly to match and—I
couldn't believe my eyes—long kid gloves! She must have
tons of money and only be working for fun. Fancy such a
vision only being an office girl.

I was just recovering from this shock when the bosses
walked in, one after another. Two big fair men over six feet
in height, and a wee dark man like Charlie Chaplin. It was the
wee man who had engaged me, and if I got a shock at sight of
my office girl the two big blond men were equally surprised
at my appearance. 'But she's a child!' I heard one say to the
other. 'I can't believe she's seventeen.'

It was a hectically busy little office, and I flew from one desk
to another, taking dictation all morning, and typed out all
the stuff in the afternoon. Patsy, the office girl, had a grand
appetite and was always willing to run round to the shops
for a pie or a cake for our mid-morning break. I don't know
if this was an official break, but she assured me she'd always
done it, and she often 'stood' the cakes or pies. I was quite
willing to believe her. I think she must have been allowed to
keep all her salary, for she had plenty of cash to spare and
never seemed to have to save for anything. I took my turn
with the cake purchases as long as my pocket money allowed
this, but even when it was finished Patsy insisted on sharing.
She was a most generous girl, and didn't have a care in the world.
The filing was in the most chaotic mess, but she seemed to
have a sort of Pelmanism which told her where everything
was. During her few odd free moments I'd beg her to put it
in alphabetical order, or at least in order of dates, but she'd
just laugh and say she couldn't be bothered, and anyway she
could always find what she wanted. 'Yes, that's all right while
you're here, Patsy,' I cried. 'but what if you're out and they
ask for something. I can't find a *thing* in those drawers.' Patsy's
method of filing was simply to thrust everything in every
available drawer, not even in folders, with a corner stuck
up here, a corner folded down there, to indicate to her the

various weeks or months when they'd arrived and been dealt with. I shuddered with dread that one day she'd be found out and sacked. And then one day the worst happened. She fell ill with 'flu, and was off. An important client arrived from the Midlands, where the head works were, and wee Mr. Brown rang the bell for me. When I went in he said, 'Oh, Miss Weir' (I was back to Miss again) 'will you just bring me in Patent and Grant's file.' I turned white, I'm sure I did, for my stomach certainly gave such a convulsive heave of fear that I felt sick. I stood in the middle of the outer office and closed my eyes in panic. Where would I look first? I opened a drawer, and papers burst out in every direction. I shut it hastily, and decided I'd start at the top drawer and work my way down, on the theory that the latest correspondence would maybe be right at the top.

The top drawer was packed so tightly with letters that I couldn't even get my wee finger in to check the dates, and when I pulled up the first lot of papers, the others closed behind them in serried ranks. Feverishly I turned over dozens of letters. Not one in alphabetical order, and all about six months old. I stuffed them back and opened another drawer. The same chaos there, but this time only about a month old. But *where* had Patsy put the most recent ones. I ran about the office opening drawers and slamming them shut again, frightened out of my wits, picturing the two men sitting in the private office waiting for me to reappear. As I didn't, Mr. Brown himself strolled in. 'Having trouble finding the letter?' he said pleasantly. 'It can't be far away—it just came in last week. Where's the file?' 'There are no files,' I blurted out miserably. I didn't want to give Patsy away, but there was no way of disguising the truth. 'No files,' he said with slight irritation. 'Don't be silly, girl, of course there are files,' and he pulled open a drawer. 'Good God!' he said, as letters sprang up in dozens, all bunched together just any old way. He pulled open every drawer in the office, and his face twitched, in fury as I thought, but suddenly to my amazement he burst out laughing. I decided he'd gone mad from the shock. But no. 'Well,' he said at last, wiping his eyes, 'like the bloke who's fiddling the books, if you have a system like this, you just must never be ill, that's all.' He patted my arm kindly and told me not to bother looking, for it was like looking for a

needle in a haystack. He gave me a conspiratorial wink.'
'Don't tell the others,' he said, 'and we'll straighten it all out
when Patsy comes back.' He was Scots, and the other two big
blond men were English, and I think he felt we Scots must
stick together. I thankfully agreed, and just prayed they wouldn't
ask me to find a letter while she was away from work. When
Patsy came back that kind Mr. Brown had a little talk with
her, and between them they started a real filing system. He
made her tackle one drawer at a time, told her it would probably take her some months, but if she wanted to keep her
job, and let him keep his sanity, then it would just have to
be done. And I was to see that she spent at least two hours
every morning and afternoon on it. Poor Patsy, I was a hard
taskmistress. By this time I'd long forgotten my awe of her
smart clothes and her ladylike appearance. Deeds, not looks,
were what counted in the long run, and I was determined
she would repay Mr. Brown's confidence in both of us, and
show a proper gratitude for not losing her job. There were no
more pies or cakes for many a long day, for I just wouldn't
let her go out, not even to buy stamps. I did that in my dinner-
hour. We did the mail between us at night, and by Christmas
we could look with pride on a really efficient filing system
where even I could find a letter at a moment's notice.

I was so glad we had worked so hard, because one day
during Christmas week our doorbell rang at home, when I
was home for my dinner, and a delivery boy handed us in an
enormous parcel. It was addressed to me. 'Are you sure it's
not a mistake?' I said. 'Are you sure it's for us?' 'Oh aye,' he
responded cheerfully, 'It's your name and it's your address so it
must be for you. It was sent from England.' 'From England,'
I said. 'I don't know anybody in England.' 'Well, somebody
knows you,' he said. 'Come on, ah've no' got a' day. Sign
for it and ah'll be on ma way.' When we opened it, it was from
the head office of my firm, and it was the biggest bird we'd ever
had inside our house. It was a goose, and it was so huge it
wouldn't go inside the oven. 'Oh my,' said my mother, 'wisn't
that lovely of them? They must think a lot o' you to send
such a grand present. It wid feed the hale o' Springburn.'
I was sent up to the big Co-operative bakers, and they promised to bake it in their big oven and we were to collect it on
Christmas Eve. We had often done this with big steak pies

if we were having a special celebration, but this was the first time we had had the pleasure of presenting a magnificent fowl to be cooked. 'By jings,' said the boy who took it from me in the Co-operative, 'It's nearly as big as you, hen. Whit a tightner you'll have aff that. It'll dae ye for a week.'

When my mother and I went to collect it, the baker had to lend us one of his big baking trays to carry home the delicious fat. 'Just the stuff for a tight chest, Mrs. Weir,' he assured my mother. 'Pit it in a big jeely jar and keep it—it's faur before ony o' yer embrocation.' And so we were able to prove for ourselves, after all, that goose fat was the very dab for winter ailments. What a beautiful bird it was. It lasted right through to Hogmanay, and filled the tastiest sandwiches for our Ne'erday visitors that any of us could have imagined. And to think it had cost us nothing, and had been a gift from a firm for whom I'd only worked for a few months. And that wasn't all, for the three bosses had clubbed together and given Patsy and myself a pair of silk stockings each, and a wee box of chocolates for the office. 'What a marvellous firm,' I thought, it was nearly as good as the Cratchit's Christmas from Scrooge, all those gifts landed in our laps so unexpectedly, and allowing us to spread our bounty so widely among our own friends because of the size of that enormous bird. I wrote to the head office, urged to do so by my mother, although my bosses said it wasn't necessary, and I told them that thanks to them we had now all tasted goose, and we had a big jelly jar full of the fat to see us through our winter colds, and they sent a very nice letter in return saying how pleased they were with my work, and thanking me for taking the trouble to write. Trouble! It was nae bother at a'. I'd have written a hundred letters for such a Christmas.

One day, when the spring sunshine transformed the dusty streets of Glasgow, and sent little motes shimmering into every bright ray, I went into the boss's sanctum to leave some letters for signing. To my dismay, for I had thought the room was empty, the younger of the two tall blond Englishmen was sitting with his arms spread over the desk, and his head sunk in them, groaning. I stood there, biting my lip, not knowing what to do. Should I say something? But what? Should I just tiptoe out and hope he hadn't heard me come in? I had no social graces at all to equip me for such a situation. I decided to retreat, and was just creeping quietly to the door, when his voice stopped me. 'No, don't go,' a strangely muffled voice said, 'I've got to talk to someone.' My heart gave a jump and I stopped, but I didn't turn round. I didn't like the sound of that voice. Could he be crying? I'd never thought a grown man could cry, and I didn't want to be proved wrong, especially by my boss, and him with such an English voice that it had taken me weeks to get used to him, and of whom I was very shy. 'Come and sit down,' he said. I kept my head down and sidled into a chair, my eyes on the floor. There was no sound now except the ticking of the wee clock on the mantelpiece. I bit my lips, and held my breath, and was terrified my stomach would make a noise, for I'd hurried all the way down Parliamentary Road, and we'd had lentil soup for our dinner, a windy food even when you took your time over it.

At last the silence was unbearable and I was forced to look up. He *had* been crying! Even now a big tear rolled down his cheek. What could be the matter? I was suffocating with embarrassment. 'Oh I'm sorry to make such an ass of myself,' he said, and then gave another frightening gulp, 'but my fiancée has just broken off our engagement.' I let out my breath, in a long sighing sound. The novels were all true. When they said, thrillingly, 'Such emotion was strong enough to make a grown man cry', I hadn't believed them, but it was all *true*! Here was a grown man crying because he had been crossed in love, and I was privileged to see it. Oh I was on familiar territory now, all right, and I sat back, as receptive and willing an ear as he could have hoped to find. I made him describe her in detail, not realising the possible anguish I might be inflicting. 'Was she tall, like you?' I asked. 'Was she English, like you?' Yes, to both questions, and that had been the trouble. They had been too much apart, with him being posted to the Glasgow office, and she had found someone else. I closed my eyes with the sheer rightness of the words. 'She had found someone else.' How often had the final words of a *My Weekly* story ended on that very sentence. There was no doubt about it, grown-ups got into the most terrible messes with their romances, and nothing was safe when not even the beautiful diamond ring he had given her had kept her faithful to his memory.

I was glad to see, though, he had stopped crying and actually seemed to have found a grain of comfort in remembering how he had never liked her parents very much. 'Oh that's terrible,' I said, 'for if you don't get on with your in-laws, it's murder. You're maybe just as well without her.' I was aghast at my own daring, when I'd uttered this so impulsively, but he didn't seem to mind. In fact with a bewildering change of mood he leaned his elbows on the desk, stared at me and said, 'Do you know, I never noticed before that you have a black spot under the pupil of your eye, like a beauty spot in the wrong place.' I jumped with embarrassment, suddenly remembering that he was my boss, and I didn't much fancy him gazing into my eyes like this. Especially when he'd just lost a fiancée. It wasn't seemly. Not seemly at all. As I sat there, hypnotised like a rabbit, not knowing what to do next, the door opened, and it was wee Mr. Brown. Oh what a relief. I leaped to my feet, pointed to the letters I'd laid on Mr. Brown's desk (how many hours ago it seemed!), and escaped to the outer office. Gosh what a strange lot the English were. I couldn't imagine a Scotsman behaving like that, whatever the novels said, but it had all been very exciting, and I couldn't wait to get home and tell my mother all about it. Strangely enough her reaction was 'Hoo auld did ye say this man wis?' 'Och I don't know,' I said, impatient at this flat response to such a dramatic tale. 'About thirty-five maybe. He's quite old.' My mother laughed. 'Aye, too old to be greetin' in the office like that—he must be a bit soft.' 'Oh, Mother,' I said reproachfully, 'he was heartbroken, so he was.' Mind you, I came to the conclusion myself he really was a bit soft, for after that when I went in for notes I'd find him staring at my eyes, as if he couldn't keep his mind off that wee black spot in the iris. It was terribly rude of him, and I wished I had the courage to tell him to get on with his dictation. That broken engagement seemed to make him go daft, right enough, for one day he actually picked me up and sat me on top of the big corner cupboard and I couldn't get down. I was scared out of my wits, because I couldn't move in case I'd crash to the floor, and he was such a tall man he could put his arms on either side of the cupboard wall and keep me trapped there. I squeaked feebly in protest, 'Please let me down, sir, oh *please*!' He didn't take a blind bit of notice, but just laughed. I could have hit him, if he hadn't been my boss. He strolled away towards the door, pretending to leave me there marooned, and when I let out a scream of fright I lost my balance and slipped forward. One bound, and he'd caught me in his arms. The next minute, Patsy had arrived and was staring as if her eyes were going to fall out. Aye, it was high time I looked for another job.

Wee Mr. Brown, my Scots boss, helped me in this decision, because, like my nice lawyer boss, he had my interests at heart. 'I don't know why you stay in a pokey place like this,' he kept telling me, 'with your speeds you could be earning twice what we are able to pay you. Why don't you try for one of the really important firms in Glasgow.'

I decided to take his advice, but I'd wait a wee while. After that generous treatment at Christmas I felt it would be most ungrateful of me to desert them so soon. I just couldn't decently hand in my notice before the Fair. By that time I'd have been with them a year, and my mother too would take it quite naturally that I wanted to move on. She'd never suspect the middle-aged English boss had helped to drive me out, because he showed every sign of going wrong in the mind.

14

THE summers were periods of blessed release from learning, for I had used my prize money, as planned, to go back to college for night classes, and the winter months were devoted entirely to study. Three nights a week at classes, one night at the Guides, choir practice, and homework filled every week from September right through to the end of May. I discovered what a marvellous help to study walking was. I walked to the office in the morning, back to it again at lunch-time, home at night, back to college, and home again after classes. The only time I rode in a tram, unless it was absolutely torrential rain, was home for my dinner. I'd never have dreamt of spending money on fares for all that travelling, and the movement of my feet and legs seemed to increase my thoughts. I did trial balances in my head for the business methods class, I translated my French exercises, I wrote every word of every shop advert in shorthand as I passed the windows, and I wrote little stories for *The Times* and for *The Citizen* and *The Bulletin*, describing all the humorous things I observed in my daily marches to and from Springburn. I had discovered also, to my surprise, that newspapers liked what I wrote and actually paid me. *The Times* gave me first encouragement. I was so inexperienced that I didn't even know I ought to enclose a stamped addressed envelope if I wanted my article returned, and nobody was more surprised than I when my brother picked up the paper one night and cried, 'Hey, is this you?', pointing to the initials M.W.W. at the foot of an article about Glasgow trams. 'Oh, they've printed it,' I shouted, and seized the paper from him. The family were stunned. I had told nobody. Tommy was particularly amazed, for he was already trying his hand at the writing game, with mixed success, and he was full of encouragement that I had hit the jackpot with my very first piece. They paid me fifteen shillings. The equivalent of a whole week's wages from the law office. I hoped I would get some more good ideas, for this seemed a great way of adding to my savings and enjoying myself at the same time, since writing was always a wonderful respite from all the hard grind of lessons and homework.

I even enjoyed taking the minutes for the Guide meetings, for not only was it good practice for my shorthand, but I could write out a précis of our discussions in my own words. The Guides were a great source of pleasure, and provided a fine outlet for my energies after nights of quiet study during the rest of the week. I was now a patrol leader, and chose the swallow for my emblem. I admired the dark blue and white of the embroidered badge, and I loved its swift darting movements in flight, and the way it never seemed to keep still. As my mother always said of me, because I never 'warmed a chair', 'it's a pity oor Molly hisnae a pair of wings', I thought the swallow particularly appropriate, and so did she. We had a great time marching up and down in our church hall, playing racing games, learning country dancing, and studying for our various badges. All my earlier childhood activities were a great help in acquiring those coveted badges. Needlework just meant doing a piece of simple sewing, and a few pieces of knitting, plus a crochet edging, all of which I had done either at home or at school. Grannie had taught me to knit before I went to school, and although I could never hope to work as fast as she did, I could turn the heel of a sock well enough to please her before I was ten years old. The cookery badge didn't give me a minute's worry, for again I had cooked with and for Grannie since I could toddle, and I felt the few things I'd been asked to do for the badge hadn't really earned me that beautifully embroidered emblem to put on my sleeve. The first-aid one was harder, though, and we had special classes from some of the big boys from the Boys' Brigade, and learned all about splints and slings, and how to cope with fainting and nose-bleeding, and such minor disasters. There were dozens of tricky questions we could be asked about the various bones of the body, not to mention the parts of the brain, and the differences between veins and arteries, and the composition of the blood. Oh how we groaned and worried over our first-aid book, and trembled in case we'd be asked something we knew absolutely nothing about. We could hardly believe it when we all got through, and we felt that that was one badge we had well and truly earned.

Our company was particularly good at maze marching, and for the big combined display at St. Andrew's Hall we were chosen to do this intricate form of marching to represent Springburn. Our captain was a really fine pianist, and we rehearsed to the splendid tunes she chose, until we knew every turn and twist and wheeling movement and could have performed in our sleep.

I washed my hair the night before the display, for an abiding passion with me has been soft, clean, silky hair. The only time any of us visited a hairdresser was to have our hair trimmed, and the very idea of paying somebody to set it in smooth neat waves round our heads was beyond imagination. We just washed it, pressed wee combs in to form some sort of wave, and let it go its own sweet way, which in my case was to stand up in a great fluffy mop which added a few satisfying inches to my small stature. I've always walked with a spring in my step, a sort of bouncing rhythm, or, as my mother tactfully put it, 'as though I were dancing'. I just couldn't walk any other way, and so I was quite unconscious of the fact that when we went into our maze marching on the stage of St. Andrew's Hall before a packed audience I presented a very comical figure, my mop bouncing in time to my springy steps. As we twisted in and out, arms swinging, heads up, forming intricate patterns for the admiration of our audience, a slight ripple of laughter started, and grew and grew. None of us could understand it. The whole audience were soon convulsed. 'What is the matter?' we wondered in panic. We couldn't utter a word of our dismay, of course, for we were too busy following our long-rehearsed movements, but we had done this marching so often that we could allow ourselves to steal glances at one another as we passed and repassed. Every eye became riveted to the hem of the opposite number, to see if anybody's knickers were falling down. No, not a bloomer leg in sight. What could it be? We were scarlet with shame and confusion, and when we came off the stage we gazed at one another in bewilderment, deaf to the applause which followed our exit. And then a patrol leader who had been watching from the audience came in, gasping with laughter. 'It was Molly Weir's bouncing walk and her hair going up and down that looked so funny,' she said. 'It was like a hairy-jock in the wind.' I blushed with mortification till the tears came to my eyes, and the others were furious that I had spoiled the effect of their neat marching. Fancy making such a fool of myself up there in front of everybody. Oh how glad I was that my mother hadn't come to see us. And then at the thought of my mother I laughed, for I remembered one of her favourite stories was of the country lassie who had gone out with the farmer's son, and during the course of the evening he had rifted right out loud in the pictures. She had laughed and laughed, for, as my mother had said, she hadn't enough gumption to hide her feelings and spare those of the young man. At last he had said, sarcastically, 'I won't bother to take you to the pictures again, since you're so easily entertained with a mere rift.' We all thought this a great joke, and a fine bit of repartee, and I suddenly thought it was equally hilarious that a whole audience could be so easily amused by a clean head of hair. If they were as daft as all that, why should I let it bother me? But I never forgot, all the same, how easily one could become a figure of fun through something in one's appearance, and how ignorant one could be of the effect of such a thing on the rest of the world. I wondered if the time would ever come when I would feel calmly sure of everything, like my mother and the minister and the Guide captain, and I longed to look into the future and see how I would turn out.

We were all getting to the age, my chums and I, and the girls I met in offices, where the future tantalised us with its mystery, and one of the great excitements of those days was having our fortune told. We knew well enough it would be *years* before any of us could afford to think of getting married. Oh we were romantic, all right, but we had first-hand evidence all round us that marriage involved rent, insurance, clothes, and that a house had to be furnished before you could live in it, and furnished from savings at that.

Everybody was far too poor to be able to count on such munificent presents as suites, or indeed any sort of furniture, and hire purchase was regarded with horror in the community where I lived. The nearest we ever got to H.P., apart from my mother's mad flight of fancy with the piano, was 'the

Menage', or 'the Minodge', as we pronounced it, to which working-class wives belonged because it meant being able to buy sheets and blankets and towels when they were needed, all essential items if the decencies were to be preserved, and which could be paid off at the rate of a sixpence or a shilling a week over what seemed like an eternity of time.

Even this mild form of H.P. was frowned on by my mother and my grannie, and we saved up and had the money in our hand, or at any rate covered by the Co-op dividend before we bought a single item.

We were prepared for the long legendary Scottish courtship, and saw nothing odd in courtships which lasted for ten or fifteen years. One enterprising couple delayed the wedding day until they had won their household equipment by their skill at local whist drives, and we all knew that they were just waiting to win the bed, and then the great day could be named. Eventually the nuptial couch was won, they were wed, and seemed none the worse for the waiting. The whole district followed those whist drives, and the couple themselves rejoiced no more with each prize than we did, watching on the sidelines.

So with such examples to keep us with a proper sense of perspective and stifle any thoughts of indecent haste in such matters, we followed the thrifty ways of our elders, but nobody could stop us from dreaming, or from seeking occult help in trying to penetrate the mysterious future which lay so far ahead. The clap-trap of the spae-wives was drunk in with almost swooning eagerness, in spite of the fact that we were all respectable attenders of Sunday School, Church and Bible Class. We saw no contradiction in believing in both, and news of a new spae-wife flashed through the young community with the speed of bush telegraph, just as it had with the advent of a new church mission bent on saving our souls. The very word 'fortune-teller' held magic for us and we clamoured to be taken to the new oracle. 'How much is it?' we demanded. If it were sixpence, we decided she couldn't be much good. Anybody with the real second sight would put a far higher value on her gift, for she would be in great demand. A shilling was more like the thing, we felt, and could be scraped together now that we were working, without too much sacrifice. We'd put the money we saved on fares towards the shilling, and we'd cut out sweeties entirely—well, except maybe for one or two Imperials to suck in church on Sunday. A spae-wife at two shillings, though, had us searching the corners of our purses, and doing frantic calculations to try to meet this enormous sum. 'She must be good,' we'd think excitedly, 'if people pay her two whole shillings.'

The spae-wives generally lived in the South Side of Glasgow, or the 'Soo-side', as it was known, alien territory to most of us. We shivered with nervous delight as we bowled along in strange, different-coloured tramcars through unfamiliar streets. We tried to keep these excursions from our mothers, but somehow they sensed that something was going on. They'd have had to have been deaf and blind not to have noticed, for we rushed about to each other's houses in frantic activity, and in a hiss of whispers, for days before the actual spae-wife visit took place. My mother was so sure we'd be murdered, or at the very least 'set upon' and left for dead in those darkly suspect districts, that she reduced me to a state of fear where I could scarcely take in my fortune when it was told to me.

The fortune-tellers were, almost without exception, Irish, with vast bosoms, over which were stretched tight hand-knitted jumpers. We talked to each other in whispers as we waited in dingy lobbies for our turn to go in, and, once confronted with the oracle, could hardly breathe as fear blended with desperation that having come this far we couldn't turn back. The rooms always seemed strangely dark, with a queer smell which I realised later was compounded of dust and sooty chimneys and drying clothes. Sometimes they read the cards, but sometimes they peered into the lines of our hands, and the heavy scent of their bodies came suffocatingly close. We chattered non-stop on the way home, like birds released from a cage, glad to be in the open air again, with safe, familiar faces round us. We compared notes on what we'd been told. Each and every one of us were told we would cross the water, but as we'd already crossed the Clyde to reach the fortune teller, we felt this was a pretty safe prediction. Secretly we were terribly disappointed at having to share even this one forecast with each other. We wanted to be unique, but, of course, as the spae-wives were Irish and had migrated themselves, they doubtless felt this was the most important thing that could happen to anyone. However, the rest of our fortune had a satisfying variety. One was to marry a tall dark stranger. Another a short, thick-set fair man. A third would be widowed early in life, which we felt was thrillingly romantic. Even the future widow liked this, and was glad she was fair, because everybody knew that widows' weeds looked far nicer on fair-haired people. None of us had even seen widows' weeds, but we'd heard our mothers and grannies speak of them, and the description sounded beautifully dramatic and tragic.

Some would have three children, some five, some were guaranteed twins, and none would be childless. We were so sure that spae-wives were right, we almost started knitting our layettes to be well prepared for our broods. Only a lack of money, and the impossibility of truly seeing ourselves as mothers, stopped us buying the wool.

We never suspected that they were frauds, every single one of them. We wanted so desperately to believe that they knew what lay ahead that we pretended to ourselves that the things they told us were coming true one by one.

All except one of my chums, who had complete faith in my mother's ability to read fortunes from tea-leaves. 'She's *faur* better than yon spae-wives,' she'd declare, 'and she doesn't charge you anything.' My mother only did this for fun, and had started it just to prove anybody could make up a fortune if she put her mind to it, and to try to stop us wasting our money on 'thae Jezebels ower at the Soo-side'. Strangely enough, many of the things she said did come true, and what had started out as a joke became her party piece, and she was in great demand by all my friends. In fact she became quite fed up with the whole business, and made every excuse to go out when she knew my chums were coming to do their sewing, or wash their hair, for she knew she wouldn't get a minute's peace until she'd read their fortunes in the tea-leaves.

We were becoming very absorbed with our grooming now, and stayed in at least two evenings a week for the sole purpose of washing our hair, doing our nails, going over our clothes and mending any straps or stockings which needed attention. We shared breathless ideas for making our hair or skin more dazzling, and these usually had to be concocted from house-hold items, for none of us wore make-up, apart from a little daring use of lipstick. One chum with beautiful hair swore by an egg-yolk mixed in with liquid green soap as *the* perfect shampoo. Another urged that oatmeal mixed with egg made a terrific face-pack and gave you rosy cheeks. My mother's scorn at this waste of good food had me rushing through the lobby to hide my meal-covered features, for I would defeat the whole purpose if I let the stuff crack by arguing. However rosy my cheeks were when I went to bed after such beautifying treatments, they wore their usual Glasgow pallor in the morning, and justified my mother's wrath at the waste of a good egg. We spent hours tidying out the solitary drawer we were allowed to use in the big chest of drawers, and checking over all our treasures. I once found tenpence stowed away in a typewriter-ribbon box, where I'd stored it for safe keeping for my holidays and then forgotten where I'd hidden it, and if I had inherited a fortune, I couldn't have been more elated.

I don't know how many times I'd lifted out that box during the many tidyings I'd done, but the pennies were packed so tightly they hadn't rattled, and the treasure within had lain unnoticed all that time. Oh I could now appreciate to the full the story in the Bible of the rejoicing which took place when that which was lost was found again. Whole tenpence! And just in the nick of time for the hat sale.

As far as we were concerned there was only one hat sale and we waited for it every summer. What the Queen's milliner was to London, Annette was to Glasgow. We could never have afforded her hats at ordinary prices during the year, and contented ourselves with mere window-gazing until sale time rolled round. She had a routine which never varied, so you knew exactly where you were.

As soon as Glasgow Fair was on, and those with money to burn had equipped themselves with their holiday and summer hats, a huge notice would appear in the window of her exclusive little shop in Sauchiehall Street. 'SALE—HATS TODAY £1.' So those with a pound to spend got the pick of the stock. Then, a few days later, when Annette felt the hats were getting a bit too battered to ask a pound for them, the second notice went up. 'SALE—HATS TODAY 10/-.' None of your gentle reductions for Annette. Prices were slashed dramatically or not at all. The exciting thing was that you didn't know just *when* she'd reduce her prices. You knew it would happen, but whether days or merely hours would elapse between one reduction and the next, only Annette herself knew. And she gave no hint. So you had to flee up to the shop every lunch-hour from office or college to check how the odds were being reduced. If you saw a hat for which your heart panted, you had to weigh the risk of it surviving the ten-shilling customers, and oh the agony of trying to decide whether to splash your savings at this stage and make sure of it, or chance it not attracting anyone and getting it for five shillings later.

If you were a gambler you waited. Inevitably, the next notice was 'SALE—HATS TODAY 5/-', to be followed a few days later by 'SALE—HATS TODAY 2/6d'. But madness really took over among the youngest fry when somebody came rushing into the cloakroom with the news 'They're down to sixpence tomorrow.' At that stage Annette put the notice in the window the afternoon before, so we had advance warning.

There was no time for leisurely eating that day. We'd snatch a sandwich on the wing, wouldn't even stop to walk, but raced up to the shop as fast as our excellently trained legs would carry us. It was like a football scrum. Sharp elbows working overtime, we dived into the centre of a milling mass of teenagers. Nobody wore a hat, for if you'd gone in wearing one, you'd never have recovered it again. Ten to one somebody would have plonked down sixpence for it and vanished before you could have protested. We had a hilarious time. Hats with veils were tried on to shrieks of laughter. Anybody with a sense of comedy paraded round in feathers, reducing the others to hysteria. But when it came to actually choosing something for our sixpence we became deadly serious and called all our chums to give an opinion.

How Annette could have allowed us to invade her shop like this I simply don't know. Maybe it made a change from the usual quiet elegance of her surroundings, and she may even have enjoyed the rapturous appreciation we gave to all her battered sales models. She stood at the back of the shop, smiling, and only volunteered a quiet word of advice when the agony of indecision was almost reducing a customer to tears. We had a glorious hour, and at the end of it each and every one of us bore off in triumph a sixpenny hat in a brown-paper bag. This would be the last hat purchase for many of us until the notice went up next year: 'SALE—HATS TODAY SIXPENCE'.

My best sixpenny bargain was a pale pink straw boater trimmed with black veiling, which was an exact match for a pink linen dress I made. I felt so grown-up I almost choked with my own importance, and my mother was amazed at the transformation it wrought. We all helped each other with our home dressmaking, and I had the great benefit of being close chums with a girl who had obtained a job with one of the top dress houses in Glasgow. She used to be allowed to bring home cuttings from the posh dresses made for the aristocracy of Glasgow and Renfrewshire, and from these she showed us how to cut leaves and petals, and stitch them into lifelike chrysanthemums and spring bouquets which we pinned to the neckline or shoulder of our home-made garments. This added a most elegant touch to our bargain remnants, and we spent hours stitching and trying on and pressing to pass the critical eye of our dressmaking chum. She also showed us how to make little crêpe-de-Chine garters, again from exquisite material obtained from her employers, and all of us eventually sported silken garters which exactly toned in with our outfits, so we didn't mind a bit when our skirts were whirled up during the active birlings of the eightsome reels and quadrilles at the church dances. Our garters were part of our outfit, after all, and it would have been a shame if nobody had caught a glimpse of them and appreciated all our hard work and dainty stitching.

Those church dances were great fun, and our mothers served behind the scenes and kept an eye on us at the same time. Instead of bags of cookies and cakes we had boxes handed out to us at the interval, and this seemed so opulent and grown-up. There would be a salmon sandwich, moist and delicious, and usually a Paris bun and one or two dainty little cakes. The mothers came round with steaming cups of tea, and we all sat round the hall, and ate every scrap. We couldn't rush back to the cloakroom to save anything to take home, and we wouldn't have dreamt of leaving anything when we'd paid for it, so there wasn't a crumb left.

The boys sat along one side of the hall, and the girls along the other wall, and the minute the orchestra struck up, there was a dash for the girl of the moment. Paul Jones' foxtrots took care of the wallflowers, and gave everybody a chance, and ladies' choice sent us off shyly to choose the boy who found favour in our eyes. At the first of these dances my mother who had romantic ideas of daintiness, had made my heart turn over with dismay by buying me a little pair of pale blue dancing pumps, dead flat like ballet shoes, to match a pale blue chiffon dress she had found in one of her mysterious sorties down by the Barrows. I hadn't the heart to disappoint her by telling her how I longed for higher heels, and how much I needed them to boost my miserably small size, and I tried to hide my feet under my chair in case nobody would dance with me because I was so wee. A few of the girls were scathing, and said they weren't proper dance shoes, but the boys didn't seem to mind, and once my embarrassment was forgotten those flat shoes were marvellous for scooshing up and down the hall during the quadrilles, and for leaping round the hall dancing the Dashing White Sergeant.

For a special Christmas dance my mother had managed to find some floral ninon dress material and some matching net, and although it was inexpensive sale material, we decided we couldn't manage such flimsy stuff ourselves and would have it made by a real dressmaker. It would have to be somebody cheap, of course, but there were plenty of seamstresses in Springburn at that time who were glad to earn a few shillings by taking orders for dressmaking. We heard of a wee woman out the Low Road, as we called the road between Balgrayhill and Auchinairn, and one foggy Friday night after my mother came home from work, and I had done my homework after my office job, we set off for the dressmaker's house. I had a picture from a newspaper which I wanted her to copy, for to me the mere word 'dressmaker' invested this unknown lady with all the qualities of *haute couture*. It was a dark wee close, with a gas-lamp which flickered from a broken mantle, and I was glad my mother was with me. We climbed the stairs and peered at all the name-plates and found the name we sought on the second floor. We rang the bell and waited. Not a murmur. We rang again, 'Maybe she's no' in,' my mother said, 'but where could she be on a night like this?' She didn't stop to reason that she and I were out on such a night, and not in our own house. I wouldn't give in, for I was dying to get my beautiful ninon and net into the hands of this expert. 'Ring again, Mother,' I urged. So we gave another yank at the bell-knob and sent a wild jingle of sound echoing down the lobby which was assuredly on the other side of the door.

We heard footsteps, the door opened, and a frightened face peered round the frame. 'Who is it?' she demanded, in a high, shrill voice. I couldn't answer, for I was too busy taking in her appearance. She looked about a hundred, and nothing like my mental picture of a dressmaker at all. We followed her through the lobby, to an icy-cold front room where she lit the gas. We hadn't managed to speak a word so far, for she had spied the parcel we were carrying and had obviously assumed we wanted her services to make a dress. 'Who is it for?' she asked, looking from my mother to me. While my mother opened the parcel, I spread out the newspaper picture and started to explain that I wanted her to copy it, but she seized my arm abruptly and called, 'Wait a minute.' She disappeared, and came back almost at once carrying something which glittered in the gas-light. 'Now,' she said, 'What is it you want?' and, so saying, she raised her arm and smartly put an ear trumpet to her ear. My mother and I stared at each other, and I could feel the laughter bubbling from the pit of my stomach, up through my chest and over the top of my head. My mother shook her head reprovingly, and pushed me towards the trumpet. I opened my mouth, placed it to the mouth of that trumpet and tried to speak. Instead of words, out came a strangled shriek of laughter which nearly blasted the poor wee woman to the other side of the room. At her look of reproach, tears of laughter and embarrassment ran down my cheeks. 'I can't, Mother,' I gasped. 'You'll have to tell her.' 'Indeed I will not,' said my mother sharply. 'You'll just control yourself and tell her yourself. I never saw such bad manners.' I gulped, put my mouth to the trumpet, tried to speak, shrieked again with hysterical laughter, then turned and ran down the stairs into the fog, leaving my mother, the dressmaker and the ear trumpet. I leaned against the wall of the close, aware of my terrible behaviour, but unable to stop laughing. At last it all ended in a bout of most uncomfortable hiccups, and still there was no sign of my mother. I *couldn't* go in and face that poor wee deaf woman again, but now I was frightened of the dark close and the flickering gas-light. I crept upstairs again and listened outside the door which I had left wide open in my flight. To my amazement my mother and the dressmaker were chatting quite amiably, and the wee dressmaker was telling all about her days as a court dressmaker to which she had been apprenticed at the age of fourteen and had only left to nurse her mother a few years back. Her mother! How could anybody so old have a mother? I wondered. The type of work she was doing now, I heard her say, was a far cry from what she had been used to, but sewing was all she knew and she had just to take whatever offered in the district. Oh how ashamed I felt, but I couldn't have returned to that room if I'd been shot for not doing so. When my mother eventually came out, carrying my dress material, I couldn't meet her eyes. When I tried to take her arm she shook me off. 'I was black affrontit,' she said. 'Fancy laughing like that, and you supposed to be a lady. I don't know what you learned in that college, but it certainly wasn't manners.'

My heart felt like lead. How could I explain to my mother that I wasn't laughing at the poor deaf woman, that it was self-consciousness at having to speak down a trumpet that had been my undoing. Miserably I realised that I was no lady. I was just like the farm servant who had laughed because somebody had rifted. No, I was far far worse, because she had just been a simple girl, whereas I at least had had the advantage of a good education. Would I ever learn to be a lady? I doubted it very much, especially after this black black episode.

My mother broke the silence. 'Well,' she said at last, 'You'll come oot o' this worst anyway, for you'll sew every stitch of that dress yourself, and then maybe you'll be sorry you lost the chance of that clever wee woman doing it for you.' She was right, of course. It was ghastly material for an amateur to work with, and many salt tears were shed over puckered neckline, stretched sleeve-seam, and uneven hem before I could wear that dress to the church dance, and every time I wore it I could see that ear trumpet, and remember my undisciplined behaviour. In the end I gave it away long before its usefulness was ended. I couldn't bear the sight of it. It was a bitter lesson.

15

At the end of that winter term of night classes the college principal asked if I would stay on for a few weeks to be coached in special high shorthand speeds in short bursts, for they wanted to arrange public demonstrations of my skill and at the same time give the college a boost. I was delighted to do this, for I owed them so much. The head teacher whose house I had visited was still the only one who could rattle off the test pieces at breakneck speed, so he and I stayed on for an hour every night, when his day classes were over and I came from the office, and soon we were zooming along at the dazzling speed of 300 words per minute. It didn't seem possible. It was comparatively easy to get up to 200, then 220, but every 20 words per minute on top became progressively difficult. I still had to perch up on my feet on the seat, and I used to feel a bit like a jockey, crouching over my book and desk, hand racing along like lightning. By this time, I didn't even have to think of an outline. I had been going over and over the teacher's course at night classes, to keep me in training for the exam, which I couldn't take till I was eighteen, and I must have drilled every outline, every grammalogue and phrase a million times since I was fourteen. In fact, I was greatly encouraged one night when, after I'd done my oral stint at the blackboard, my teacher said laughingly, 'If you give them this sort of example when you go for your exam, they'll hand you your teaching certificate as you walk out of the door!' I may say when the exam did come I was just as terrified as if I'd never looked at a book. And when the results came out, and I knew I'd passed, I was so exhilarated I could have done cart-wheels all over Glasgow.

My high-speed demonstrations to parents and would-be students were part of a campaign to boost the numbers enrolling at the college, and as an added personal draw I came in for a week of my holidays and enrolled the students who were to start after the summer term. How business-like I felt, standing behind the counter on the first floor, welcoming each new arrival, taking details of name, address, previous school, what subjects they would study, and finally their payment for the course. I whirled round date-stamps with great authority, signed with a flourish the copperplate receipts given to me by the principal, and handed over with fitting solemnity a folder giving all details of the books required. The principal christened me Peter Pan, as I flew from desk to counter, back to desk again, round to his office to hand over the money, and back to the desk again to take care of the next student. I thoroughly enjoyed this taste of officialdom, and was astounded when at the end of the week the old man pressed a ten-shilling note into my hand. For what? For being allowed to play at running the whole college? Fancy getting money as well as such fun. Whole ten shillings too, to add to my savings.

Although they were very pleased with my speeds and were frighteningly certain I'd get through the teacher's exam with flying colours, the college heads took another look at me and came to the conclusion that with my tiny proportions of 4 ft. 11½ in. height and a weight of under seven stones I'd need some backing to give me authority over heavy-weight pupils. They decided that the thing for me was to do was to have professional voice coaching. I didn't even begin to suspect that it might also be to iron out the broad Springburn accent, which I was hardly aware of now, for I was using my posh office voice all the time, being careful not to be too lah-di-dah, of course. It was almost worse being too 'pan-loaf' than being too rough in accent.

By a strange coincidence, I had actually heard of the voice teacher whom the college suggested. Months before this, Patsy, my sophisticated office girl, had come in one morning full of enthusiasm for a concert she'd enjoyed the previous evening. With my interest in everything to do with acting, I drank in every word, and before the morning was over she had taught me two poems by A. A. Milne which she'd heard at the concert. If she was terrible at filing, she had a wonderful memory for words. The performers had all been pupils of this marvellous teacher. I envied them from the bottom of my heart. And now, to my delight, the college were suggesting I take lessons from this very teacher. It was too good to be true. And then the harsh facts of life brought me back to earth. How would my mother and I pay for the lessons? Although we weren't quite so hard up, I still had only thirty shillings a week, and there were books, and clothes, and fares, and Guide subscriptions, and a dozen other calls on my pocket money of five shillings a week.

My mother thought I was daft enough paying to join the Scottish Clerks' Association, just to get my teeth looked after, in case I would one day be an actress and need a perfect smile—she herself would have run a mile from any dentist—so how could I ask her to pay for voice lessons? The very idea of paying to learn how to *speak*, when she thought I was a lovely speaker, would have seemed like throwing good money down the drain.

I was still very shy of those elderly college men, and didn't know how to tell them that I had no money to help me to follow their lovely suggestion, but they sensed the difficulty and said they would put in a word and see that I had specially advantageous terms. They might seem especially advantageous to the college, I thought, but any charge at all would seem impossible to us, who hadn't a penny left over for such frivolities.

Suddenly I saw a possibility. This was maybe the right moment to look for a new job with better money. I'd promised myself I'd only stay where I was till the Fair anyway, and if I got one right away, I'd have from the Fair till September to save, for there was no hurry to start the voice coaching until the autumn term. It would be perfect timing, for I'd also be into the final winter session before the shorthand teacher's examination, and I'd be able to make immediate use of my voice training. I began looking at the advertisements in the newspapers that very night, as soon as my mother had finished with *The Times*. There were several which took my fancy, but the most interesting one was for a shorthand typist required by a huge steel company's head offices in Oswald Street. They asked for 'exceptionally good speeds in shorthand and typing. Must be over eighteen. Good salary to right applicant.' I knew I had exceptional speeds in both shorthand and typing, but I wasn't even eighteen, much less *over* eighteen. I ground my teeth in frustration. Should I have a try anyway? I wondered. What was age, if I had the speeds? It was a good thing they hadn't put 'must be over five feet,' for I certainly couldn't have done anything about my height. I could grow older, but I seemed to have stuck in height and was still far too small to impress anybody with my office efficiency. Ah well, nothing beats a good try, I said to myself, and I wrote out the applictaion. To be on the safe side, I also wrote to several other firms, and I begged all of them the favour of an interview.

Every night when I came home I flew to the chest of drawers to see if there was a letter for me lying on the top, beside the wee dish with the buttons in it and my mother's best brooch. 'There's been nae post the day,' my mother would say irritatingly. She wasn't at all sympathetic to my wish to change offices. She hadn't forgotten that beautiful goose they'd given us for Christmas, and she had a great loyalty to those who were 'good to us'. I hadn't breathed a word about my crazy, lovelorn boss, but I had told her that the college felt I should have voice lessons to 'hold my own' with the big boys I might find in my classes when I taught shorthand, and that I'd have to find the money for such lessons. 'Well, maybe they'll give you a rise where you are,' my mother suggested. 'Och, Mother,' I said, 'it's *time* I moved to a bigger office. Anyway, they can't afford to pay any more where I am, so if I want to better myself I'll just have to move.' My mother pursed her lips. 'You've hardly been wi' thae nice folk ony time at a', and here you are wantin' tae shift. Well, you'll no' find onybody that'll think ony mair o' ye than they dae.' My mother had a great desire to be thought well of. This was far more important to her than money, and she couldn't understand why I couldn't be content to remain where I was, happily basking in approval and popularity. She was nervous of my ambition, but she respected the advice I obtained from the college heads, and she knew if voice lessons had been suggested for me I'd move heaven and earth to try to get them.

A week passed, and I decided the steel firm didn't want anybody so young as myself. I had had two interviews with smaller firms, but I explained that I wanted the experience of a large company and the chance of promotion and a good salary. And then one morning, by the first post, a letter arrived from the steel company offices. Beautiful thick, crackling notepaper. They would be pleased to see me at three o'clock the following afternoon. I'd have to ask time off for the interview, but I knew wee Mr. Brown was on my side, for he had told me often enough I was wasted where I was. I showed him the letter as soon as he came in that morning, and he was enthusiastic. 'A marvellous firm,' he assured me, 'you will do well there.' 'But they'll maybe not have me,' I said, 'for they wanted somebody of eighteen.' 'Well,' he laughed, 'they'll be mad if they don't take you on. I'll give you a letter if you like, and tell them I can thoroughly recommend the employment of this mighty atom!' He was a bit of a coughdrop, I decided, but I refused the letter. I didn't want my prospective employer to think I had been working for lunatics. Fancy handing anybody such an unbusiness-like note! Anyway, you didn't receive a reference until after you left your job.

I was glad it was summer for this interview, for it was so much easier to look nice and neat and tidy in a striped cotton dress than in a well-worn winter coat and maybe stockings splashed with rain. It was a lovely warm sunny day, and I checked the appearance of my blue and white 'Kodak' dress in each shop window that I passed between our office and Argyle Street. I wore a little white jockey cap and my best Sunday shoes, and I decided I must look pretty grown-up because I got a few encouraging whistles from the lorry-drivers as I bounced down Hope Street.

The offices were huge. Red sandstone rose to a height of three storeys ,and they actually had a lift entirely for themselves. In fact the whole building was theirs. I was to go to the second floor, to the office of the company secretary. A middle-aged lady in the outer office bade me wait, as Mr. Stewart wasn't quite free. I sat with my feet tucked neatly under the chair, not moving a muscle, but my eyes darting round this splendid office. Beautiful panelling half-way up would have pleased my mother with its quality, and above the panels ran opaque glass, giving a pleasant light look to the place. The door fittings were all of the best, and the typewriter, files and paper were everything that I could have desired. No shortage of anything, I decided. A very rich company.

Then the door leading to the inner office opened, and a very tall elderly gentleman beckoned me through. He looked surprised at my appearance, checked that I really was as much as seventeen, said I was younger than they had wanted, but in view of my speeds they had decided to see me, and give me a test. My heart warmed to him. This was the sort of reasoning I liked. I simply hated being dismissed as 'too young' before being given a chance to prove that I could do the work. He handed me a shorthand notebook, dictated three letters of varying lengths, and asked me to go outside and type them. The elderly lady showed me where paper and carbons were, and I sat down at the machine and polished them off, returned to the inner office, and handed them over. Mr. Stewart seemed to be concealing a smile as I bounded back to his side with the letters. 'Well, that's an impressive display of speed,' he said. 'Let me just see how you've set the letters out.' He put his head on on side. 'Well, young lady' (lady! my heart gave a bound), 'I don't think we can let you go. I also think we'll have to make an exception in your case about salary. We normally pay according to age, and at seventeen you'd only be entitled to thirty shillings a week. Clearly you're not going to change jobs for the same money, and clearly such speeds merit a special reward. You will start at the rate for a twenty-one-year-old, but you must not tell anyone of this, or it will create discontent. You will start at two pounds a week, with a yearly rise in salary in line with our policy.' Two pounds a week! Ten shillings more than I was getting. Och it would easily be enough to give my mother a bit extra, and leave me something to put towards my voice lessons. I ran back to the office on air, gave Mr. Brown my notice, and felt I couldn't wait for the summer to be over to begin my voice lessons and to meet my very first elocution teacher.

The new office was bewilderingly different from anything I had known. I was attached to the export department on the third floor, and the men and women worked strictly separately, apart from the actual time taken for dictation. The men worked at desks in a large open-plan room, and the typists were placed in a long narrow room leading off this main office. It was panelled up to eye-level, and had glass above this height, so that one could see into the main office when one stood up. Two typists were allocated to each section, and whoever was free answered the summoning bell. In case of emergency, or extra pressure of work, we all worked for anyone. There were about ten of us in each typing room, and the combined clatter of the machines in that narrow space was terrible. I'd never worked in such close proximity with other machines, and wondered if I would ever get used to the din. The head typist handed me a list of branch offices, and foreign offices, and details of the category of letter which would require three carbon copies, or four carbon copies or even six carbon copies, and I had to learn these by heart so that I would know at once how many copies were required. I could ask at first, of course, until I got used to things. I was shown where to get supplies of paper, and carbons, and ribbons, and pencils and rubbers. It was like a wee shop. It even had a lady in charge, who handed you out the materials you needed, and for which you signed a chit. Fancy an office doing so much work that there was a constant job just handing out materials! And office girls were kept busy all day long, emptying our baskets of finished work and taking them to the section heads for signing and despatch. Commissionaires dealt with them at this stage, and they were in constant touch with the postal department. I was fascinated. All the jobs Patsy and I used to do between us were handled by separate departments in this office, and some of those grand typists with whom I now worked had never filed a letter or done a trial balance. They knew nothing but their own little cog in this vast machine. I began to realise what a splendid experience a small office was, when you just had to know how to do everything if the wheels were to turn smoothly. In spite of their poshness, I comforted myself that I knew a whole lot more about office routine than those fashionable typists. And I began to feel it was just possible that I was even worth my two pounds a week. I didn't let on, of course, that that was what I was earning, and I took my place as the most junior of junior typists, for I was by far the youngest in the typing room. Although I had been told to ask anything I wished to know for the first few weeks, I soon realised that those elegant young ladies didn't mean a word of it. Each time I queried a foreign market, or an Asiatic spelling, eyes would be cast heavenwards, and a voice dripping sweet-sour tones would say, 'You don't mind asking a great many questions, do you, Miss Weir?' I didn't recognise the sarcasm at first and replied innocently, 'Oh no, for you told me to ask.'

But after I'd intercepted a few amused glances I shut my mouth, and asked the bosses instead, and they didn't mind telling me anything I wanted to know, for they were charmed with the speed with which I rattled off their letters and specifications. In fact, I soon earned another nickname from them, and was known throughout the building as 'The Flying Scotswoman'.

Oh but I longed to be as assured and sophisticated as my typing companions. I had thought my accent was pretty acceptable until I went into this office and listened to the voices of girls who had been educated at the best schools, and for whom the expressions of workaday Glasgow were a source of rippling amusement. They would send each other into shouts of laughter by parodying their 'dailies', and saying, 'I was *that* annoyed', or 'Oh she was *that* nice'. How could I laugh when I lived among people who spoke like that every day of their lives, and when I wasn't above saying such things myself? Feeling I was speaking a foreign language, I began forcing myself to say, even at home, 'Oh it was *so* nice, Mother,' and to my surprise the heavens didn't fall, and nobody seemed to notice. I had been afraid people at home would think I was stressing inadequacies in their own speech, but my altered vocabulary went right over their heads. I was so glad. I'd have hated to have hurt them, but I did want to fit into my new smart office background. Other expressions culled from those oft-quoted dailies were 'I'm a done day this wumman', and if they were in a rush in the afternoons they'd exclaim, to peals of laughter, 'Two o'clock and no' a peenie on the wean', or 'Two o'clock and no' a wean washed'. I hadn't realised such expressions were comical; to me they were quite normal, for I'd heard the women in the back courts use them all my life. I was base enough to curry favour by adding one of my own, which I'd heard from my brother, and which even struck us as being funny, although we knew perfectly well what was meant. Our typists had to have it translated. Describing a bus conductor who'd infuriated him, one of my brother's mates had said, 'He wis wan o' thae fullas wi' eyes a' sewn wi' rid worset.' When I translated this as 'One of those fellows whose eyes were all sewn with red wool', a perfect description of red-rimmed eyes, the typists fell about holding their sides, and making such a noise with their gasping laughter that the boss on the other side of the glass rapped it to make them be quiet. But on that warm gale of laughter I was admitted to their friendship. I was accepted as one of them. I knew I wasn't, and I hoped they would never think of coming to Springburn, where nobody knew what a 'daily' was, and where they said without a blush, 'Oh I'm *that* hoat', or 'I'm fair sweetin' '.

There were some in that fine office, though, who knew coarse Springburn words. I was walking along the corridor with an old commissionaire one day, to recover something from Postal Department, and he said, observing a plump young girl walking ahead of us, 'My the young lassies nooadays have awfu' big bums!' I jumped in fright. I was absolutely scandalised. Fancy hearing such a word in the office. I pretended I hadn't heard him. But my heart sank. I betted to myself he would never have used such a coarse word in front of any of the other typists in my room. He obviously knew I was from the tenements, like himself, and that he needn't choose his words, as he'd have to have done if I had been a lady. Just wait till I had my elocution lessons, though, he'd soon change his tune.

By the time September came, I had saved enough for my first quarter with the elocution teacher. I raced home from the office, swallowed my tea, and walked back the mile and a half to her house 'down the town', in a very swanky area. To my surprise the first thing I had to do was to learn to breathe. I thought everybody breathed as a matter of course, but it was a highly complicated performance, with ribs having to be held out, diaphragm allowed to extend, and stomach gently lowered. All this without raising the shoulders. I got into a terrible fankle, and was sure the talented elocution teacher would give me up as a bad job. I thought she was quite quite perfect. Beautifully dressed, with soft brown wavy hair, rosy cheeks, good teeth, and, best of all, a lovely voice. I had expected a good voice, of course, but this was a deep, warm, carrying voice which sent tingles down my spine. I had always had a husky voice, and because it was so different from the voices of my chums, I was inclined to whisper when I was with grown-ups. Miss Mitchell changed all that. She taught me to recognise the different qualities of my voice—to use middle register, lower register, and top register, and said I was very lucky to have such a wide range. We did 'Mee, moh, mah', and 'Mah, may, mee', and I breathed out and in till I was dizzy and had to hold on to the chair. Far too soon the hour was up, and I was to go home and practise all she had told me, and see how improved I would be the next week.

I danced up the road on air. It was difficult. It was strange to have to begin to examine so intensely something I had taken for granted all my life, like breathing and speaking. But instinctively I knew that this was going to be a great asset to me in my future life, and not only for the teaching of short-hand. Oh if only I could learn to speak like Miss Mitchell I would be indistinguishable from all those posh typists, and I would be able to speak out loud in public just as they did, with the confidence bestowed by an impeccable accent. I hoped I wasn't getting too big for my boots, but I had a passionate desire to 'fit' wherever I was.

I rushed home and showed my mother and my brothers how to breathe, and walked about the kitchen shouting 'Mee, moh, mah', and they thought that teacher earned her money gey easy if that was what elocution meant. 'Ye canny go aboot sayin' thae things,' my mother said, 'I hope she knows whit she's daein'. I wouldnae like tae think ye were wastin' yer two pound twelve-and-sixpence.' My mother still hadn't got over spending this fortune on a quarter's lessons, paid in advance. She kept equating it with all the useful things we could have bought with it. A new pair of blankets for the bed. A pair of shoes and a hat maybe. A winter's coat, or at least a good bit towards one. But she began to think I might be getting a bit of value for my money when I started reciting poems instead of making unintelligible 'Maw, moh, moos'. I hadn't imagined for a moment that this bonus would be added to the vocal exercises, and when Miss Mitchell handed me a book one night, and asked me to read a poem, I thought she was just giving me a break from the monotony of all those sounds. Instead it was the start of drama coaching for me. Rudyard Kipling was followed by W. D. Cocker, and then Walter Wingate, and de la Mare, and, to my joy, A. A. Milne. We found that the light range of my voice was just like a little boy's, and Miss Mitchell decided I was going to be Christopher Robin at her annual performance by her pupils. The shorthand goal was forgotten, and as the performance date drew near,

I was introduced to the other pupils and plunged into the dizzy excitement of plays and sketches. These rehearsals were pure joy, and a perfect relief from the monotony of the shorthand studies which occupied my other evenings, but I had to discipline myself to stick rigidly to my little time-table pinned up beside the kitchen range, and devote the proper time to my shorthand theory, including psychology, or it would have been only too easy to spend every free moment learning my poems and my part in the sketches and plays.

We were to perform in a real concert hall, with proper footlights and curtains, and Miss Mitchell arranged all our costumes, partly from our own clothes, and partly from a huge trunk of 'props' she possessed. I'd never heard the word used before, and I thought it held the very savour of the theatre. She decided my own little red-and-white gingham dress would do for Christopher Robin, plus a floppy straw hat to hide my hair, to pretend I was a boy, and little white socks and plimsolls would complete the childlike effect. For once my tiny build was going to be a positive asset. She even had a backcloth painted with all the A. A. Milne characters, and I was to do the whole thing as a solo performance, starting off with 'Where am I going, I don't quite know', and finishing up with 'In the dark', where the poem ends in sleep.

All this rehearsing and reciting had robbed me of my diffidence when speaking to this beloved teacher, and one night when I was chattering away she startled me by asking me if I had no father. When I said I hadn't, she exclaimed, 'I knew it!' How did she know it? I wondered. 'Well, you have an unusual independence and vigour, and I just felt you had always had to stand on your own two feet. You've had very little cosseting, and that always shows.' Fancy all Grannie's teaching being so obvious to this clear-sighted teacher. For Grannie had always said, 'Bairns have to learn to stand on their own two feet, for they never ken whit's in front o' them.' Wouldn't Grannie have been pleased to know this teacher had used her very own words, and had seemed to approve of my independence? Mind you, clever as my grannie was, I doubt if she would have known what an elocution teacher was. After all, I'd hardly have got within spitting distance of one myself if I hadn't wanted to teach shorthand.

During the final rehearsals before the concert Miss Mitchell again surprised me by saying, 'Can I ask you something?' My heart always gave a lurch at such questions, for I never knew what was coming next, and I hoped Christopher Robin wasn't going to be taken away from me, or that I'd be asked to pay an impossible subscription to help finance the concert. To my utter astonishment, all she wanted to ask me was to remove a ring from my middle finger and transfer it to my fourth finger! With great delicacy she explained that it looked rather unladylike where it was, and it lent a grace to the hands if worn on the fourth finger. I was most impressed with this tender care for my feelings, and I realised there was far more to being a lady than I had ever dreamed. I began to respect my mother's values when she used the words 'She's a real lady', and now knew this was a true accolade to somebody very different from me.

On the night of the concert I was absolutely sick with nerves. How I worked in the office during the day I simply don't know. The hours at work passed like a dream, and I have no recollection of taking a single note or typing a single letter that day. My entire imagination was pinned on the concert, and my first appearance on a real stage. I didn't recognise it as just an end-of-season display of pupils' work. This was the stage, the theatre, and we'd be acting for an audience. Friends of Miss Mitchell made up our faces, and I had mine creamed and powdered and coloured by the famous Scottish character actress Miss Elliot Mason. I didn't know her then, but later hugged to my heart her praise for my performance.

My first appearance was to be in the Christopher Robin characterisation, and while I was waiting back-stage with Miss Mitchell we both paced up and down in complete silence. At last she turned to me. 'Do you know, Molly, this is a sign of the true artistic temperament—this silent tension—I think you may have your future in the theatre, and not in the schoolroom.' And then she groaned, 'Mind you, it's a terrible price to pay—it's so much easier if you can take it all in your stride, and be more light-hearted about it, but I'm afraid you're stuck with this sort of artistic temperament, just as I am.'

So that was why I felt so sick! It wasn't because I had been too excited to take my tea, to my mother's annoyance, and whose dire predictions that I'd upset my stomach had followed me all the way down the stairs and through the close to the street.

Everyone had a programme, so there was no announcement before the items. Just a programme note: 'Molly Weir as Christopher Robin'. The curtain rose, the footlights were blinding, and my heart raced so hard I thought I'd never get a word out. And then suddenly I was hopping across the stage and my mouth was opening and shutting, and I could hear A. A. Milne's words and knew I must be saying them. The first ripple of laughter took me by surprise, for I hadn't thought of A. A. Milne's poems as being very funny, just deliciously childish and true. It couldn't be the St. Andrew's Hall and the maze marching all over again, could it? It *couldn't* be something in my appearance that made them laugh? No, it was the words, for here it came again, and this time I saw what had amused them. Oh the sweet sense of power in finding myself able to make an audience laugh because of my acting.

This new awareness was my undoing later in the evening, alas. We had a little one-act play about a grandmother taking a crowd of youngsters to the theatre, and as they perch in the gallery waiting for the performance to begin, Grannie's comments and the children's behaviour form the play. The girl who was playing Grannie was marvellous, and she had us all in hysterics at rehearsals. We were just to do anything irritating or appropriately childish between our brief bits of dialogue, and show enough animation to make us look naturally obstreperous. During the performance I found, to my delight, that Grannie had a lipstick in her handbag, a hangover from her private life, and I was inspired to draw a cupid's bow on myself, then squiggles and scrolls all over my face. The audience were convulsed. They were riveted, wondering what I'd do next. Not a word of Grannie's rehearsed dialogue was heard. All her subtleties drowned out on gales of laughter. We exited to warm, strong applause, and I was fairly carried away with excitement in discovering I was a comic. I thought Miss Mitchell would have been delighted with our success. Instead she looked at me thoughtfully, and told me, oh so tactfully, that I had done a most unprofessional thing. That I had, by my 'business', diverted attention from the dialogue and had changed the entire nature of the play. That all our rehearsing had been for nothing, rendered ineffective by my broad comedy. That 'the play was the thing'. I could feel the colour drain from my cheeks, and the shaming tears rise to my eyes. I hadn't known! I had thought I was pleasing her, and that it was a good thing to make an audience laugh. But I had been wrong, it seemed. I had been carried away with my own power. It was at this black moment that Elliot Mason came to wipe off my make-up and mop up a few tears at the same time. 'You have a real gift for comedy, Molly,' she told me cheerfully, 'you just have to learn to keep it under control. That's not hard to learn, you'll find. The main thing is that you *have* it, and it's not a bad thing to make people laugh.' I gulped gratefully, as she went on: 'You must just remember there are other people on the stage with you, and it's also a gift to know when to be quiet.' I never forgot that lesson, a lesson which was to stand me in great stead in later years when I was privileged to work with some of the greatest comics in this country.

16

I T had been a hectically busy year, culminating in the two-day shorthand teachers' examination which would decide whether or not I would be able to add the initials P.C.T. after my name. I had to have two days off work for this marathon, and it seemed so strange to be back at a school desk in the daytime again. Thank goodness the desks were lower in the huge rooms where the examination was held, so I didn't have to sit up on my feet. In spite of four years' preparation the concentration demanded by the stiff papers was terrific, and my head was throbbing when I went out at lunchtime to eat my piece. I didn't speak to anybody, for they all seemed quite old to me, and many of them seemed to have enough money and enough light-heartedness to go and actually drink coffee before the afternoon session. I wandered about the streets until it was time to go back again, and didn't even look in the shop windows, for I didn't want to divert my mind from thoughts of the exam.

It was the oral next day, plus one other paper, and I was thankful for the elocution lessons when I came to give my lesson in front of the blackboard, for the examiner walked about the floor, sometimes facing me, sometimes with his back to me, and I had to be very clear and loud and interesting to hold his attention. I finished by the middle of the afternoon, and nobody had given a sign as to whether or not I had done well, not even the man who took the oral exam. He had just asked a few questions, nodded curtly, and dismissed me. What if I failed, after all this hard work, and all the money we'd spent on my lessons? I had a terrible sense of anticlimax and a great tiredness in every limb. I seemed to have been running forever. All that winter and spring whenever I'd come home from the office I'd swallow a meal and walk back to the town for my classes or rehearsals. My brothers used to say, 'How can you bear to race home from work and rush out again like this every night? You never sit down.' As my mother watched me darting about collecting my tammy and my satchel, she'd say, for the thousandth time, 'Aye, it's a peety she hisnae a pair o' wings. She hisnae got time tae live, that yin.' I had just laughed, because I hadn't recognised the existence of weariness in my eager pursuit of all the new and marvellous things I was learning.

How was it then, when both the concert and the exam were over, I could feel so tired? I couldn't even sleep when I went to bed at night, and even if I went to bed early there was no peace, with my brothers and their friends playing the radio, or having endless discussions on politics long after midnight. People in the tenements were so used to all activities being carried on in the warm kitchen that it wouldn't have crossed anybody's mind to go through to the cold room, the best room, for amusement or discussion, especially just because somebody wanted to go to bed. What a daft idea.

I drooped and grew pale, and when my 'peelie-walliness', as we called my wan looks, could no longer be ignored, we visited the doctor. We hadn't really wanted to go, but again, just as they had done after Grannie's death, the neighbours kept saying, 'My, I hope Molly's no' gaun into bad health'—this was their polite understatement for consumption, a disease which hadn't been conquered when I was a young girl, and which had taken off the wee chum in the next close. That was enough. 'We'll just go along and see the doctor on Sunday,' my mother said. 'Maybe ye need a wee tonic efter a' that night school on top of your job.'

The doctor never even mentioned a tonic. What he did say sent us into a flurry of amazement. We were so open-mouthed that he said it again, watching our astonished faces, 'Yes, she must have some place where she can be quiet and sleep, without disturbance from the rest of the household. She needs a room of her own.'

These were revolutionary words, and seemed to us as fantastic as though he had recommended regular rides in our own Rolls-Royce! But the seed was sown in my mind. A room of my own. 'What bliss, oh what bliss,' I thought.

To be able to go to bed and put out the light when I wished.

To end the pressing weariness of trying to shut out the lively noise of the kitchen as I tried in vain to sleep. To be able to read in peace. The doctor's words revealed unsuspected currents, for I had had no idea I longed for privacy with such intensity.

Although we were a happy family, this craving for solitude must have been there all the time. I realised it now. The doctor was suggesting a reprieve from having to live in the constant whirl of family life in our wee room and kitchen, which he said was slowly undermining my nervous health. I hadn't known what I needed until I heard those words, and I knew now I'd never rest until I had that room.

But how would I set about it? We hadn't a hope of the only sort of accommodation we could afford, a Council house, roomy and cheap. With only four of us the Corporation would laugh in our faces, for we certainly didn't qualify on the grounds of hardship. We had two rooms, hadn't we, and according to the standards of our neighbourhood, this was verging on the luxurious. If fourteen folk could live in a boxroom and kitchen in the close, we hadn't a case, so we could save our breath to cool our porridge and not bother the Corporation with trifles.

All this was going on inside my head, for my mother had listened to the doctor's advice without having the slightest intention of doing anything about it. She was astounded when I started to coax her to 'ask the factor' if he could find us a bigger house, one with two rooms and a kitchen. 'A two-room-and-kitchen,' she echoed. 'Hiv ye ony idea whit the rents are for a hoose of that size?' She banged down the kettle in irritation. 'I wish I'd never taken you near that doctor. There's many a family twice oor size would be glad of the chance of oor room and kitchen.'

'But, Mother, the doctor *said* I needed peace and quiet, and I would help with the extra rent. I won't have so many classes next winter, so my fees will be lower, and that will leave a few spare shillings I could give you to help pay for my room.'

'I ken somebody who's no' gaun tae get ony peace and quiet and that's me,' said my mother grimly. She had no idea of the fire that had been kindled in my mind by the mere possibility of privacy, and she was truly bewildered by what seemed a sudden desire for a bigger house, just because of a few words spoken by the doctor because he couldn't find anything wrong with me for which a tonic could be prescribed.

We both set the cups and saucers on the table in silence, but I could see she was thinking about what we'd said. 'And where would we get the extra furniture for a bigger hoose?' she said, playing her trump card. I felt this was no time for argument, but for cunning and coaxing. 'Och we'll get a wee bit of furniture here and there,' I said vaguely. 'And,' I swallowed desperately, carried away by my own boldness, 'I'll pay for the decorating myself. I'll save up.'

So now, as well as saving for Christmas, birthdays, holidays, insurance, elocution fees, fares, clothes, and my precious Scottish Clerks' Association. I would just have to start saving for paper and paint for my dream room and for some wee bits of furniture to fill it.

I took out a ruler and drew an extra column in the book where my savings were zealously noted. I headed it 'For my room' and noted down 'two shillings', the first instalment towards paradise.

I wouldn't be able to save much on fares, for I walked practically everywhere. Still, I could save the odd ha'penny by walking to the fare stage even when it poured with rain. I could let my hair grow, and the one-and-six saved on cutting would go into the column 'for my room'.

I changed my mind about going to Aberdeen and tasting the splendour of a boarding house for my summer holidays, and decided to go to the cheaper Girl Guide camp instead. That would be a terrific saving.

And I had a marvellous piece of luck when a neighbour asked me if I would teach her daughter shorthand as a private pupil, and she would pay me half a crown for each lesson of an hour. I practically danced down Parliamentary Road to the office that day. A whole half-crown! My shorthand teaching was proving its worth at just the right moment. It would be sheer profit, for I'd never expected a pupil to land in my lap like this. And if I had my own room I could teach my pupil there, and we could be utterly quiet on our own away from the rest of the house. Even my mother saw the extra room as a source of profit if I could get shorthand pupils, and best of all she was getting used to the idea that it might be possible after all.

At last, one never-to-be-forgotten day, the factor told us he had a flat he thought might do for us, and I rushed my mother round to see it in my lunch hour. There was a large kitchen, a really fine sitting room, a lovely square hall, a *bathroom*, and—the best point of the flat as far as I was concerned—a long, narrow bedroom with a lofty window.

My mother had only gone along to see the flat to humour me, but I could see the extra space everywhere was having a telling effect, and she fell in love at first sight with the scullery, an amenity she'd never enjoyed before. 'Where's the sink?' she'd asked the factor, as she looked round the big kitchen, with its high wide windows. He flung open a door dramatically, revealing a neat little scullery with white sink, well-scrubbed draining boards, and useful, roomy dresser. My mother gave a gasp, and turned to me, starry-eyed. 'Oh whit a handy wee place,' she enthused. 'Just fancy, if onybody came in and ye hidnae done the dishes, you could just shut that door and naebody would be ony the wiser.'

The factor looked out the window, whistling, while we anxiously worked out whether we could afford the extra rent. I'd just had a five shillings rise from the office, and that, plus the two shillings I had been putting away for furnishing the room, plus the half-crown from my shorthand pupil, would just about cover it. This flat wasn't far from our present house, so we'd be able to carry the small items round ourselves, and just have to hire a van for about an hour. That wouldn't cost much, and my mother thought she could manage it. She'd forgotten all her opposition to a two-room-and-kitchen and I laughed to think how she had gradually come round to my point of view without even knowing it.

We took the flat. 'Oh my, ye could haud a dance in that big lobby,' my mother said happily, and did a little 'Pride of Erin' step as we moved to the front door.

Now it was up to me to see about the decorator, for much as I loved my room, I wasn't blind to the fact that it was dull and dark and dingy with its scuffed brown paint. A friend heard of a decorator who was starting his own business and who was looking for work, and I felt very excited and grown-up when I took him round and showed him the room and discussed colour schemes. I'd never dealt with a real tradesman before, and it was most thrilling. My nest-egg was very small, and my heart thumped as he narrowed his eyes, looked round the walls, totted up the amount of paper and paint we'd need, and quoted me £2 10s. for papering and painting. I hadn't counted on paying so much, for I hadn't any idea how much these things cost. My mother usually just had a neighbour in to help her when she papered our kitchen, and as they did it in their spare time, we seemed to be in a mess of paper and paste for weeks. I couldn't ask her to tackle the lofty walls of this room, and anyway I had said I would pay for it, and pay for it I would.

But £2 10s.—it was an awful lot of money. I bit my lip, and then I remembered that hardly anyone in our tenemen s paid outright in cash. Young as I was, I knew the value of a lump sum.

'Two pounds in cash outright,' I said, my heart hammering at daring to bargain with a big grown man. He looked at me, and made up his mind. 'Done,' he said. There need be no delay in starting, for the house was already empty.

I chose pale yellow wallpaper, and duck-egg blue for the paintwork, this at a time when colour schemes everywhere in our Glasgow tenements were fawns and browns and strong dark greens. Everyone dismissed this flight of fancy as sheer madness, but the pastel effect in that murky atmosphere was charming, and those who came to scoff stayed to admire when the painter had finished, I kept running in and gazing round the room, almost swooning with pleasure. The bright colours had made it all look so *big*, and it was twice as bright with all the reflected light.

But I still had to face the problem of furnishing the room. My little nest-egg consisted of about six pounds now, and I was furiously puzzling how best to allocate it when I had another piece of luck, although it was a sad occasion for my benefactor. One of the older women in the office lost her mother, and as her only brother lived in England she decided to move there to set up house with him and share his expenses, so a lot of her mother's old stuff was superfluous. This was a gift straight from heaven, and I wasted no time.

I was invited out to her house in the South Side of Glasgow, and it was an Aladdin's cave of treasures for me. My office friend kept apologising because everything was fairly shabby, for it had all been used for years and years in their kitchen, but what did I care? I could see my room filling before my very eyes, and the bargains I was getting seemed to me beyond the dreams of avarice. Fancy having all this stuff to sell, at practically give-away prices. My goodness, they must have been very rich. You could have furnished three Springburn tenements with the things they described as odds and ends.

The old kitchen chest of drawers was mine for five shillings, and with a coat of duck-egg-blue paint became my dressing chest. The marble-topped washstand which they'd used for a baking top, changed hands at three-and-six, and you'd never have recognised it when it too received its transforming coat of duck-egg-blue paint and was tastefully draped with a matching cotton frill, to become my dressing-table. What a marvellous sound that was—a dressing-table, I who had never owned more than one drawer in the family chest of drawers. This was opulence indeed. A small very shabby plush-covered chair changed hands for two shillings, and a little rug was valued at seven-and-six. An upholsterer friend of my mother re-covered the wee chair in brown velvet for us for nothing, using a piece of velvet left over from another job, and my mother was loud in her praise of the chair. 'My word, it's as nice as yon wee chairs you see in the good antique shops,' she enthused. And so it was. Its shape was delightful, and I used plenty of elbow grease to give the wooden edging a satin gleam, and the quiet browns made a soft focal point against the pale walls and paintwork.

My mother vanished towards the Barrows just before we flitted, and returned to announce that she had managed to get a bed for two pounds, and as she had always been prudent and kept a good stock of bed linen, this was no problem. There would be sheets and blankets galore for my two-pound bed. There was still the floor to cover, though. We decided to have a wander round Bows Emporium—'Bows Implore 'em', my mother called it—and to our delight, although there wasn't a sale on at the time, they did have one blue linoleum square 'slightly off-pattern' which had been reduced to a pound. This was a marvellous buy, for it was real linoleum, and as my mother said, could be lifted again and again without cracking, for future flittings. Future flittings! And we weren't even into our two-room-and-kitchen yet! But I knew what she meant. It was the quality which impressed her, and even if it was never moved from my room, the fact that it *could* be lifted was a great comfort. Fancy getting such a reduction in price just because a flower was out of place, and it would be hidden under the two-pound bed anyway. How lucky we were. We celebrated this victory, as usual, with a coffee and a cake, this time in the D. & F. Stores at Glasgow cross, before walking home on air.

Hoeys in Springburn yielded a little imitation copper kerb for the fireplace, and a grass-fibre-top stool in blue for fifteen shillings the two. I was so excited about these that I wouldn't let them deliver, but carried them across Springburn Road myself, in case they would come to any harm in the van.

My mother unearthed a pair of curtains which, with a little alteration, fitted my window. A tremendous excitement filled me as I ticked off the items in my mind's eye. I had done it! I was furnished!

I gave my mother what was left of my six pounds to help with the flitting, and I forced myself to help with the dull ordinary arrangements for the rest of the house.

It was a great flitting. Great.

It was quite different from all the other Weir flittings. For one thing, the outgoing tenants had departed weeks before, and the house had lain empty, because of the poor demand for a house of that size, with its comparatively high rent. People in tenements were so used to being crowded together that there seemed no advantage to be gained from paying good money which was needed elsewhere for the mere luxury of a bit more room to spread out. This vacancy allowed us the unaccustomed treat of being able to go round there at every spare moment to clean the house in readiness for the flitting. And to be able to place her things in a house which had been cleaned and scrubbed from end to end was unalloyed bliss for my mother.

The normal practice was for outgoing and incoming tenants to move practically in unison, and my mother used to be in a frenzy, overseeing the packing of her precious 'cheenie' and ornaments at the house she was leaving, and, if the new house wasn't clean enough for her liking, racing like the wind ahead of the cart carrying the furniture, and trying to fit in a frenzied bit of cleaning before the linoleum could be laid down or the furniture set in place. As soon as this was done, she'd race back to the original house again, and lend a hand to the women who had remained there, to make sure of a spotless house for the incoming tenant. The highest praise which fell on the ears of a departing tenant was 'Aye, she left a hoose that clean, you could have ta'en yer tea off the floor.' And my mother made sure those words were spoken of her after all our many flittings. This frantic activity completely exhausted her, but we didn't know any other way, and took it all as part of the fever of changing house.

If the new address was too far away for my mother to find time or opportunity to achieve a spotless background, then when we moved everything was kept in boxes or cartons until the place was properly scrubbed. My strongest recollections of such occasions were of wakening in the morning after the flitting, to a tug on my arm and a hoarse voice whispering in my ear, 'Where's my galluses?' My brother would be standing by my bed, holding up his trousers and urging me awake. 'In the button box,' I would answer automatically, 'in the top drawer of the chest of drawers.' I had been the winner of so many 'Kim's games', where articles have to be memorised in one minute, that my photographic memory was relied upon by every member of our family. I would be falling asleep again when my other brother tugged me awake. 'Where's ma bunnet?' 'In the jelly pan under the bed,' and a triumphant 'Goat it' would assure me that was just where it had been stowed. And then it would be my mother's turn. 'Molly, waken up, do you know where I put the store book.' 'Aye, it's in the darning basket in the lobby.' By this time I would be thoroughly awake, and staring with dismay at the chaos which faced us, and which would only be cleared up when my mother had made certain that not a speck of dirt left behind by the old tenant remained.

This time there would be no such awakening, for we had all made sure the new house was as clean as soap, scrubbing brushes, and elbow grease could make it. The flues of every chimney had been cleaned. The windows sparkled. We had laid the new bargain linoleum square in my room, and covered it with papers in readiness for my second-hand furniture, which was to arrive ahead of the main flitting. When I had been knitting my brows, wondering how I would get this furniture from the South Side to Springburn, my good-hearted office colleague had come to the rescue. She knew a friend who had a van, and as she was giving him so much work in connection with her move to England, he would move my stuff without extra charge. I think she was so staggered at my elation over her mother's old furniture, and so infected by my enthusiasm, she wanted to make her own contribution to this room of mine. So, a whole week before our actual flitting from the old house, my second-hand bargains were transferred from the grandeur of their bungalow setting to our Springburn tenement. Help was freely given by male friends, and as freely accepted, to rub down this old furniture with wire wool, to apply undercoats and topcoats of paint, and never a minute wasted, to make sure it would be completely dry by the end of the week. While the boys were painting, I stitched three yards of blue-and-white gingham at sixpence a yard into a petticoat which would be draped round the marble-top washstand. When at last the curtain wire was slipped through the top hem, and snapped into place, held by two screws on the back legs of the washstand, the frill cunningly concealing the fact that there was no linoleum underneath. I was quite dazzled by the effect. Oh it was so feminine and dainty, and so unlike the usual bed-pawn that I could have sung an anthem in praise of it. 'Don't craw sae crouse,' I could hear Grannie's voice admonish me. 'Don't craw sae crouse.' But it was no good. I had to exult over my good fortune or I would burst!

When the last paintbrush had been cleaned in turpentine we removed the papers from the linoleum square, and pushed the pale blue painted furniture into place.

The little blue stool from Hoeys stood snugly beside the imitation copper kerb. The newly upholstered brown velvet chair repeated the warm tone of the kerb, and looked almost elegant against the pale wallpaper. The chest of drawers and the marble-top dressing-table gleamed like pale blue satin, and nobody but us knew that the drawers had sprung a little with the years of standing in a steamy kitchen far from Springburn.

All was now in readiness for the big flitting.

It was a lovely dry evening for it, and as soon as I got home from the office I joined the usual army of helpers who attended the Weir flittings, and packed china in newspapers, wrapped blankets and sheets round the crystal bowl and the overmantle, to cushion them against damage, then raced round with the others with fire-irons, pots and pans, wee stools, and other small items which were light enough to be carried by hand. We were like a colony of ants as we passed and re-passed one another, shouting instructions and checking everything as we ran. All the pals joined in, willing as ever to enjoy the bustle and fun of a flitting, with all the time in the world to lend a hand where needed.

What a difference it made, though, moving to a bigger house. There seemed to be tons of room, and our helpers were loud in their appreciation of 'how rer and easy it wis' with space to move freely and no banging into one another, and, best of all, no awkward corners or tight bends to negotiate when handling the wardrobe and the big mahogany chest of drawers. And, of course, this house had the great advantage of being in the close, which meant no tricky stairs to worry about either. We'd never lived in a close before, in fact we'd never been nearer the ground than two storeys up, and we hoped we would like it. Still, there were half a dozen steps up to the close from the pavement, so folk passing along wouldn't be able to look into the rooms. We wouldn't have relished being continually overlooked by every passer-by, having always lived so high above the streets.

The van was loaded and unloaded in record time, the old house swept and tidied, and I laid the rest of my personal possessions on my newly installed bed. I didn't want to arrange them just then. I wanted to take my time, to enjoy every second of the completion of my room.

I would stop now and give my attention to the feasting. There were at least eight hungry helpers waiting for the fish-and-chip party which was the only reward they expected or were given for having lent their brawn and advice in effecting this successful flitting. While they were washing themselves in the much praised little scullery, and having great fun shutting the door between that and the kitchen, pretending they required complete privacy. I ran round to the special fish-and-chip shop off Keppochhill Road, the one with the clean tiled walls which my mother favoured, although they weren't too generous with their helpings. I waited patiently in the queue for my huge order. 'Oh, have you been flitting again?' enquired the big pleasant woman behind the marble counter. She knew as well as everyone else that nobody bought that amount of fish and chips unless a flitting had taken place. 'Imphm,' I nodded happily. 'We've just moved into a two-room-and-kitchen and I've got my own room now.' Her eyes widened. 'My,' she said, 'you're ferrly comin' oot yer shell.' Then, as she handed me my parcel. 'You're no' lookin' for a lodger, are you?' The very idea. 'No fear,' I said, and ran home with the large, savoury-smelling parcel. My mother had spread the big white cloth over the kitchen table, and had cut a whole square loaf for the hungry helpers who sat round, faces shining with soap, waiting for their reward. Only then did I realise that I was starving, and we all fell on those delicious fish and chips as if we'd not seen food for a month. We even had two kinds of sauce, a fitting touch of luxury to celebrate our elevation to a two-room-and-kitchen. I chose tomato, which I'd learned to like on my infrequent visits to city tearooms, but the boys were happy with H.P., and my mother had to make two lots of tea to quench everybody's thirst.

At last they all went and the flitting was over. I was free to attend to the rest of my tidying. Oh the joy of arranging my little possessions. Reverently I laid jerseys, undies, hankies, poems, plays, shorthand books and Girl Guide treasures in the capacious drawers of my beautiful five-shilling chest. My hairbrush and comb seemed absolutely at home on top of the pale blue marble top. My shoes were hidden behind the sixpence-a-yard frill. I had thought this move was special because of the extra room, but it was special in another way I could never have dreamed. It was to be the last flitting we would ever do as a complete family. From this house, two of us would be married. I would become a stage and radio actress, and I would hear the sound of bombs dropping and witness the break-up of the world as we had known it. But all that was hidden in the future and not even the most expensive spae-wife could have foretold it.

But I had no notion of any of this as I gazed round my room on that first night. I had done it! The doctor had applied the spur and I had galloped into action. It had taken a lot of planning and saving, but it had been done. In less than a year.

I wondered what Grannie would say if she could see those yellow walls. Would she say, as I'd heard her say so many times, in scathing comment of some high-falutin' finicky notion of mine, 'Aye, that yin should ha'e been born wi' a silver spoon in her mooth.' What a long, long way I seemed to have come since I cooried into her back in the hurley bed. I wished I could tell her that I could now write the initials P.C.T. after my name. But I knew my grannie well enough to appreciate she wouldn't give a 'thank you' for the initials themselves. It would be the hard work which went into getting them which would always earn her praise. I wondered, if she could see me now lying in a whole bed all to myself, if she would be pleased with me. I remembered reading that Barrie's mother never envied the wife of a great man, but always said, in praise of a special quality, 'Oh I'd love to have been that man's mother.' We knew our mothers felt like that too, and our pride would have known no bounds if somebody had wanted to be our mother.

My grannie would never have said it in so many words, but it would have been a crowning joy to have seen it in her eyes. 'I'm pleased to be that bairn's grannie the night.'

I put out the light—my light—and felt the peace and quietness gradually steal away the excitement which twitched at my toes. I grew drowsy, and at last fell into the first of the deep sleeps which were to restore me to full health and vitality in that delightful room of my very own.

Peace and privacy, those desirable twins whose company I was always to cherish, were mine at last.